THE COSMOPOLITAN LYCEUM

THE COSMOPOLITAN LYCEUM

LECTURE CULTURE AND THE GLOBE IN NINETEENTH-CENTURY AMERICA

Edited by

Tom F. Wright

University of Massachusetts Press
Amherst & Boston

Printed in the United States of America

ISBN 978-1-62534-059-7 (paper); 058-0 (hardcover)

Designed by Jack Harrison
Set in Adobe Minion Pro with Linotype Centennial display
Printed and bound by the Maple-Vail Book Manufacturing Group

Library of Congress Cataloging-in-Publication Data

The cosmopolitan lyceum : lecture culture and the globe in nineteenth-century America / edited by Tom F. Wright.
pages cm
Includes bibliographical references and index.
ISBN 978-1-62534-059-7 (paper : alkaline paper) —
ISBN 978-1-62534-058-0 (hardcover : alkaline paper)
1. Lyceums—United States—History—19th century.
2. Lectures and lecturing—United States—History—19th century.
3. Cosmopolitanism—United States—History—19th century.
4. Popular culture—United States—History—19th century.
5. United States—Intellectual life—19th century.
6. United States—Relations. I. Wright, Tom F., 1981–
LC6551.C67 2013
374'.97309034—dc23
2013040191

British Library Cataloguing-in-Publication Data
A catalogue record for this book is available from the British Library.

Contents

Part III: Internationalism or Imperialism?

Conclusion: Cosmopolitan Medium

Acknowledgments

Many of the experts working on this field, across a range of academic disciplines, were able to come together at a special two-day conference at the American Antiquarian Society in Worcester, Massachusetts, in September 2011. This book has emerged from the lively exchange of ideas that took place at that event, which was kindly supported by the Antiquarian Society and the University of Oxford.

For making that initial exchange of ideas a success, I thank all the contributors to this volume and other speakers at the event, including Paul Dahlgren of Georgia Southwestern University, Carolyn Eastman of Virginia Commonwealth University, and Tom Heeney of the College of Charleston. Particular gratitude also goes to Jay de Prima of Worcester State, who thoroughly stole the show with an appearance as Henry David Thoreau, performing the lecture "Economy."

Numerous people deserve further thanks for their practical assistance. The hospitality and generosity of Barbara McCarthy of Worcester Polytechnic Institute, Eugene McCarthy of the College of the Holy Cross, and Murray Wheeler Jr. of the Yale Club of Boston was invaluable. Above all, the event would not have taken place, nor the subsequent book exist, without the intellectual and practical energies of Paul Erickson, director of academic programs at the Antiquarian Society.

Clark Dougan and Carol Betsch at University of Massachusetts Press, and the astute comments of anonymous readers of the manuscript, have helped make the process of publication as smooth as possible. Finally, the support of Angela Ray of Northwestern University has been exemplary throughout. Her willingness to submit lyceum culture to the most critical standards of scholarly scrutiny has inspired the book that you hold in your hands, the conversations that it represents, and the dialogues it hopes to provoke.

THE COSMOPOLITAN LYCEUM

Introduction

Tom F. Wright

During the nineteenth century, the word *cosmopolitan* evolved from a noun to an adjective. Attempting to establish where and when the shift occurred, the *Oxford English Dictionary* cites a Boston lecture hall and Ralph Waldo Emerson's 1844 talk titled "The Young American."[1] In that speech the word appears at the head of a moment of prophetic rhetoric:

> [With] a heterogeneous population crowding on all ships from all corners of the world to the great gates of North America, namely, Boston, New York, and New Orleans, and thence proceeding inward to the prairie and the mountains, and quickly contributing their private thought to the public opinion, their toll to the treasury, and their vote to the election, it cannot be doubted that the legislation of this country should become more catholic and cosmopolitan than that of any other.[2]

"Cosmopolitan" becomes the terminal point in a paradoxical national narrative. An increasingly mixed population, Emerson argues, will make more receptive laws and culture inevitable; it will make a republic more reflective of "all corners of the world." Because the open spirit of the nation is opposed to "the defensive, the conserving, the timorous, the lock and bolt system," he continues, "it seems so easy for America to inspire and express the most expansive and humane spirit."[3] In full cultural-nationalist register, this most atypically political of Emerson lectures associates the drama of immigration with the triumph of liberal principles.[4] As everywhere in his writings, here the rhetoric turns on the rival demands of individualism and community, this time filtered through the paradox of the ancient Greek coinage: simultaneously bound to *kosmos* and *polis.* But the novel grammar of this passage is crucial. As his periodic sentence unfolds and resounds from the lectern of Boston's Odeon auditorium, it resolves on an adjective and concept in flux, coalescing from a noun of individual attainment to a descriptor of national character. Whereas for previous generations. becoming "a cosmopolitan" was essentially a strategy of self-definition, in Emerson's hands we see it crystallize into a collective potential. Transcending the national was to be the culmination of nationhood.

This *OED* citation is striking in two ways. First, the date surprises, because 1844 seems an unexpected time for the reemergence of what Martha Nussbaum has called "the very old ideal of the cosmopolitan."[5] Most modern accounts suggest that the "world spirit" that had been so much a part of the intellectual and sociopolitical landscape of the previous century was on the wane during the nineteenth, a victim of the newer forms of loyalty and identity that took hold during this great age of nation building.[6] Second, the venue is unexpected because the culture of the American popular lecture is often seen not as an incubator of global ideas, but as one of the patriotic icons of nationalist identity. During this period, thanks to the growth of the lyceum movement, the popular lecture became a force in the media ecology of public life, possessed of an uncertain cultural agency that was both resisted and embraced. Many at the time recognized it as a medium that was helping to unify an emerging national public. And as the dictionary entry suggests, one way in which the lyceum movement tried to unify was by providing a common discursive space in which speakers and audiences could contemplate the ambivalent relationship of the republic to the world beyond its borders.

The resonances of this Emersonian moment provide a useful point of entry into the problems addressed by the essays in this book, which place the United States' culture of popular lecturing in an international context. Past studies have demonstrated the ways in which Americans built a coast-to-coast circuit of lectures and performances and, in turn, created a culture of self-education that contributed above all to nation building. However, nineteenth-century audiences were in thrall to both the exotic and the vocal, and this book shows that lecturing was as much about looking outward as inward. Orators frequently rose to speak to their fellow Americans in order to help them understand their connection to the world beyond the nation as well as to ways of life distinct from a dominant British American culture, thus shaping their sense of what national community might mean. As this book reveals, these diverse and frequently paradoxical connections raise an intriguing set of questions: Was the lecture hall a space where one went to become more American, or did the ways in which lecturers held up the globe for analysis or entertainment change how citizens thought of national identity? Did attending and reading about lectures encourage audiences to develop, in the words of an influential book on cosmopolitan thought, ways of "thinking and feeling beyond the nation"?[7] Was there something about the lyceum format that cultivated cosmopolitan values and desires?

The ten essays that follow bring a range of original research to these problems, drawing on methodologies from rhetorical, literary, and historical studies, reaching from the 1830s to the early 1900s, and introducing us to performers renowned, obscure, exotic, and domestic. Rather than providing a comprehensive overview, these contributions use a series of case studies to illuminate a complex phenomenon while leaving some aspects consciously unaddressed. For example, the essays do not directly consider the international lecture circuit and, for the most part, do not add to the already extensive scholarship on major stars of the transatlantic platform, such as Charles Dickens, Robert Ingersoll, Mark Twain, and Oscar Wilde. Moreover, though the term *lyceum* was shorthand for organizations and buildings that, at least initially, hosted a range of discussion functions, this book is limited to exploring so-called lecture culture: a cluster of practices of speech, listening, watching, and reading that constellated around a certain type of vocal performance. Through a consciously diverse emphasis on multiple genres, types of speakers, and location, we intend to sketch as broad a picture as possible of the curious and contradictory aspects that made up a cosmopolitan lyceum.

Lecture Culture and National Project

Popular lecturing in the United States was a diverse and unruly phenomenon. It was at once a formative class practice, a market transaction, an instrument of reform, and a marker of civic identity. The array of spaces both grand and humble that nineteenth-century Americans called "lecture halls" was a fusion of academy, church, and theater, unique arenas of sociability and part of a dynamic infrastructure of knowledge. As Thomas Augst notes in the closing essay of this book, lecturing represented "a constellation of sites and practices . . . a contested field of cultural production, where a traditional genre of learned discourse with roots in the medieval university was democratized, where middle-class audiences cultivated tastes for self-improvement and entertainment, and where forms of intellectual and literary labor" found a brief window of mass expression before the rise of organized higher education. Furthermore, lecture culture helped redefine the relation between oral and print media. Through the widespread practice of recording and transcribing talks in local and national newspapers, the lecture report became its own rhetorical form, making lecture culture a phenomenon that involved both an active body of attendees and a broader private reading public. Lectures could therefore fit into the lives of cultural consumers in multiple ways, becoming as much a practice of the study, the oyster house, and the railway carriage as of the auditorium.

Uncertainty about how to approach such baffling heterogeneity perhaps lies behind the phenomenon's surprising scholarly neglect. After Carl Bode's pioneering 1956 book, *The American Lyceum,* it would be another generation before a series of articles by Donald Scott revisited the field and expanded our understanding of popular lecturing; apart from intermittent work on the careers of individual speakers, the phenomenon attracted little subsequent attention.[8] Since the early 2000s, however, the lyceum has seen something of a revival. Angela Ray's 2005 book *The Lyceum and Public Culture in the Nineteenth-Century United States* provided a timely synthesis that reconfigured the importance of these institutions and their lecture-sponsoring activities as a "culture-making rhetorical practice."[9] Building on their foundational work on the social history of reading in early America, Ronald J. and Mary Saracino Zboray have turned their attention to the lyceum in an attempt to chart the inner life of the lecture-going public; and from a cultural-historical perspective, Augst has shed light on the significance of lecture-going in the moral life of antebellum America men.[10] This rediscovery of the lyceum forms part of a wider revival of interest in American studies concerning oral practices of earlier generations. Americanists are no longer content to rely solely on print culture, and some of the most exciting work on the early republic is being undertaken at the intersection of orality and literacy. In doing so, scholars are developing new methods of understanding what Peter Gibian has called an "explosion of American speech" that reverberated in the lyceum among many other cultural spaces.[11]

One strand that has united lyceum scholarship has been a focus on its nation-building impulse. For Scott, the achievements and energies of early-nineteenth-century lecturing "expressed a national culture" and was "one of the central institutions within and by which the public had its existence."[12] Similarly, for Ray, nation-building agency depended on a collective turn inward: "the lyceum," as she states in her essay in this book, "was about nation building." Broader narratives of nineteenth-century cultural and reform movements have also tended to invoke a consciously "national" American lyceum.[13] In part, this narrative was established by F. O. Matthiessen's classic act of literary canon formation in *American Renaissance* (1941), which held up the popular lecture as the solution to Emerson's "quest for form" and an engine of literary emergence.[14] But even when recent accounts, such as those of Lawrence Buell, have been far more attuned to lecturing as part of a transatlantic "proliferation of media," the sense still remains of a domestic forum whose emphasis on theorizing and forging the consciousness of the new republic was made possible by turning its back on global influence and models.[15]

Foundational accounts by practitioners and champions of lecture culture certainly bear out this theory. In 1857, an article in New York–based *Putnam's* magazine argued that lecturing was "the American amusement which is most congenial to our habits and tastes."[16] In 1864 the *Atlantic Monthly* deemed it the "most purely democratic of all our democratic institutions."[17] In a lyrical account for a British reading audience in 1868, Thomas Wentworth Higginson hailed it as the capstone of a continent-wide infrastructural mission:

> Across the prairies of the American continent, five hundred miles west of the Missouri river, and about midway between the Atlantic and Pacific shores, there moves westward into the wilderness a railway construction train of eighty vans. There is no house within a hundred miles, nor sign of human existence, save that connected with the new railway itself. . . . It is the measured footstep of advancing civilization. With each day's sunset more than two additional miles of this habitable globe have been permanently girdled and possessed by man. These iron rails once laid, all else follows, all the signs and appliances of American social order: the farm, the workshop, the village, the church, the school-house, the *New York Tribune*, the *Atlantic Monthly*, and the popular Lecture-system.[18]

In this way, the nineteenth-century lecture hall was frequently idealized as fundamental to a certain view of midcentury Northern expansion and civic identity and the means by which "social order" could be achieved and acquired. Attending lectures held the promise of a shared experience, a form of literary consumption that linked village, town, and metropolis, in which diverse peoples could hear, read, and argue about the same things. It was both a "sign," or iconic emblem of social order, and the "appliance." or discursive framework through which the ideology of that order could be sustained. It was, in other words, an institution concerned primarily not with engaging the globe but in self-consciously defining and securing a national culture.

This assessment also seems true of the kinds of lectures that dominated lecture courses throughout the nation. For example, themes of self-improvement in various forms were a signature theme of the circuit, and audiences who flocked to be chastened and uplifted by such moralists as the preacher Henry Ward Beecher or John B. Gough, a reformed drunk, encountered minimal consideration of global issues. Efforts to embody a world spirit or to model forms of urbane connoisseurship seem far from many performers' minds, and the insistent thematic focus on individualism and the conduct of practical life commends a view of lecturing as a mostly straightforward nationalist enterprise. Even when lecturers offered representations of "the world," these frequently involved a limited Anglo-Saxon or Eurocentric horizon; and even when audiences were invited to think about other cultures, the emphasis was frequently less about sincere intellectual engagement than about diversion and spectacle. It is easy to see why we might mistake such a milieu for an entirely solipsistic and inward-looking enterprise.

Nevertheless, the more one examines the period's lecture culture, the more one is struck by how lyceums were one among many spaces that provided an interface with world cultures. More often than we might assume, a night at the lyceum meant thinking about people, things, and ideas from beyond the United States. As the classical pretensions of its Aristotelian label suggests, the lyceum was a self-consciously foreign import, and its arrangement represented an adoption of Scottish Enlightenment experiments in public adult education with roots in eighteenth-century Glasgow. Several speakers who commanded sizable audiences on the circuit were foreign-born scientists, writers, and reformers, such as the Harvard botanist Paul Du Chaillu, or periodically newsworthy statesmen, including the Hungarian revolutionary Lajos Kossuth or the Irish nationalist Thomas F. Meagher. Above all, the record of subjects reveals a significant appetite for information and tales from a range of cultures, traditions, practices, and peoples, both familiar and unfamiliar, far-flung in geography as well as history. The essays in this book explore this neglected terrain and show how many of the ideas that found expression on the lyceum circuit were far from straightforwardly patriotic. In cumulative fashion, what follows reminds us how, in foregrounding its nationalist energies and imperatives, we tend to obscure an important dimension of lecture culture and simplify the ambiguities of its handling of international themes.

Cosmopolitan Nationalism

In particular, seeing the lyceum as a vessel of American exceptionalism stands in the way of an appreciation of how its contradictory engagement with the globe played on the interaction between cosmopolitan and nationalist impulses. As Bruce Robbins has powerfully argued, "cosmopolitanism sometimes works together with nationalism rather than in opposition to it."[19] In pursuing a revised picture of lecture culture, the contributors to this book aim to flesh out this insight in more or less explicit ways. By doing so, they contribute to a burgeoning critical discourse on the topic of cosmopolitanism, an idea and practice that has returned as a crucial concept in the contemporary humanities and a term that, as Kwame Anthony Appiah reminds us, remains "the name not of a solution, but of the challenge."[20] Yet a more nuanced grasp of the challenges it contains is needed to embark on an exploration of how such ideals worked on the lecture platform. As Ray frames the problem in her contribution to this book, "How would we recognize a cosmopolitan lyceum if we saw one?"

In the most comprehensive survey of the concept to date, Gerard Delanty and David Inglis trace three primary articulations of cosmopolitanism in modern Western thought: moral, romantic, and cross-civilizational.[21] The first, associated with the tradition of Immanuel Kant, embraces an aspiration toward transnational political community and the ethical goal of global human loyalty that Appiah has revived in terms of "universal concern."[22] Romantic cosmopolitanism embraces traditions of heroic individualism associated with a peripatetic intellectual class, centering on the idea that the horizon of a given culture can be broadened to include the perspective of others. Crucially, this tendency was also made possible by modern information revolutions and the proliferation of societies, journals, and meeting places that have helped disseminate global ideas through the public sphere. Finally, cross-civilization cosmopolitanism characterizes the aspiration to maintain a dialogue between different and sometimes unexpected parts of the globe, such as the nineteenth-century dialogues between East and West. Any given articulation of the cosmopolitan impulse will enfold differing combinations of the above, for, as Robbins asserts, "like nations, cosmopolitanisms are now plural and particular. . . . Cosmopolitanism is *there*—not merely an abstract ideal, like loving one's neighbor as oneself, but habits of thought and feeling that have already shaped and been shaped by particular collectivities."[23]

In all three strands, cosmopolitanism was an underacknowledged force in the particular collectivities that made up the nineteenth-century United

States. Romantic, moral, and cross-civilizational currents underpinned major touchstones of national expression, from Thomas Jefferson and Washington Irving through Margaret Fuller and William Sanders Scarsborough.[24] The cosmopolitan character of American culture and letters from the era prior to the transatlantic milieu of Henry James has often been caricatured as a one-dimensional worldly expression of elite privilege, largely disingenuous in its claims to transnational affinities. However, recent scholarship has attempted to reconsider what lay behind these "Genteel" sensibilities and asked us to reexamine figures like Henry Wadsworth Longfellow as key players in a surprisingly unfamiliar American story of sincere international engagement.[25] This book adds to this reassessment, using the history of lecture culture to develop a more nuanced sense of the ambivalent role that aspirations to worldliness in its various forms played in the nineteenth-century American imagination. In some chapters, we find an affinity with the wider world that was markedly critical of American national culture and its shortcomings and that resisted what Nussbaum calls "the comforts of patriotism and its easy sentiments."[26] Equally, in others we encounter a pure sense of ethical obligation to know about, learn from, or develop connections with those outside or on the margins of the nation.

But as Robbins suggests, expressions of engagement with the outside world cannot always be meaningfully separated from nationalist sentiment. "In the past," he notes, "[*cosmopolitanism*] has been applied, often venomously . . . to a luxuriously free-floating view from above," and such detachment was clearly part of the life of the lyceum goer.[27] A desire to engage with the world could be voyeuristic and chauvinistic at the same time as it was academic and ethical. Nineteenth-century Americans who cherished or flaunted their international attachments and sensibilities might inhabit cosmopolitanisms that were conservative as well as radical, using affinity with the world less as social ideal than as mere exercise in cultural capital. Learning about the achievements of distant cultures could help address local shortcomings; educating oneself on distant inequalities could catalyze pride in American freedoms; becoming worldly could reinforce superiority. These contradictions were acutely felt on the lecture circuit for several reasons: the unpredictable thematic scope of lecture courses made eclecticism part of a lyceum sensibility; an emphasis on self-education licensed an acquisitive individualism that was both outward and inward; and the reliance upon spectacle reinforced social, political, and ethical distance. Above all, as Ray maintains in her essay, "Americans construed the world through social performance," and the dramaturgical medium of the lecture platform placed the competing claims of national belonging and global consciousness vividly on display.

Cultivating Cosmopolitanism

The contributions to this book are grouped in four thematic sections relating to audiences, authorship, ideology, and media. The first group explores the extent to which lyceums fostered a public culture of cosmopolitanism, and it begins with a provocative overview by Ray, whose title pointedly asks "How Cosmopolitan Was the Lyceum, Anyway?" Her essay is skeptical on this point. As she puts it, her work has been concerned with the "ritual practice" of lecturing as a manifestation of the American public, viewing the lyceum as an "institutional structure that helped to create, promote, and sustain what would count as American values and American popular knowledge." Considering various potential meanings of the word *cosmopolitanism,* Ray revisits her earlier claims about national identity and thinks about how lyceum events operated as social practices that encouraged Americans to turn their gaze outward. Touching upon various subsets of lyceum activity, from scientific talks to costumed impersonation, Ray considers four ways that the lyceum represented the world: as a resource for knowledge, as an arena for political decision making, as a source for comparative ethnographic data, and as inspiration for embodied performance. In doing so, she shows how certain definitions of *cosmopolitan* do apply to lyceum participants, even though she thinks that much lyceum discourse involved processes of national definition created through contrast. Most lyceum lectures, she insists, approached international subjects from a distinctly "American" point of view and functioned as an arena for national decision making or expressions of national citizenship. "As a site for studying the mix of the national and cosmopolitan," she concludes, "the lyceum manifests the possibilities and limitations of that interaction."

The next essay, "Women Thinking: The International Popular Lecture and Its Audience in Antebellum New England," by Ronald and Mary Zboray, is more sanguine on these possibilities. The authors draw upon a deep archive of women's private diaries to present a vision of the lecture form as a potent stimulus to cosmopolitan attachments, revealing what a cosmopolitan lyceum could mean for its relatively disenfranchised audience members. They demonstrate that New England lecture-going women cherished the lyceum and recaptured it in diary entries as a socioliterary experience, imbibing through the lyceum a kind of cosmopolitan relativism and a sense of obligation to world of strangers. The authors see women's imaginations transported to distant places as they became—or at least *thought* they became—"citizens of the world," even if their rights of citizenship were limited at home. Their analysis reveals how individuals invested time, money, and imaginative energy in global culture and shows that internationally inspired lectures allowed women to fashion a worldly identity and develop a distinctively feminine culture of lecture going, becoming "highly active listeners" who "justified and fiercely defended a cosmopolitan outlook."

This was an audience whose eclecticism was cultivated through not just educational talks but also broader performance-based events. As one magazine editorial conceived it in 1850, lecture culture was "a protest against the theatre," arising from a "desire to substitute something more wholesome in [its] place" while ultimately working "something in the same line."[28] This paradox has been a characteristic of the lyceum from the outset. As early as 1838 a Boston reporter realized that "it has been discovered that the two objects of entertainment and improvement may be united in one pursuit."[29] By the time of the postwar circuit, distinctions had become even more blurred, and such increased interplay is explored by Sara Lampert in "Bringing Music to the Lyceumites: The Bureaus and the Transformation of Lyceum Entertainment," which turns to a late-century vogue for musical acts on the lyceum stage. In her essay, Lampert challenges the long-held narrative of the apparent decline of the postwar lyceum, providing evidence for the vitality of a forum that was "no longer a pure medium for lecturing—if it had ever been." Instead, it had become a multimedia experience that expanded the market for international artists and provided a new avenue for American musicians. Through this shifting composition of lyceum entertainments, a new culture emerged whose cosmopolitan eclecticism repositioned Americans as participants in an international culture of musical celebrity.

Cosmopolitan Authorship

Of course, audiences of the kind sketched by Lampert and the Zborays were simply more active members of the wider reading public. The next group of essays considers how the interplay between orality and print culture had an impact on the expression of cosmopolitan ideals. In "Mr. Emerson's Playful Lyceum: Print Culture and Polyvocal Promotion on the Lecture Circuit," Robert Arbour focuses on what one contemporary observer called the Sage of Concord's "genteel way of swindling" lyceum audiences. Through an analysis of certain "polyvocal" performances of the 1840s, including "The Transcendentalist" and "The Times," Arbour explores the phenomenon of Emerson as "oratorical curiosity" as well as the paradox of the inept speaker as lyceum star. He argues that this particular performer was willing to fail on the lyceum circuit in ways that had profound implications for wider issues of cosmopolitan personae and promotion in lecture culture. In Arbour's analysis, cosmopolitanism emerges as an individual posture of ambiguous or ambivalent authorship, a way of deliberately wrong-footing an audience with an ambiguous cocktail of stimulus derived from world literature and thought in a way that opened up a space for personal and rhetorical experimentation.

In "With Press and Paddle: William H. H. Murray's 'Adirondack' Lectures and the Making of a Wilderness Guide," Virginia Garnett considers a comparable postwar figure. Introducing us to William Henry Harrison Murray, the "renowned pastor, gamesman, and writer" of guides to the mountainous upstate region of New York, her essay situates Murray's performances within a discourse on travel whose ubiquity on the late-nineteenth-century platform made both the lecture and the travel narrative sites "where Americans worked through ideas of authority and knowledge transmission." Garnett's focus on the stability and authority of orality over print provides a stark and intriguing contrast with Emerson's sense of the flexibility or anti-authority of orality in the lyceum context. Through a close examination of the interaction of voice and text in the reception of "Adirondack Murray," she offers a vision of the platform as testing ground for the relationship between private study, literary expression, and cosmopolitan realities of lived experience.

In "William James's 'True American Theory': *The Varieties of Religious Experience* and Transatlantic Intellectual Culture," Paul Stob provides an intensive examination of an exemplary cosmopolite delivering his work as part of the 1901–2 Gifford Lectures held at the University of Edinburgh. Reconnecting us thematically and geographically to the spiritual origin of the lyceum in the public sphere of Scotland, Stob situates James's lectures within the rhetorical dynamics of their historical moment. As we are told, James used this foreign lecture platform to demand a place for a distinctly cosmopolitan approach to philosophy with an American "style of thought." In contrast to the many examples in this book of performers urging cosmopolitanism on an American public, James is shown to champion a form of empathetic transatlanticism back to a distant, British audience. Through close rhetorical analysis of text and context, Stob explores how such edifices as the Gifford series helped build a more cosmopolitan perspective on religious experience and how the text's formal qualities helped define versions of American oratory, cosmopolitanism, and pragmatism at this transitional moment in intellectual life.

Internationalism or Imperialism?

In Part 3, the ideological tensions beneath lyceum rhetoric and content are more directly addressed. The essays of Susan Branson, Gibian, and Evan Roberts reflect on the types of complicity that lecturers showed with the imperialistic attitudes of an expanding nation. In her essay "'Barnum is undone in his own province': Science, Race and Entertainment in the Lectures of George Robins Gliddon," Branson introduces us to this former vice consul to Egypt and prominent scholar and collector of antiquities who toured antebellum lecture halls displaying ancient artifacts in theatrical fashion. Inevitably, his live unwrapping of mummies was often compared to the crude show culture of P. T. Barnum. However, resituating Gliddon's activities "within the context of the lyceum movement," Branson argues, "illuminates this otherwise puzzling association of culture with spectacle." Her account of the content and reception of these multimedia performances makes a case for the cultural work of this speaker's comparative imperative, placing American society in a global framework, blurring the boundaries of performance culture, lyceum practice, and lyceum ideal. Crucially, she presents Gliddon's material as energized by discourses of race that starkly illustrated the realities underpinning the cosmopolitan tastes of the lyceum audiences that are the focus of the Zborays' analysis.

Chief among the figures usually seen as meeting this cosmopolitan appetite was the diplomat, poet, and adventurer Bayard Taylor. One of the most famous men in the antebellum republic, this "Great American Traveler" had reportedly experienced more of the world than almost all of his fellow countrymen, having embarked on extended forays into Africa, Asia, and Europe and accompanying Commodore Perry on the commercial opening of Japan in 1854.[30] On returning from each voyage, he toured the nation and lectured on his travels; from the 1840s through the 1870s, he was one of the most notable stars of the circuit, renowned for dressing in the costume of the country about which he was speaking. Gibian's essay, "The Globalizing Lyceum: Bayard Taylor's Travel Lectures and the Legacy of Washington Irving's Cosmopolitan Vision," charts a shift from the cross-culturalism and hybridity of Irving and Longfellow to Taylor's own immersive approach, seeing in the latter a more conflicted and contradictory identity, simultaneously willing to "enter the spirit" of the exotic other and yet reluctant to lose ties to a native home. This most prominent of midcentury cosmopolitans posed fundamental questions to his audiences: Could a person *become* the other? What were the benefits of immersion in exotic cultures? And how would such transformations be recognized by others not in possession of such romantic foreign experience? Gibian shows how, to our own age, he raises a different set of questions. He was a symbol of incipient American empire whose representations of the peoples and customs of the globe cast an influence over his audiences that was often far from benign. Addressing such difficulties head-on, Gibian offers a nuanced examination of the specific qualities of the globalized ideology that Taylor brought to the platform through lectures such as "The Arabs" and "Moscow," revealing a cosmopolitanism that was nationalist and internationalist, imperialist and mediating.

The years after Bayard Taylor's midcentury heyday saw a marked increase in the interconnectivity of the republic both internally and externally, in its links to a wider world. As one commentator noted in 1898, "the fact that we are now intellectually almost one country and not several differing provinces . . . has stripped lecturers of something of the glamour that attached to that which is foreign. His message has preceded him."[31] In this age of greater exposure to foreign nationals, the role of the lecturer as global mediator became increasingly marginal as audiences were increasingly able to learn about the world from "exotic" performers themselves. Such talks had been a part of lyceum culture since the appearances in the 1840s of Native Americans such as George Copway (Kah-Ge-Ga-Gah-Bowh); however, as Roberts's essay reveals, when thc lecture circuit evolved into the Chautauqua summer-season tent shows in the northern states, this kind of international star performer became a mainstay of platform life. In "The Peripatetic Career of Wherahiko Rawei: Māori Culture on the Global Chautauqua Circuit, 1893–1927," Roberts elaborates on "the shift of the lyceum and Chautauqua movement from principled search for educational and spiritual uplift to a form of mass entertainment." Moreover, with cultural links between Australasia and the United States bolstered during the fin de siècle by a recognition of a shared colonial encounter with indigenous populations, the essay notes how the attention and commentary that Rawei's evolving performances attracted provide a series of rich insights into racial and ethnic ideas in a new century. In doing so, Roberts establishes a productive dialogue with Gibian's analysis of Taylor. Rawei's savvy use of self-exoticization to make money and affirm white Americans' sense of their own cultural superiority not only echoes some of the strategies of Taylor but also *qualifies* Taylor's claims to be able to embody "the Other." Roberts's material helps frame our period, for we witness the transition to a distinct modern cosmopolitan sensibility. It also takes us to the limits of a nineteenth-century performance culture that, with moving image supplanting the values of embodied live performance, seems to mark the close of a chapter of popular lecturing as mass media phenomenon.

Cosmopolitan Medium

Exactly how to speak of this "medium" has always been a matter of dispute. To the *Christian Review* in 1850, lecturing was simply a belletristic achievement, a "species of literature of comparatively recent origin"; to others, it was a straightforward subgenre of oratorical performance; to the skeptics, it was theater by any other name.[32] But the real picture was far less stable. This mass form, through which citizens could speak directly to more of their fellow citizens than via any other medium, had introduced a dynamic interplay between oral and print expression and between values of pedagogy and performance, transformations that speak to twenty-first-century concerns with the ways in which new media revolutions restructure perception. As Augst makes clear in the wide-ranging essay that concludes this book, a great deal can be learned by considering the lyceum as part of a web of competing nineteenth-century media formulations. Thinking about lecture culture in this way sheds light on contemporary platforms of knowledge, about the interaction of emergent and established media, and about how such a media ecology can help us comprehend global culture in an age dominated by professionalized knowledge.

In "Humanist Enterprise in the Marketplace of Culture," Augst asks what "the institutional history of the lyceum [might] teach us about building social infrastructures for advanced literacy in the contexts of mass communication, about forms and values of humanist enterprise in multimedia environments." Thinking about lecture culture in terms of civic institution, media platform, and pedagogic tool, he situates the rise and fall of the platform within a broader transformation of the public sphere driven by "social and economic developments of capitalist modernity" that demanded educational entertainment to discipline and distract the aspiring middle-class masses. Elsewhere in his work on institutions of learning in midcentury America, Augst has written of the period's libraries and reading groups as "conduits of refined cosmopolitanism," but here he presents the lecture hall as a parallel conduit whose handling of worldly themes must be understood in terms of both an emergent higher education specialization and the incipient pressures of the market.[33] In a gesture that underlines the commercial dimension, his essay equates the cosmopolitan impulse with consumerist imperatives: "As its traditional civic mission was overtaken by commercial motives, the lyceum had become just another system of mass consumption. The lecturer himself had become just another standardized product," and the cosmopolitan experience itself was reduced to a type of market transaction.

In marking this transition, Augst draws on several elegies for the golden years of the lyceum that were published during the 1890s. In these backward glances, he observes, "the platform would become a site of nostalgia, not only for a lost sense of civic mission but for *shared* experience of communication that had been so intimately tied to the human body." A central question for Augst, and for the scholars of this book collectively, is the meaning of the comparable sense of nostalgia that our own contemporary moment seems to exhibit toward the lecture culture of early America. What do contemporary scholars champion when charting, recovering the complex civic mission, moral authority, and human presence of the lyceum platform? For at least some modern scholarship, Augst suggests, the act of reviving the culture of the lyceum appears as a way of recovering a loss in much the same way that Walter Ong's classic account of the "technologizing of the word" articulated an elegiac nostalgia for the vanished world of orality, which had been supplanted by the literacy of modernity. In reflecting on the continuing draw and fascination of a "hybrid genre of learned communication" such as the popular lecture, his afterword reaffirms how "we are still affected by cultural economies that emerged in the nineteenth century."

To many of the people and performers described in this book, lecturing represented a fortuitous fit of market, media, and mission. The cosmopolitanism of the medium, in other words, could express its own message. In concluding with this idea we might productively return to the rhetorical flourish of Emerson's "Young American" lecture with which this introduction began. Read more closely, his gesture becomes not only a commentary on "cosmopolitan" national destiny but also a parable of citizenship that celebrates the potential of an emerging public sphere and a triplet of civic institutions: "the treasury" and "the election," but first and most suggestively, "the public opinion." The process by which "a heterogeneous population" might "contribute their private thought" to collective discourse was central to Emerson's view that national coherence rested on collective habits of engagement made possible by the social ritual of the lecturing medium.[34] The growing network of lyceums and halls formed a web of culture through which itinerant speakers could usher into being an open-minded national audience. Along with cities such as Boston, New York, and New Orleans, the lecture hall was one of the "great gates" of North America, serving as a medium through which cosmopolitan ideas could gain entry into public culture.

The romantic cosmopolitanism of the transatlantic Enlightenment saw global belonging as the result of the circulation of texts and ideas across national borders, and the line from Emerson that found its way into the *Oxford English Dictionary* enshrines the lecture hall as a privileged space in which this kind of exchange took place. In this way, the original oral context remains essential to the passage's meaning. The day after the debut of "The Young American," for instance, readers of the *Boston Evening Transcript* were met with Emerson's words reframed in print columns that retained the palpable rhythms of oral speech and noted that "there was no resisting his tones—no dozing through his startlingly homely similes."[35] Recording, re-creating, and potentially reciting these "tones" of delivery and the dynamism of shared encounter were central to the secondary audience of lecture culture. Subsequent printed and published versions of this spoken text pointedly retained the record of origin—"delivered before the Boston Mercantile Library Association, 7 February 1844"—drawing power from the resonance of oral performance as a shared art form offered up to a symbolic public whose presence is felt each time we read Emerson's text.[36] Through lyceum performances and subsequent print renditions, Emerson enacted for listeners and readers a form of civic engagement, the philosopher-orator as agent of both interconnection and global consciousness.

In 1843, a year before the lecture, Emerson delivered a talk entitled "New England" in which he made an even more explicit plea for the potential of the "Lecture Room as the true Church of the coming time":

> I please myself with the thought that this may yet be an organ of unparalleled power for the elevation of sentiment and enlargement of knowledge . . . as other nations have each their favourite instrument, as Spain her guitar, and Scotland her pibroch, and Italy a viol, and as we go eastward, cymbals and song, let the reasoning, fact loving, and moral American, not by nature a musician, yet with a hunger for eloquence, find his national music in halls opened for discourse and debate, the one leading to the other.[37]

The moment is another self-reflexive cosmopolitan gesture, reeling off a melodious series of symbolic artifacts to flatter audience awareness of global tradition, securing a form of what Robbins calls the "(re)attachment" to the world, and claiming the lyceum as part of the carefully demarcated continuity of international culture.[38] In Emerson's conception of "national music" we receive a metaphoric projection of a harmonious public sphere whose melodies are both national and global. His grand ambitions for the "church of the coming time" were to prove unfounded, for the institution had evolved beyond almost all recognition by the time of Rawei. Yet during the century covered in this book, spending an evening at the lecture was an electric experience to so many precisely because the "national music" of the lyceum contained the potential to change how audiences thought about the largest questions in life. In keeping with this impulse, the essays that follow provide a meeting ground allowing "discourse and debate" to spark across disciplinary boundaries in order to test how secure this notion of a "national music" really is. The collective insights sharpen our understanding of American popular education, entertainment, self-fashioning, and national identity and help us ask new questions about the role of public speech. By casting a skeptical eye over the dramatic medium of lecture culture, *The Cosmopolitan Lyceum* suggests ways that the performative character of the public sphere can shape understandings of identity and community in a globalizing world.

NOTES

1. *Oxford English Dictionary,* 2nd ed., s.v. "cosmopolitan."

2. Alfred R. Ferguson, ed., *The Collected Works of Ralph Waldo Emerson* (Cambridge: Belknap Press of Harvard University Press, 1971), 1:229–30.

3. Ibid., 1:230.

4. For a substantial discussion of the intellectual importance of "The Young American," see Nikhil Bilwakesh, "Emerson and American Cosmopolitanism" (PhD diss., City University of New York, 2008).

5. Martha C. Nussbaum, "Patriotism and Cosmopolitanism," in *For Love of Country: Debating the Limits of Patriotism* (Boston: Beacon Press, 1996), 4.

6. Gerard Delanty and David Inglis, *Cosmopolitanism,* Critical Concepts in the Social Sciences Series, vol. 1, *Classical Contributions to Cosmopolitanism* (Oxford: Routledge, 2011), 6.

7. Pheng Cheah and Bruce Robbins, eds., *Cosmopolitics: Thinking and Feeling beyond the Nation* (Minneapolis: University of Minnesota Press, 1998).

8. Carl Bode, *The American Lyceum: Town Meeting of the Mind* (New York: Oxford University Press, 1956); Donald Scott, "The Popular Lecture and the Creation of a Public in Mid-Nineteenth-Century America," *Journal of American History* 66, no. 4 (1980): 791–95; Donald Scott, "Print and the Public Lecture System, 1840–1860," in *Printing and Society in Early America,* ed. William L. Joyce et al. (Worcester, MA: American Antiquarian Society, 1983); and Donald Scott, "The Profession That Vanished: Public Lecturing in Mid-Nineteenth-Century America," in *Professions and Professional Ideologies in America,* ed. Gerald Grierson (Chapel Hill: University of North Carolina Press, 1983). As an example of articles treating individual speakers, the following have focused on Emerson: Mary Kupiec Cayton, "The Making of an American Prophet: Emerson, His Audiences, and the Rise of the Culture Industry in Nineteenth-Century America," *American Historical Review* 92, no. 3 (1987): 597–620; Sallee Fox Engstrom, *The Infinitude of Private Man: Emerson's Presence in Western New York, 1851–1861* (New York: Peter Lang, 1997); and Bonnie Carr O'Neill, "'The Best of Me Is There': Emerson as Lecturer and Celebrity," *American Literature* 80, no. 4 (December 2008): 739–67.

9. Angela Ray, *The Lyceum and Public Culture in the Nineteenth-Century United States* (East Lansing: Michigan State University Press, 2005), 2.

10. Ronald J. Zboray and Mary Saracino Zboray, *Everyday Ideas: Socioliterary Experience among Antebellum New Englanders* (Knoxville: University of Tennessee Press, 2006); Ronald J. Zboray and Mary Saracino Zboray, *Voices without Votes: Women and Politics in Antebellum New England* (Durham, NH: University Press of New England, 2010); Thomas Augst, *The Clerk's Tale:*

Young Men and Moral Life in Nineteenth-Century America (Chicago: University of Chicago Press, 2003); Thomas Augst, "Temperance, Mass Culture and the Romance of Experience," *American Literary History* 19, no. 2 (Summer 2007): 297–323.

11. Peter Gibian, *Oliver Wendell Holmes and the Culture of Conversation* (Cambridge: Cambridge University Press, 2001), 16. Examples of this "new orality" in American studies include James Fleigelman, *Declaring Independence: Jefferson, Natural Language and the Culture of Performance* (Palo Alto: Stanford University Press, 1993); Christopher Looby, *Voicing America: Language, Literary Form, and the Origins of the United States* (Chicago: University of Chicago Press, 1997); Sandra Gustafson, *Eloquence Is Power: Oratory and Performance in Early America* (Chapel Hill: University of North Carolina Press, 2000); Mark M. Smith, *Listening to Nineteenth Century America* (Chapel Hill: University of North Carolina Press, 2001); and Carolyn Eastman, *A Nation of Speechifiers: Making an American Public after the Revolution* (Chicago: University of Chicago Press, 2009). For a critical survey of such work, see Sandra Gustafson, "American Literature and the Public Sphere," *American Literary History* 20, no. 3 (Fall 2008): 465–78.

12. Scott, "Popular Lecture," 808–9.

13. See Richard D. Brown, *Knowledge Is Power: The Diffusion of Knowledge in Early America, 1700–1865* (Oxford: Oxford University Press, 1989), 289–90.

14. F. O. Matthiessen, *American Renaissance: Art and Expression in the Age of Emerson and Whitman* (Cambridge: Harvard University Press, 1941), 23–24.

15. Lawrence Buell, *Emerson* (Cambridge: Harvard University Press, 2003), 23.

16. "Lectures and Lecturers," *Putnam's Monthly,* March 1857, 321.

17. J. G. Holland, "The Popular Lecture," *Atlantic Monthly,* March 1865, 362.

18. Thomas Wentworth Higginson, "The American Lecture-System," *Littell's Living Age,* 4 April 1868, 630.

19. Bruce Robbins, "Actually Existing Cosmopolitanism," introduction to Cheah and Robbins, *Cosmopolitics,* 2.

20. Kwame Anthony Appiah, *Cosmopolitanism: Ethics in a World of Strangers* (New York: Norton, 2006), xiii. Examples of recent attention to cosmopolitanism include Cheah and Robbins, *Cosmopolitics;* Catherine Lu, "The One and Many Faces of Cosmopolitanism," *Journal of Political Philosophy* 8 (2000): 245; and Martha C. Nussbaum, "Toward a Globally Sensitive Patriotism," *Daedalus* 137 (Summer 2008): 78–93. Cf. Nussbaum, "Patriotism and Cosmopolitanism," *Boston Review* 19, no. 5 (October/November 1994), reprinted in Garrett Wallace Brown and David Held, eds., *The Cosmopolitan Reader* (Cambridge, UK: Polity, 2010), 155–62. Delanty and Inglis, *Cosmopolitanism.*

21. Delanty and Inglis, *Cosmopolitanism,* 1:1.

22. Appiah, *Cosmopolitanism,* xi.

23. Robbins, "Actually Existing Cosmopolitanism," 2.

24. See Peter Gibian, "Cosmopolitanism and Traveling Culture," in *Blackwell Companion to Herman Melville,* ed. Wynn Kelley (Oxford: Blackwell, 2006), 19–35.

25. For example, the revised verdict on so-called genteel culture is defended in Christoph Irmscher, *Longfellow Redux* (Champaign: University of Illinois Press, 2006).

26. Nussbaum, *For Love of Country,* 4.

27. Robbins, "Actually Existing Cosmopolitanism," 2.

28. "Popular Lecturing," *Christian Review,* 1 April 1850.

29. "Interesting Lectures in Boston," *New Bedford Mercury,* 2 November 1838.

30. For a discussion of Taylor's lecture career, see Tom F. Wright, "The Results of Locomotion: Bayard Taylor and the Travel Lecture in the Mid-Nineteenth-Century United States," *Studies in Travel Writing* 14, no. 2 (June 2010): 111–34.

31. Mark Lee Luther, "The Bygone Lyceum," *Dial* 25 (1 November 1898): 291–93.

32. "Popular Lecturing," *Christian Review,* 1 April 1850.

33. Thomas Augst, introduction to *Institutions of Reading: The Social Life of Libraries in the United States,* ed. Thomas Augst (Amherst: University of Massachusetts Press, 2007), 7.

34. As Buell points out, attendance at these venues was a mixed affair, "ranging from teens to elders of both sexes, professionals to tradesmen. Not that audiences were social microcosms . . . but to a comparably sheltered, well-bred Bostonian like Emerson, . . . this was real diversity"; Buell, *Emerson,* 24.

35. "Mr. Emerson's Lecture," *Boston Daily Evening Transcript,* 9 February 1844, 2.

36. Alfred R. Ferguson, ed., *The Collected Works of Ralph Waldo Emerson* (Cambridge: Belknap Press of Harvard University Press, 1971), 1:229.

37. Ronald A. Bosco and Joel Myerson, eds., *The Later Lectures of Ralph Waldo Emerson, 1843–1871,* vol. 1, *1843–1854* (Athens: University of Georgia Press, 2001), 48.

38. Robbins, "Actually Existing Cosmopolitanism," 3.

PART I

CULTIVATING COSMOPOLITANISM

1

How Cosmopolitan Was the Lyceum, Anyway?

Angela G. Ray

In 1980, historian Donald M. Scott wrote in the *Journal of American History* that the lyceum lecture system in the mid-nineteenth-century United States "not only expressed a national culture; it was one of the central institutions within and by which the public had its existence."[1] Drawing on the scholarship of Scott and others, as well as my own investigation of primary materials, in 2005 I described the lyceum as a "culture-making rhetorical practice."[2] By that I meant that through the regular performance of communal ritual—such as participating in or watching debates, delivering or listening to public lectures—Americans in cities on the Eastern seaboard and in hamlets on the frontiers of European settlement acquired habits of mind that created cultures. It is unmistakable that the cultures I thought they were creating were local manifestations of an ideal called "an American public." I found especially compelling the metaphor of Thomas Wentworth Higginson, who in 1868 wrote of the role of the lyceum lecturer as a "living shuttle" on a weaver's loom, "moving to and fro . . . to weave together this new web of national civilization."[3] The characteristics of that imagined and performed nation were affected by region, politics, religion, race, gender, and class, for what was called "America" in public discourse about the lyceum bore the hallmarks of the rising middle class of white Protestant New England and often invoked the sensibilities of the Whigs and their descendants. In 2005 I saw the lyceum as an institutional structure that helped to create, promote, and sustain what would count as

American values and American popular knowledge. Ample empirical evidence supported such a claim, from the model citizen that emerged in the pages of Josiah Holbrook's Boston-based journal *The Family Lyceum* to the tenets of American exceptionalism heralded by even an incisive social critic like Frederick Douglass. The lyceum, I said, was about nation building.

Yet the contributors to this book propose to discuss something called the "cosmopolitan lyceum." English usage sets the word *cosmopolitan* in opposition to the nationalistic, denoting the former as "free from national limitations or attachments."[4] So the title of this book seems prima facie to challenge the emphasis on American national identity that characterizes much earlier scholarship on the lyceum, including my own. How are we to interpret the title? Is *cosmopolitan* meant as a descriptor of the whole (the lyceum was a cosmopolitan phenomenon), or does it signal a subset of practice, those lyceum activities that were somehow cosmopolitan? Are we interested in lyceum events designed to develop participants into people who were polished and urbane or those who had a sense of global responsibility? Or do we want to trace the resonance of international topics in popular nineteenth-century venues? In our scholarly investigations, how would we recognize a cosmopolitan lyceum if we saw one?

Of course, consensus is not required for this book to contribute to new understandings of nineteenth-century culture. Indeed, the power of the title may rest in its ability to balance centripetal and centrifugal forces: openness to pluralism in artifact selection and interpretive approach combined with collaborative attention to common problems. I read the title as an invitation to revisit my conclusions about national identity and to inquire into the ways in which lyceum events might be interpreted as social practices that encouraged Americans to turn their gaze outward. To explore these subjects, I begin with the title's constituent elements, *cosmopolitan* and *lyceum,* and then describe four distinctive ways in which I believe that nineteenth-century lyceums represented the world: as a resource for knowledge of nature, as an arena for political decision making, as a source of comparative ethnographic data, and as inspiration for embodied performance. Although this list does not exhaust the possibilities, the range of lyceum practice creates the basis for a provisional argument: the nineteenth-century U.S. lyceum was characterized by a dynamic interplay of nationalism and cosmopolitanism. In other words, through repeated cultural performances, people had the potential to perform their own identities as citizens of the nation and denizens of the cosmos, and even to imagine worldliness as a fundamental characteristic of American national identity. At different times and places, this interplay of national and global belonging might entail curiosity and a willingness to be educated about difference, or it might imply an imperialist impulse to expand the nation by engulfing the world. Therefore, as a site for studying the mix of the national and the cosmopolitan, the lyceum manifests the possibilities and limitations of that interaction.

The *Cosmopolitan* Lyceum

The twenty-first century has witnessed a resurgence of interest in cosmopolitanism as scholars and nonscholars alike experience increasing interconnection across the globe and grapple with the problems of climate change, the threat of infectious disease or international violence, and widespread financial crises. Cosmopolitanism as a moral and political philosophy traces its roots to the ancient world, particularly to the Cynics and Stoics of Greece; in the modern era, the writings of Immanuel Kant invigorated cosmopolitan political theory. Today the term *cosmopolitanism* can imply multiple goals, ranging from increased amity to a world government. Contemporary scholars especially emphasize moral and political dimensions, with political scientist Catherine Lu, for example, writing that cosmopolitanism is based on "the acknowledgement of some notion of common humanity that translates ethically into an idea of shared or common moral duties toward others by virtue of this humanity." In a related vein but a different linguistic register, philosopher Kwame Anthony Appiah notes that "cosmopolitanism shouldn't be seen as some exalted attainment: it begins with the simple idea that in the human community . . . we need to develop habits of coexistence: conversation in its older meaning, of living together, association." Scholars who focus on cosmopolitan education tend to view its purpose as distinct, even opposite, from the patriotic or nationalistic, although legal ethicist Martha Nussbaum, following the nineteenth-century Italian revolutionary Giuseppe Mazzini, recently proposed that patriotic sentiment, in its appeals to a commitment beyond the self, might be a catalyst for global justice.[5]

Because cosmopolitanism as a political idea has a substantial intellectual history, one way to study something called a "cosmopolitan lyceum" would be to trace philosophies of cosmopolitanism prevalent in the nineteenth century, whether moral, political, legal, or economic, and then to explore the ways in which cosmopolitan ideals became an explicit topic of discussion in lyceum practice. According to the *Oxford English Dictionary*, the first use of the word *cosmopolitan* as an adjective occurred in Ralph Waldo Emerson's lecture "The Young American," delivered before Boston's

Mercantile Library Association in 1844. Emerson predicted a universally inclusive form of legislation that would arise in the republic, owing to the "heterogeneous population" arriving "from all corners of the world."[6] Although a study tracking the usage of the word through lyceum history would be fascinating, it is only one possibility for investigation. If we are motivated by concerns of the cosmos that are common in our own time, then how might we shape those interests into a historically informed study of nineteenth-century cultural practice? Before envisioning additional possibilities, it is important to consider what we mean by the title's second term, *lyceum*.

The Cosmopolitan *Lyceum*

If the word *cosmopolitan* harnesses multiple potential meanings, then *lyceum* is no less dynamic.[7] The Latin term, derived from Greek, recalls the Lyceum in ancient Athens that became the hearth of Aristotelian learning. The word was in use in the United States well before the mid-1820s, identifying, for example, the Lyceum of Natural History in New York, which was founded in 1817 and continues today as the New York Academy of Sciences; the Detroit Lyceum, a debating and lecture society established in 1818; and the Gardiner Lyceum, a manual labor school incorporated in Maine in 1822 to prepare boys not for college but for "agriculture and the mechanical arts."[8] Yet in the origin story that we currently tell, 1826 remains a key date. In that year, Connecticut-born teacher and scientific lecturer Josiah Holbrook helped a group of Massachusetts farmers and mechanics to establish Millbury Branch Number 1 of the American Lyceum. This origin story could use further scholarly exploration, the better to identify precursors and to contextualize the activity in Millbury, but the moment remains significant. Holbrook's tireless promotional activity coalesced impulses for intellectual culture, self-improvement, and camaraderie into what literary historian Carl Bode called "a social institution," a burgeoning movement.[9]

By the early 1830s, similar local organizations had sprung up throughout the country. Some groups commenced owing to Holbrook's direct involvement; for example, his 1831 visit to the town of Jacksonville, Illinois, is credited with fomenting the establishment of lyceums in that state.[10] Others began without Holbrook's input. Many early lyceums were debating clubs; some combined debates with public lectures that had an educational emphasis, such as travelogues, historical narratives, or biographical reports. Members were often the up-and-coming young men of a locale, the white Protestant professionals, merchants, and skilled laborers, although many lyceums admitted women as spectators and some allowed them as members. Free African Americans, especially in urban areas, established and ran lyceums for themselves.[11]

Most early lyceums lasted only a few years, but a few survived for decades. The Concord Lyceum in Massachusetts is particularly unusual, lasting a century. The group began in 1828 as a forum for debates and lectures, but after about a dozen years it became entirely a lecture-sponsoring association.[12] This shift in a general way represents a national trend; by midcentury many lyceums were primarily venues for the sponsorship of public lectures, sometimes delivered by local people and sometimes by lecturers brought in from elsewhere. The midcentury platform offered a lucrative source of income to dynamic and entrepreneurial speakers, helping to establish the occupation of lecturer as a profession in its own right.[13] In the Old Northwest, officers of lyceums forged alliances to lure prestigious lecturers from eastern cities and to ensure annual programs of lectures attractive to local fee-paying audiences. Such cooperative efforts prefigured the postwar commercial management bureaus in such cities as New York, Boston, and Chicago.[14] Although the dual functions of education and entertainment persisted, the entertainment function grew increasingly prominent in the postwar period as the lyceum made room for humorists, vocalists, musicians, and dramatic performers. In 1912, the president of the Chautauqua Institution, in claiming a contrast with the lyceum, criticized it for being too commercial, too flashy, and insufficiently religious.[15]

Even in the late 1820s the term *lyceum* was ambiguous, connoting classical letters and the study of the natural world, and meanings altered further as time passed, owing to the activities of groups called lyceums. Today, the term is most often used in a historical context to describe an antebellum debating club or a midcentury lecture-sponsoring society. Yet buildings called lyceums also exist, such as those in Salem, Massachusetts, and Alexandria, Virginia; both structures were built in the nineteenth century by local lyceum organizations.[16] The activities that occurred within these buildings, whether or not they were directly sponsored by the lyceums, are often remembered as "lyceum events." The term also occasionally designates present-day schools or theaters.

The meaning of the word *lyceum*, then, is not self-evident. When I use it here, I intend to signal an organized, local voluntary association of the nineteenth or early twentieth century that sponsored activities for the intellectual and social benefit of its members and the broader public. I also use *lyceum* to denote something more amorphous: the collection of these associations as a nineteenth-century cultural phenomenon. By *lyceum activities* or *lyceum practices,* I usually mean debates or lectures, both of which involved direct participants (debaters or lecturers) and indirect participants (the spectators who interpreted and evaluated the performances). I do not use the term *lyceum activities* to refer to events that occurred in buildings named Lyceum unless those events were sponsored by voluntary associations identifiable as lyceums. At the same time, because nineteenth-century print sources sometimes use *lyceum* generically, I do not restrict its use only to those associations that included the word in their names. Thus my analysis encompasses such groups as the Farmers and Mechanics Association of Holden, Massachusetts; the Henry Institute of Camden, New Jersey; and the Young Men's Association of the City of Milwaukee, Wisconsin, all of which acted as lyceums.[17]

Although a precise and comprehensive definition remains elusive, discernible parameters can be established. *Lyceum* is not a synonym for "nineteenth-century oratory." A lyceum lecture was distinct from a sermon, political speech, legal argument, commencement address, or Fourth of July oration. The lyceum ideal implied a popular audience—a cross-section of "the public"—even if actual lyceum audiences may have been more narrowly circumscribed. For that popular audience, the term *lyceum* implied that what was heard was meant to be useful, by provoking thought and discussion or a better understanding of human experience. For my own purposes, I find helpful the felicitous phrasing of Bode, who wrote that the word *lyceum* stood, "grandly if a little vaguely, for learning."[18]

Using this characterization, we can understand all lyceum activity as cosmopolitan in a limited sense: the lyceum was a site designed for nineteenth-century individuals to embrace learning, to grow in knowledge outside their ordinary sphere, to transcend parochial or provincial tendencies, and to become worldly, that is, fully functioning members of a social economy, literate in the knowledges and morals of that culture. This meaning invokes a metaphorical sense of worldliness and highlights the potential for self-fashioning, for the creation of an individual subjective understanding of oneself as a social and intellectual being.[19] In contrast, a literal reading of the term *cosmopolitan* may also prove productive, allowing for an exploration of how the lyceum offered participants an image of themselves as citizens of the world and, hence, how it represented what that world was.

The World as a Resource for Knowledge of Nature

First, especially in some of its early iterations, the lyceum promoted a sense of the world as the natural, physical world, susceptible to comprehension through observation and analysis for those with the requisite knowledge and skills to identify and characterize its important features. Learning in this way was a practice of reading, and the world was often described as the book of nature, the direct counterpart of the book of revelation, that is, the Old and New Testaments. For example, *The Family Lyceum,* Holbrook's periodical of 1832–33, exhorted readers to study lizards, hummingbirds, corals, truffles, and the stars of the firmament in order that these might "plainly evince to the contemplative mind the wisdom and power of the Creator."[20]

By the 1840s Holbrook was promoting what he called the Universal Exchange Lyceum, a system whereby young and old alike could exchange rocks, minerals, shells, botanical specimens, paintings, needlework, and other scientific and artistic "productions" with others from around the world. Writing in his periodical *Self Instructor* in 1840, he noted that such worldwide exchanges encouraged participants "to respect the rights and to promote the interests of each other, and of the whole human family."[21] The following year he praised international scientific exchanges based in France and Austria.[22] Then in March 1846, on the eve of the U.S.-Mexican War, he published testimonials from diplomats and teachers, including the Brazilian and Venezuelan consuls and Juan Nepomuceno Almonte, by then the Mexican secretary of war, who had written in 1844 that "the system . . . of scientific exchanges . . . is, in my opinion, calculated to promote an enlightened and pacific intercourse among nations." Holbrook also quoted a Turkish ambassador as saying that "exchanges of the intellectual faculties" would increase mutual understanding between peoples, leading "to the abolition of national prejudices, arising from ignorance and egotism."[23] Fleetingly, Holbrook's promotional materials, which elsewhere supported religious proselytization and hierarchies of humanity, configured the peoples of the world as participants in a venture of collaborative learning.[24]

The impulse to scientific study in lyceums was not confined to Holbrook's periodicals. In 1840, for instance, Wisconsin engineer and naturalist Increase Lapham delivered a lecture to the Milwaukee Lyceum on natural history and the rationale for its systematic study. He described mineralogy, geology, botany, and zoology and briefly highlighted the utility of scientific study for mining operations. He also mentioned that the "beauties of nature" and "the wonderful works of the great Creator" could guard against immorality in young people. The mechanism for this protection, he said, was the "pure and unaloied [*sic*] pleasure" of learning, which he explained at length, providing examples of European and American scientists and explorers who pursued knowledge from mountain wilderness to polar ice. Lapham urged his fellow lyceum members to begin a museum for local specimens of minerals, fossils, and antiquities, saving "the natural productions" of the Territory of Wisconsin for local use and following the lead of scientific societies in the East.[25] Early lyceums regularly heard similar lectures on science, with men like Amherst geologist Edward Hitchcock and Cincinnati astronomer Ormsby Mitchel delivering popular lectures on the subjects of their expertise in the 1850s.[26]

In these types of lyceum activities, the world was a resource for action, a vast array of riches that might result in economic gain, renewed piety, increased safety, or new friendships but that would surely produce joy through the generation of knowledge. The world was a book just waiting for the careful reader.

The World as an Arena for Political Decisions

Although scientific lectures occurred frequently, and for decades institutions like the Lyceum and Natural History Association in Worcester, Massachusetts, collected cabinets of specimens, many lyceum members did not share the passion for scientific learning promoted by Holbrook and other enthusiasts.[27] Even Lapham began his 1840 lecture by noting that in the year since its founding, the Milwaukee Lyceum had ignored its professed goal to support the natural sciences in favor of sponsoring lectures, debates, and a library and reading room.[28] Lapham's observation appears applicable nationally: records of antebellum lyceums demonstrate that many focused attention on members' debating of political, social, and historical issues.[29] Surveys of debate questions, drawn from lyceums run by white men in select locations from Rhode Island to Illinois between the late 1820s and the mid-1840s, suggest that these debates tended to represent the world not as a source of knowledge but as an arena for political decision making by powerful leaders, whose choices debaters evaluated and whose mantle of power they hypothetically assumed.

Only rarely did lyceum participants frame questions that had worldwide reach. Exceptions included a debate in Alexandria, Virginia, in 1841 that asked "Should the government of Nations, in any case, be entrusted to Females?" and another in Canton, Ohio, in 1842 on the question "Would a Congress of Nations Be Beneficial?"[30] However, most questions clearly situated debaters in their roles as citizens of the United States, not citizens of the world, and the language usually assumed American self-interest. At the Concord Lyceum in 1837, for example, members asked "Is the territory of the U.S. with her national domains too large to insure permanent prosperity?" Three years later, the lyceum in the unincorporated village of Naperville, Illinois, debated a related question: "Would a greater extent of territory be dangerous to the Union?"[31]

Similarly, many questions concerned boundaries: lyceum members debated rationales for establishing or expanding state and national borders, and they argued about controlling such borders. The topic of Texas and its annexation was one of the most popular lyceum debating questions of the day. In 1830 debaters in Concord asked whether it would "be expedient for the United States to purchase Texas"; between the establishment of the Republic of Texas in 1836 and its annexation by the United States in 1845, the Concord Lyceum, as well as groups in places as distant as Providence, Rhode Island, and Springfield, Illinois, debated "whether Texas ought to be admitted into the Union." The Franklin Lyceum in Providence debated this question five times over nine years.[32] Other topics concerned the expansion of the American empire across the continent, as evidenced in two debates held in Providence in 1837 and 1843 on the question "Are the Indians entitled to be treated as independent nations?" and another in Downingtown, Pennsylvania, in 1843 that asked "Has the United States a Clear Title to the Oregon Territory?"[33] Some questions invited a moral evaluation, such as those probing the ethics of the conquest of native peoples, but many were framed to emphasize legal, political, and economic factors.

When lyceum debaters looked outside their own continent, they tended to focus on U.S. government policy in relation to foreign peoples or nations, and they framed most of their questions as general inquiries, such as whether laws should limit immigration to the United States or whether tariffs on imported goods were desirable.[34] Questions related to specific foreign governments were less common. When such debates did occur, they were often a response to immediate events, such as the Franklin Lyceum's 1839 discussion of the question "Ought the crew of the *Amistad* to be surrendered to the Spanish Government?" or the debate in Lincoln, Massachusetts, in early 1842 that argued "If Great Britain Persist in holding the disputed land on our eastern frontier, will it be policy in the United States to engage in War?" in reaction to ongoing conflict over the border between Maine and New Brunswick.[35]

Only rarely did lyceums debate questions of contemporary international relations that were not directly related to U.S. policy. An unusual instance occurred in Providence in 1845, when debaters asked "Is it better for the Irish nation to have the union between England & Ireland dissolved?" (The lyceum concluded it was not.)[36] But even the question of the dissolution of the Act of Union, which Irish Catholic leader Daniel O'Connell was promoting through his Repeal Association, was linked through the Providence debates with direct American involvement. Two years earlier the lyceum had inquired, "Is it right for the people of this country to interfere in the Irish repeal Agitation?" At that debate, members did not reach a decision and substituted a different, unrelated question for debate.[37]

Some lyceum debates placed members in the position of judging European rulers of past ages, inviting imaginative rethinking of historical decisions. These included the ever-popular questions of whether Queen Elizabeth was right to execute Mary, Queen of Scots, and whether Napoleon's banishment to Saint Helena was justifiable.[38] The French Revolution also provided occasional topics, and classical antiquity supplied such questions as "Was Brutus justifiable in the part he took in the assassination of Caesar?" and "Was the Governmental policy of Athens preferable to that of Sparta?" both debated in Naperville, Illinois, in 1843.[39]

Appraisal of debate questions from the late 1820s through the mid-1840s demonstrates that antebellum lyceums were places in which issues of international scope were sometimes discussed, although debates on such themes were far fewer than those on domestic issues, from banking policy to the emancipation of slaves, from the role of public charities to the abolition of capital punishment.[40] Yet questions that do have an international component reward our attention: as this brief survey shows, lyceums typically framed such questions in ways that invited debaters to imagine and practice discourses of leadership, situating them in postures to make choices about political, military, and economic policies. Questions often presumed American self-interest as the basis for decision making. Although research may well uncover different types of questions for analysis, it now appears that lyceum debating societies run by white men in the antebellum era were more often places for the inculcation of solidarity with a nation than for the development of a commitment to humanity writ large. Indeed, debate questions tended to enforce a distinction between the nationalistic and the cosmopolitan. At the same time, the presence of questions on international topics also signaled lyceum members' imaginative involvement in world politics, not isolationism; although debaters positioned themselves as national citizens, they still saw the nation as a constituent of the cosmos.

The World as a Source of Comparative Ethnographic Data

When we turn our attention from debates to lectures, we can perceive a shift from political policy to comparative cultures. In some nineteenth-century lyceum lectures, the world was a source of ethnographic data. These addresses were often based on analogies between the United States and the nation or people being discussed; that is, many lyceum lectures that offered descriptions of foreign places and peoples did so in the service of making meaning through comparison and contrast.

Lyceums supplied abundant fare for audiences fascinated with the history and culture of exotic locales. In the 1830s, for example, the lyceum in Salem, Massachusetts, sponsored public lectures titled "Present State of Greece," "History of India," "South Sea Expedition," and "English Female Writers of the Last Century."[41] Three decades later, in the winter of 1867–68, Chicago lyceum audiences heard explorer Isaac Hayes relate his exploits in the Arctic, naturalist Paul Du Chaillu tell of meeting West Africans and tracking gorillas, English agitator Henry Vincent describe social and political movements since the Battle of Waterloo, and Boston minister George Hepworth relate tales of the French Revolution.[42] Reporters for the *Chicago Tribune* linked these primarily descriptive lectures with postwar American ambitions, writing that Hayes's lecture "closed with . . . the hope that our flag would not be allowed to halt until the very [North] pole is within the compass of our widely extending empire."[43] So much for Canada. Less than a year after the U.S. government agreed to purchase Alaska from Russia, the expansionist fervor was amply in evidence, contrasting sharply with those debates of the antebellum era that had questioned the advisability of territorial gain.

If some midcentury lyceum lectures represented an incipient ethnographic impulse, then the archetypal participant observer was the writer, traveler, and lecturer Bayard Taylor.[44] As a correspondent for the *New York Tribune,* Taylor taught American youth how to see Europe on the cheap in the mid-1840s, covered the California gold rush in 1849, traveled through North Africa, the Middle East, and South and East Asia in 1851 and 1852, and sailed into Japan's Edo Bay with the expedition of Commodore Matthew Perry in 1853; he later continued his travels through northern and eastern Europe. A celebrity in his own time, he is remembered today partly for his sympathetic depiction of male homosexual love in the 1870 novel *Joseph and His Friend.*[45]

In the 1840s and 1850s Taylor published extensive reports for the *Tribune,* generated lengthy books on the same themes, and delivered lectures to considerable popular acclaim. Most of his lectures described specific trips—"The Arabs," "Japan and Loo Choo," and "Moscow"—but he also gave more abstract, ruminative lectures, such as "The Philosophy of Travel."[46] Sometimes appearing on the platform in costumes like those worn by the people among whom he had traveled, Taylor performed the paradoxes of mid-nineteenth-century American cosmopolitanism: a fascination with human variety combined with an almost blasé attitude, an assumption of white American exceptionalism matched with a warning to his compatriots about an excess of superior feeling.[47] In a recent analysis, Tom F. Wright notes development over the course of Taylor's lecturing career, observing the decline of an "early reductive emphasis on racial hierarchy" in favor of "aesthetic stimulation through vivid geographic sketches."[48]

Yet even picturesque description had the potential to change public opinion through implicit comparison. Recognizing the possibilities, President Abraham Lincoln wrote to Taylor on Christmas Day 1863 to suggest that he prepare "a good lecture or two on 'Serfs, Serfdom, and Emancipation in Russia.'" Although Taylor did not take the suggestion, his response to Lincoln indicated his deep understanding of the power of cross-cultural analogies. He wrote, "There are only slight resemblances between Russian serfdom and slavery in the southern states, although they rest on the same basis—property in Man—but the complete success of the scheme of emancipation in Russia has much significance for this nation at the present time."[49] As he did in his lectures, Taylor spoke with authority gleaned from his own travels, and he endorsed the president's observations about the potential for greater understanding of domestic issues by shifting focus outside the nation to allow for more detached, analogical reflection on topics of immediate concern at home.

Although few could speak of places and peoples across the globe with the same eyewitness authority that Taylor could marshal, international analogies were ubiquitous in lyceum lectures. For example, lecturers who supported women's rights derived evidence of capability from world history. In the early 1850s, lecturer Elizabeth Oakes Smith detailed the life of Cleopatra, carefully rejecting the Egyptian queen as a model of womanhood but linking harsh judgments of her with criticisms of contemporary women of competence.[50] In the late 1860s Anna Dickinson, who had been called a Joan of Arc during the Civil War, made a similar connection as she dramatically narrated Joan's military prowess. Dickinson said:

> Of the man, the world says, "What august power! What commanding genius!"
>
> Of the woman, under precisely similar conditions, it cries, "Why what a lucky accident it was, she should happen to hit upon that plan."[51]

Although in this passage Dickinson was comparing interpretations of Joan of Arc and Napoleon, the broader point about gender roles remained unmistakable. Situating contemporary problems in analogical relation to events and people in other places and times created the potential for new insight by throwing familiar themes into bold relief.

The ubiquity and variety of international subjects in nineteenth-century lyceum lectures promise exceptionally fertile ground for exploration. Many scholars will investigate global themes in the performances of individual lecturers; others will track representations of particular places through the work of various lecturers. Tom Wright, for example, recently analyzed interpretations of Great Britain as presented on the midcentury U.S. lecture circuit.[52] Still other scholars may focus on the work of lecturers who themselves represented foreignness for U.S. audiences, including Anatolian-born author Christopher Oscanyan, English novelist William Makepeace Thackeray, or Chinese-born American journalist Wong Chin Foo. Oscanyan toured the United States several times in the antebellum era, Thackeray had a successful speaking tour in the 1850s, and in the 1870s Wong gave lectures such as "Domestic Life in China" and "The Doctrines of Confucius."[53] Following the pioneering work of Ronald J. Zboray and Mary Saracino Zboray, some researchers will recover further evidence of audience reception of nineteenth-century lyceum events, from the skeptical to the celebratory, the better to understand the impact of the lyceum and its connection with other practices of cultural literacy.[54] Even as scholarship in these bountiful fields continues to grow, I think it likely that analogy will persist as a primary interpretive device in lectures on international themes and commentary about them, with the foreign and the homely situated as the key analogical pair.[55]

The World as a Resource for Performance

In any discussion of lyceum activity, the significance of bodily performance demands attention. If lectures and lecturers with international linkages are ubiquitous, then I proffer as a final example the work of a unique performer who illustrates the potential for understanding the world not only as a source for knowledge or comparison but also as a resource for artistic embodiment. The performances of the lyceum impersonator Helen Potter went several steps further than Taylor's costuming, with Potter presenting herself as one who could embody exemplary individuals of the world.

Potter was born in central New York in 1837, and as an adult she became a teacher of elocution and a platform performer.[56] Especially from 1874 through the mid-1880s, she traveled throughout the country, sometimes with a company of musicians, presenting shows at lyceums, schools, and churches. The best-known feature of these performances was Potter's costumed impersonations. During an evening's program, she typically impersonated four contemporary orators and actors, dressing in costume and reciting short excerpts from their most famous speeches or roles. Over time she developed a considerable repertoire, and in 1891 she published a book detailing her process of simulating her contemporaries. Potter insisted that her impersonations were reverent, not satirical, and she wrote of her artistry as a technology of preservation, as a means by which the ephemeral presence of what was best in culture might not be lost forever on the winds of time.[57] She aimed to generate an authentic imitation, and newspapers praised her for doing just that.[58]

Potter impersonated several American-born orators and actors, including Susan B. Anthony, Edward Loomis Davenport, Anna Dickinson, Elizabeth Cady Stanton, and the Reverend T. DeWitt Talmage, but many of her subjects were European, such as Polish-born actor Helena Modjeska, English actor Adelaide Neilson, and Irish playwright Oscar Wilde. Her most frequent and best-loved performance was as John B. Gough, the English-born temperance orator who was one of the lyceum's most successful and most dramatic lecturers.[59] Just as her platform work combined the genres of oratory and theatrical performance, so it eroded national distinctions, for Potter regularly mixed individuals from different cultures on a single program and presented American actors performing roles from European sources. She enacted Edwin Booth as Hamlet, for example, and performed Charlotte Cushman as Meg Merrilies in a dramatization of Sir Walter Scott's novel *Guy Mannering*.[60]

Potter also performed in the native languages of her subjects. As "Bernhardt mania" swept the country in anticipation of Sarah Bernhardt's first U.S. tour, scheduled to begin in late 1880, Potter traveled to Paris to observe the actor firsthand and have clothes made by her couturier, Charles Frederick Worth. Then, speaking in French, Potter performed as Bernhardt slightly before and then concurrent with Bernhardt's own American performances.[61] Thus did personal travel support a celebrity culture, a commercial enterprise, and a means to embrace—and compete with—the world.

One of Potter's impersonations creates particular discomfort for present-day interpreters. In an era of profound ethnocentrism, violence against Chinese workers, and federal legislation that first contracted and then suspended immigration from China, Potter performed onstage as a mandarin.[62] In her 1891 book, she described a character study of "a Chinese man of rank" rather than an identifiable individual, but in the 1870s, advertising circulars, programs, and newspapers connected the performance with the contemporary singer and stage performer Chin Foo (a different person from Wong Chin Foo, the journalist).[63] A circular from the Redpath Lyceum Bureau, Potter's promoter, identified her subject as the "Heathen Chinee," a common epithet also incorporated into newspaper reports.[64] For this impersonation, Potter dressed in an embroidered robe and a skull cap and carried a peacock-feathered wand. She sang and recited in a high-pitched tone, in syllables recognizable as Chinese. Although her characterization exhibits ethnic stereotyping that is easy to label Orientalist, her performance was notably more sensitive than many portrayals of the Chinese by white Americans of her day.[65] Even a sympathetic portrayal, however, can participate in naturalizing an unmarked position from which a white, native-born performer can observe and assess the world for audiences comfortable with race and class privilege.

Potter's dramatic performances leave us with probing questions about a cosmopolitan lyceum. Is such an adoption of markers of difference a salutary openness to human variation and artistic excellence? Or is it an example of hubris, an assumption of power to select and define the key attributes of others? Does such a performance honor or erode meaningful human experience and cultural expression? The difficulty of answering these questions demonstrates the fruitfulness of studying lyceum practice as it relates to global themes, highlighting the salience of similar issues in our own lives.

The Lyceum in National and Global Contexts

So how cosmopolitan was the lyceum, anyway? I remain convinced by available evidence that much of lyceum practice promoted nation building. But reflecting on the subject can productively place lyceum practices at the nexus of a dynamic tension between nationalism and cosmopolitanism, highlighting the ways in which national self-definition is created through contrast. In contemplating the global, lyceum participants could learn to identify particular values, beliefs, and knowledges as quintessentially American.[66]

If the cosmopolitan is one who joins directly with others around the world in a mutual enterprise, then only in the rarest instances, such as Holbrook's appeals for scientific exchanges in the 1840s, can the nineteenth-century lyceum be imagined as cosmopolitan. If, however, the cosmopolitan is an urbane and polished observer or a person with specific moral and political commitments, then ubiquitous examples allow us to ask how such social mores were inculcated or suppressed in lyceum venues.

Inquiring into the dynamics of a cosmopolitan lyceum demands consideration of the ways in which nineteenth-century Americans construed the world through social performance. Lyceums represented the world variously: as the book of nature, as an arena for political decision making by self-interested elites, as a source of comparative ethnographic data about human cultures, and as a resource for embodying a paradoxical collapse of distinctions by manifesting the trappings of difference. Participants learned about their world through a performance of direct observation or instruction, through forensic exploration in debate, and through subtle enthymematic reasoning that made use of comparisons, contrasts, assertions, and artistry.[67] Within the nineteenth-century lyceum, it is possible to locate traces of the ways our predecessors made sense of the world and of themselves—as local, national, international, transnational—and occasionally of the ways they enfolded forms of cosmopolitanism into their perceptions and performances of what it meant to be American. The evidence of what they did and what they thought offers instruction, as we in our turn make judgments about them and, by implicit analogy, about ourselves and the worlds that we inhabit.

NOTES

1. Donald M. Scott, "The Popular Lecture and the Creation of a Public in Mid-Nineteenth-Century America," *Journal of American History* 66 (1980): 808–9.

2. Angela G. Ray, *The Lyceum and Public Culture in the Nineteenth-Century United States* (East Lansing: Michigan State University Press, 2005), 2.

3. Thomas Wentworth Higginson, "The American Lecture-System," *Every Saturday*, 18 April 1868, 490.

4. *Oxford English Dictionary*, 2nd ed., s.v. "cosmopolitan."

5. Catherine Lu, "The One and Many Faces of Cosmopolitanism," *Journal of Political Philosophy* 8 (2000): 245; Kwame Anthony Appiah, *Cosmopolitanism: Ethics in a World of Strangers* (New York: Norton, 2006), xix; Martha C. Nussbaum, "Toward a Globally Sensitive Patriotism," *Daedalus* 137 (Summer 2008): 78–93. Cf. Nussbaum, "Patriotism and Cosmopolitanism" (1996), reprinted in *The Cosmopolitan Reader*, ed. Garrett Wallace Brown and David Held (Cambridge, UK: Polity, 2010), 155–62.

6. Alfred R. Ferguson, ed., *The Collected Works of Ralph Waldo Emerson*, vol. 1, *Nature, Addresses, and Lectures* (Cambridge: Belknap Press of Harvard University Press, 1971), 229–30.

7. Ray, *Lyceum and Public Culture*, 3–6.

8. Carl Bode, *The American Lyceum: Town Meeting of the Mind* (Carbondale: Southern Illinois University Press, 1956), 19; Richard L. Weaver II, "Forum for Ideas: The Lyceum Movement in Michigan, 1818–1860" (PhD diss., Indiana University, 1969), 1–22; "Gardiner Lyceum," *Christian Register*, 17 January 1823, 92.

9. Bode, *American Lyceum*, 19–20.

10. Thomas F. Schwartz, "The Springfield Lyceums and Lincoln's 1838 Speech," *Illinois Historical Journal* 83 (1990): 46.

11. Benjamin Quarles, *Black Abolitionists* (New York: Oxford University Press, 1969), 106; Shirley Wilson Logan, *Liberating Language: Sites of Rhetorical Education in Nineteenth-Century Black America* (Carbondale: Southern Illinois University Press, 2008), 58–95.

12. Kenneth Walter Cameron, ed., *The Massachusetts Lyceum during the American Renaissance: Materials for the Study of the Oral Tradition in American Letters: Emerson, Thoreau, Hawthorne, and Other New-England Lecturers* (Hartford, CT: Transcendental Books, 1969), 155–56.

13. Donald M. Scott, "The Profession That Vanished: Public Lecturing in Mid-Nineteenth-Century America," in *Professions and Professional Ideologies in America*, ed. Gerald L. Geison (Chapel Hill: University of North Carolina Press, 1983), 12–28; Ray, *Lyceum and Public Culture*, 36–38.

14. Ray, *Lyceum and Public Culture*, 39–40; John R. McKivigan, *Forgotten Firebrand: James Redpath and the Making of Nineteenth-Century America* (Ithaca, NY: Cornell University Press, 2008), 113–52.

15. Andrew C. Rieser, *The Chautauqua Moment: Protestants, Progressives, and the Culture of Modern Liberalism* (New York: Columbia University Press, 2003), 103.

16. On the lyceum in Salem, see Cameron, *Massachusetts Lyceum*, 5–25. On the Alexandria Lyceum, see Benjamin Hallowell, *Autobiography of Benjamin Hallowell*, 2nd ed. (Philadelphia: Friends' Book Association, 1884), 128–29; Philip C. Brooks, "The Lyceum Company, 1838–1990," in *Historic Alexandria Antiques Show* (Alexandria, VA, 1990), 32–39.

17. Holden Lyceum, Record Book, 1849–1853, American Antiquarian Society, Worcester, MA (hereafter, AAS); Philip English Mackey, ed., *A Gentleman of Much Promise: The Diary of Isaac Mickle*, 2 vols. (Philadelphia: University of Pennsylvania Press, 1977); Ray, *Lyceum and Public Culture*, 77–111.

18. Bode, *American Lyceum*, xii.

19. Thomas Augst, *The Clerk's Tale: Young Men and Moral Life in Nineteenth-Century America* (Chicago: University of Chicago Press, 2003), 129.

20. "The Book of Nature," *The Family Lyceum*, 8 December 1832, 68.

21. *Self Instructor and Family Cabinet—Extra*, November 1840, 6; see also 7–8, 12.

22. *The Self Instructor, and Journal of the Universal Lyceum*, November 1841, 7.

23. *Self Instructor—Extra*, March 1846, 6, 8; cf. *Self Instructor*, May 1840, 3.

24. Ray, *Lyceum and Public Culture*, 57–65; *The Self Instructor, and Journal of the Universal Lyceum*, November 1841, 9.

25. Increase A. Lapham, "Lecture Delivered Jan'y 23, 1840," 13, 11, 14, in box 20, folder 2, Increase A. Lapham Papers, 1825–1930, Archives, Wisconsin Historical Society, Madison.

26. Ray, *Lyceum and Public Culture*, 90–99, 104, 204; David Mead, *Yankee Eloquence in the Middle West: The Ohio Lyceum, 1850–1870* (East Lansing: Michigan State College Press, 1951), 133, 199.

27. See Worcester Lyceum and Natural History Association, Worcester Local Institutions Collection, AAS.

28. Lapham, "Lecture Delivered," 1. The Milwaukee Lyceum was established on 10 January 1839; "Lyceum Meeting," *Milwaukee Advertiser*, 19 January 1839, 1.

29. Angela G. Ray, "The Permeable Public: Rituals of Citizenship in Antebellum Men's Debating Clubs," *Argumentation and Advocacy* 41 (2004): 1–16; Angela G. Ray, "Learning Leadership: Lincoln at the Lyceum, 1838," *Rhetoric and Public Affairs* 13 (2010): 349–87.

30. "Lyceum," *Alexandria Gazette*, 9 February 1841, 3; Mary Whiteford Graham, "The Lyceum in Ohio from 1840–1860" (PhD diss., Ohio State University, 1950), 317.

31. Cameron, *Massachusetts Lyceum*, 146–47; Minutes of the Naperville Lyceum, ca. November 1836–15 March 1843, entry for 25 November 1840, Naper Settlement, Naperville, IL (hereafter, NS).

32. Cameron, *Massachusetts Lyceum*, 118, 147; Regina C. McCaughey-Silvia, "Lectures and Discussion Questions of the Franklin Lyceum: A Guide to Attitudes and Ideas in Nineteenth Century Providence" (PhD diss., University of Rhode Island, 1991), 303, 306, 313, 315, 316; *(Springfield, IL) Sangamo Journal*, 25 November 1837, 3; Ray, "Learning Leadership," 360.

33. McCaughey-Silvia, "Lectures and Discussion Questions," 304, 312; Robert Carl Martin, "The Early Lyceum, 1826–1845" (PhD diss., Northwestern University, 1953), 376–77.

34. On immigration, see Cameron, *Massachusetts Lyceum,* 137, 199; Journal of the Upper Alton Lyceum, 20 October 1836–19 March 1839, entry for 9 December 1836, SC 24, Abraham Lincoln Presidential Library, Springfield, IL; George H. Chapman, Journal, 1839–1842, entry for 12 November 1841, Archives, Wisconsin Historical Society, Madison; Minutes of the Naperville Lyceum, 12 October 1842, NS. On tariffs, see McCaughey-Silvia, "Lectures and Discussion Questions," 310, 313, 314; Minutes of the Naperville Lyceum, 13 January 1841, 25 January 1843, NS.

35. McCaughey-Silvia, "Lectures and Discussion Questions," 306; Cameron, *Massachusetts Lyceum,* 208.

36. McCaughey-Silvia, "Lectures and Discussion Questions," 318; minutes of this lyceum do not indicate how decisions were reached, whether on the merits of the question or of the argument (278). Cf. Ray, "Permeable Public," 5.

37. McCaughey-Silvia, "Lectures and Discussion Questions," 313.

38. McCaughey-Silvia, "Lectures and Discussion Questions," 301, 306, 317; Martin, "Early Lyceum," 352–54; Minutes of the Naperville Lyceum, possibly 1837–38 season, question 5, NS.

39. Minutes of the Naperville Lyceum, 4 January, 1 March 1843, NS.

40. Ray, "Permeable Public," 10–13; Ray, "Learning Leadership," 360–61. Although it falls outside the temporal and geographic scope of this survey of debating clubs, the San Francisco Lyceum, later called the Pacific Congress, is an interesting exception to the general pattern, with its considerable focus in the 1850s on international questions; Angela G. Ray, "Global Analogies and Social Knowledge: Nineteenth-Century Americans Learn about the World," in *Proceedings of the 4th Tokyo Conference on Argumentation,* ed. Takeshi Suzuki, Takayuki Kato, Aya Kubota, and Shusuke Murai (Tokyo: Japan Debate Association, 2012), 88.

41. Cameron, *Massachusetts Lyceum,* 16–17.

42. *Chicago Tribune,* 7 December 1867, 4; 18 December 1867, 2; 18 January 1868, 4; 14 February 1868, 4.

43. *Chicago Tribune,* 7 December 1867, 4.

44. Scott, "Popular Lecture," 803.

45. Scholars note in his earlier travelogues a same-sex admiration passing for descriptive reporting; see Robert K. Martin, *The Homosexual Tradition in American Poetry* (Austin: University of Texas Press, 1979), 98; and Angela G. Ray, "Popularizing Imperialism: Bayard Taylor and the U.S. Expedition to Japan, 1853," in *Proceedings of the 2nd Tokyo Conference on Argumentation,* ed. Takeshi Suzuki, Yoshiro Yano, and Takayuki Kato (Tokyo: Japan Debate Association, 2004), 210.

46. Tom F. Wright, "The Results of Locomotion: Bayard Taylor and the Travel Lecture in the Mid-Nineteenth-Century United States," *Studies in Travel Writing* 14, no. 2 (June 2010): 111–34; Ray, "Popularizing Imperialism," 207–12.

47. Wright, "Results of Locomotion," 121–26.

48. Ibid., 121. Historian Susan Nance argues that Taylor offered audiences a representation of authentic experience that "could inform their own identities as cultural relativists"; Nance, *How the Arabian Nights Inspired the American Dream, 1790–1935* (Chapel Hill: University of North Carolina Press, 2009), 66.

49. Roy P. Basler, ed., *The Collected Works of Abraham Lincoln,* 9 vols. (New Brunswick, NJ: Rutgers University Press, 1953–55), 7:93.

50. Elizabeth Oakes Prince Smith, "Cleopatra," box 2, Papers of Elizabeth Oakes Prince Smith, Accession #38-707, Special Collections, University of Virginia Library, Charlottesville; Angela G. Ray, "What Hath She Wrought? Woman's Rights and the Nineteenth-Century Lyceum," *Rhetoric and Public Affairs* 9 (2006): 199.

51. Karlyn Kohrs Campbell, ed., "Anna E. Dickinson's 'Jeanne d'Arc,'" in *Texts in Context: Critical Dialogues on Significant Episodes in American Political Rhetoric,* ed. Michael C. Leff and Fred J. Kauffeld (Davis, CA: Hermagoras Press, 1989), 293–94. On feminist advocacy in the lyceum,

see also Lisa Tetrault, "The Incorporation of American Feminism: Suffragists and the Postbellum Lyceum," *Journal of American History* 96 (2010): 1027–56.

52. Thomas Fitzpatrick Wright, "Britain on the American Popular Lecture Circuit, 1844–1865" (PhD diss., University of Cambridge, 2010).

53. Nance, *Arabian Nights,* 54–64; *The Adventures of Thackeray in His Way Through the World,* online exhibition, Houghton Library, Harvard University, posted 2011, accessed 11 October 2011, http://hcl.harvard.edu/libraries/houghton/exhibits/thackeray/; "Extracts from a Chinese Lecture," *The Friend,* 24 March 1877, 252–53.

54. Ronald J. Zboray and Mary Saracino Zboray, *Everyday Ideas: Socioliterary Experience among Antebellum New Englanders* (Knoxville: University of Tennessee Press, 2006), 197–220.

55. Angela G. Ray, "Making History by Analogy: Frederick Douglass Remembers William the Silent," in *Exploring Argumentative Contexts,* ed. Frans H. van Eemeren and Bart Garssen (Amsterdam: John Benjamins, 2012), 97–114; Ray, "Global Analogies," 85–92.

56. Elsie M. Wilbor, "Helen Potter," *Werner's Voice Magazine* 12 (May 1890): 113–14; G. Paul Smith, "Helen Potter," *Talent* 16 (January 1906): 1–4.

57. Helen Potter, *Helen Potter's Impersonations* (New York: Edgar S. Werner, 1891), x.

58. "Miss Helen Potter," in *Redpath's Lyceum,* circular of the Redpath Lyceum Bureau, season of 1875–76 (Boston: By the Bureau, 1875), AAS.

59. Potter, *Impersonations,* 12–16 (Anthony); 129–30 (Davenport); 190–91 (Dickinson); 91–94 (Stanton); 95–97 (Talmage); 72–77, 165–74 (Modjeska); 78–82, 179–81 (Neilson); 195–97 (Wilde); 1–11 (Gough).

60. Potter, *Impersonations,* 158–64, 152–57.

61. Smith, "Helen Potter," 3; "General Mention," *New York Times,* 26 October 1880, 5; "Central Music-Hall" and "M'Vicker's Theatre," both in *Chicago Tribune,* 18 January 1881, 3. On Bernhardt mania, see Susan A. Glenn, *Female Spectacle: The Theatrical Roots of Modern Feminism* (Cambridge: Harvard University Press, 2000), 1–39.

62. Andrew Gyory, *Closing the Gate: Race, Politics, and the Chinese Exclusion Act* (Chapel Hill: University of North Carolina Press, 1998).

63. Potter, *Impersonations,* 47–49; *Lyceum and Natural History Association: Recitations and Personations by Miss Helen L. Potter, Worcester, Oct. 21, 1875: Programme,* broadside [Worcester, MA: 1875], AAS; *Helen Potter Pleiades: Impersonations: McClellan Opera House, Georgetown [CO], Friday and Saturday, June 24 & 25 [1881],* broadside, Western History Collection, Denver Public Library, Denver, CO; Wilbor, "Helen Potter," 114.

64. Joseph E. Baker, *Miss Helen Potter, in Her Personations of Celebrities,* drawn and printed for the Redpath Lyceum Bureau by Armstrong and Co., lithographers, Riverside Press, Cambridge, MA (Boston: Redpath Lyceum Bureau, [ca. 1872–76]), AAS; "Lyceum News," *Boston Globe,* 26 July 1875, 5.

65. "The Pleasures of Looking: Women as Performers," in *Beauty, Virtue, and Vice: Images of Women in Nineteenth-Century American Prints,* online exhibition, AAS, posted 2009, accessed 13 September 2011, www.americanantiquarian.org/Exhibitions/Beauty/pleasures.htm.

66. Cf. Bonnie Honig, *Democracy and the Foreigner* (Princeton: Princeton University Press, 2001).

67. I am grateful to Ronald J. Zboray for suggesting this framing of the claims developed herein.

2

Women Thinking

The International Popular Lecture and Its Audience in Antebellum New England

Ronald J. Zboray and
Mary Saracino Zboray

On the evening of December 11, 1838, Bostonian Annie Lawrence walked over to the Masonic Temple in the bustling city center to hear the first in a course of lectures on the "domestic manners and habits of the Turks."[1] It was to be given by Christopher Hatchik Oscanyan, a New York University student who was a recent Armenian immigrant from the Ottoman Empire. The hall was packed to the gills with New Athenians who had perhaps read about his stint in New York, where he had spoken on Constantinople.[2] But this night in Boston he would focus on the Osmanli Turks. He told the crowd that "it was his object . . . to disabuse those who might favor him with an attendance of his lectures, of . . . erroneous notions" about this people. He appealed to auditors' sympathies by invoking British authors Fanny Kemble, Frances Trollope, and Basil Hall for their "shamefully inaccurate accounts" of American manners.[3] Annie was entranced. She thought he was "a handsome man . . . exceeding graceful in his movements," and she fastened on his every word, even though "he occasionally made a droll mistake," despite his fluent English. After returning home, she wrote a lengthy synopsis of his lecture:

> He spoke much of the *Harem* & the erroneous ideas we had formed of it. The word itself Harem being Arabic signifies home, a place of rest & reserve—where the women & children remain, indeed the same word is applied to the

> cabin of a steam boat or any place appropriated to women. . . . He showed the pipes used with the Houkah . . . & contradicted the notion we have that the Turks smoke opium with tobacco; . . . they also had formed the same wrong idea that we mixed opium with our bread. He showed also the tiny cup in which they drink their coffee & the manner by which they prepare it for use.

"On the whole," she concluded, the lecture "was instructive." After returning the next week for his second talk, she wrote another substantial summary in her journal.[4]

Eighteen-year-old Annie said little, if anything, that was ethnocentric about Oscanyan or the Turks. She embraced the speaker's relativism and set aside preconceived stereotypes about harems and the hookah.[5] She peered beyond her own privileged horizons as a Boston Associate's daughter and into an exotic world about which she knew very little. After hearing Oscanyan's talk, she yearned for wider vistas. That winter she took up Italian, attended a lyceum debate on "whether nations could subsist & prosper on the principle of Non-Resistance," and, despite a "wretched headache," listened to a talk on Burma at the Odeon by American missionary Howard Malcom. At the Masonic Temple she heard Francis C. Gray on "English Language and Literature" and later took in a performance by Christophorus Plato Castanis (fig. 2.1) on "the Massacre of Scio."[6] Within three months she had contemplated Burmese customs and the *Canterbury Tales,* heard out both Greeks and Turks, and wondered if pacifism was tenable in a tumultuous era of revolutions. The agility with which she rebounded after lecture upon lecture, topic upon topic, is astonishing. She wanted to imbibe as much as she could about the history, ethnographies, and arts of diverse cultures. The public lecture fostered in her a spirit of cosmopolitanism.

Many literate women throughout New England developed a similar cosmopolitanism by regularly auditing public lectures. Yet their worldliness has been as neglected as their prodigious showing. Women thinking about worldwide topics were everywhere. When Ralph Waldo Emerson referred to "Man Thinking" in his "American Scholar" address, delivered before Harvard's Phi Beta Kappa Society on August 31, 1837, he probably little thought about the women who had read his book *Nature* and attended his lectures.[7] But his "Man Thinking" might easily have been a woman. After all, the college-educated male scholar risked "becoming the parrot of other men's thinking," according to Emerson. So who better embodied his para-institutional intellectual than a woman, denied access to halls of higher learning? "Woman Thinking" was not so unthinkable after all.[8] As a sometime pieceworker wrote in 1852, "Have attended lectures &c. and have read considerable, and thought some."[9] It was a natural combination.

FIGURE 2.1. Christophorus Plato Castanis in native dress.
Courtesy American Antiquarian Society.

"Thinking women" have been recognized, but largely underrepresented, by historians who leave unexplored the implications of the female audience for lectures. Carl Bode, Donald M. Scott, and Mary Kupiec Cayton, who situate the lyceum within the Jacksonian era's so-called universal suffrage and democratization, summon concepts such the "democratic spirit," "Man Thinking," "the common man," and "self culture," thus implicitly racializing and gendering the institution as white and male.[10] But what did the lyceum mean for the disfranchised? Angela Ray has given African

Americans and "thinking women" a greater profile and notes that the latter were in Josiah Holbrook's mind when he founded the movement. That a fictitious "Harriet"—not a "Henry"—embodies the "invoked audience" in Holbrook's *Family Lyceum* says something, according to Ray. That its pages brim with women's original "lecture-essays" and sketches of powerful historical female figures says even more. Given its feminine clientele, Ray argues that the lyceum was an attractive vehicle for advocates for women's rights.[11] Beyond Ray and our own 2006 book *Everyday Ideas,* which analyzes both men's and women's reception of antebellum public lectures within the larger context of reader response, little systematic study has been done specifically on female audiences for the public lecture and what its cosmopolitan iterations meant to them.[12] So we ask here, what were these globally conscious "thinking women" thinking about?

To find out, we examined four thousand manuscript diaries and letters written by a diverse set of about nine hundred New England women and men (who reported on women) who lived between 1830 and 1861.[13] Women cherished the lyceum and wrote about it to recapture the experience or to fix, with paper and ink, speakers' ephemeral words. They also wanted to convey to distant loved ones the new ideas they heard. Where other scholars, notably Tom F. Wright, have studied lyceum reception through printed sources,[14] we consulted personal papers, which insofar as they were unintended for publication, promised greater insights into ordinary people's sentiments. Although most of the women in our study were white and lower middle class, we also encountered (and here represent) women laborers, including an African American schoolteacher, a pieceworker, and a factory hand, as well as mechanics' and tradesmen's daughters and wives. We discovered that, for many women, listening to lectures could supplement and even replace reading or, in the case of overtaxed seamstresses, other eye-work.[15] But they were hardly passive consumers of what contemporaries jestingly called "pills for the people"—easily digestible, painlessly administered knowledge.[16]

Not only did women attentively listen, they transcribed copious lecture notes into their journals, criticized orators' style, effectively evaluated their arguments, and assessed audience response.[17] But they also developed a consciousness about foreign nations and exotic cultures, refined an appreciation for European literature, discerned international networks of reform, and witnessed global repercussions of political and economic movements, all within the confines of their locales. Transported by the New England public lecture into worlds untraversed by them, they could transcend the "bonds of womanhood" that circumscribed their horizons to home, church, and family.[18] In many ways, what they imbibed through the lyceum can be seen as akin to the cosmopolitan relativism and senses of obligation to the "world of strangers" that Kwame Anthony Appiah outlines in his book *Cosmopolitanism.*[19] Furthermore, they arguably developed, in Anne Mellor's words, a "critical detachment from particular national or cultural allegiances."[20] Conceivably, they fashioned a mental universe of the cosmopolitan in which they could imagine themselves as citizens of the world.[21]

To be sure, the lecture hall was not the only stimulus to women's cosmopolitan outlook. Reading also fostered it. Arguably, popular authors like Lydia Maria Child, Frances Trollope, Charlotte Brontë, Elizabeth Barrett Browning, Madame de Staël, Maria Edgeworth, and Catherine Sedgwick explored the cosmopolitan sensibility in their texts.[22] Histories, biographies, foreign news columns, and travel literature also informed women.[23] Travelogue-like letters from acquaintances abroad likewise opened up new vistas. Besides reading, home decorating also nurtured the cosmopolitan. Kristin Hoganson has argued for a later time that domestic spaces were necessarily "loci of interaction with the wider world" in that decorative styles and furnishings were often imported.[24] In the early nineteenth century, Cantonese exports became commonplace facets of the Northeastern seaboard's household material culture.[25] Even earlier, everyday stationery items manufactured from globally produced materials were ubiquitous in the home.[26] Amid this world of goods that women selected, purchased, and consumed were lyceum tickets. One woman's 1839–40 account book, for example, juxtaposes expenditures for "[George] Combe's lectures" with "Printed French calico" and a "Volume of German Fables."[27] Whether women deployed domestic items to claim imaginary "imperial outposts" or, instead, to nurture virtual salons remains debatable.[28] But when it came to consuming international public lectures, New England women could fancy themselves *salonistes.*[29]

In this essay we show how these internationally inspired lectures allowed women to fashion a cosmopolitan identity. We first outline the types of lectures and speakers they heard within the context of a distinctly feminine culture of lecture-going. We then look at women's responses to lectures to determine why they attended and what they got out of the experience. Finally, we consider the cosmopolitan sensibility, including religious eclecticism and humanitarian reform, that women projected in their responses to speakers and their presentations. We argue that these highly active listeners justified and often fiercely defended a cosmopolitan outlook, even when speakers would not.

Types of Lectures and Speakers

Women audited a remarkable array of lectures about different parts of the world. Many of them mentioned lectures about China, Switzerland, France, Turkey, Palestine, Italy, or Rome.[30] Talks on Jerusalem and India were especially popular.[31] These presentations, which included the travel lecture, encompassed, according to Tom F. Wright, "several modes of expression and inquiry" including "natural history, popular anthropology, [and] comparative politics."[32] Women reveled in the intellectual bounty. Charlotte Forten, an African American schoolteacher from Salem, delighted in the expansive scope of one 1854 lecture on Ecuador: "[I] received much useful information concerning that beautiful country, the variety of its climate, soil and productions; the grandeur of its mountain scenery; the splendor of its capital, and the character, dress, and manners of its inhabitants." The idea that a lecture should be informative was commonly voiced.[33] Women wanted to learn something new, to explore parts of the world they had not seen. If it could be gotten from a book, they asked, "what was the point?"

Women were fascinated by traditionally male topics: politics, history, science, and philosophy. Martha Osborne Barrett, a Danvers, Massachusetts, boot-and-bonnet pieceworker, went to an 1855 "Eastern Question" talk by Reinhold Solger, a German refugee.[34] Abigail Lummus, a Lynn apothecary's wife, braved a winter storm to hear about the "History of England," while Lowell millworker Mary Hall ventured out one December night to audit a lyceum lecture on "Ancient Rome."[35] Two New Haven sisters were deeply interested in foreign missionary Robert Baird's course on nations in conflict that included "Russia & Poland," "Turkey and Greece," and "Great Britain and Ireland."[36] Thinking women tackled Socrates, Epicurus, and Immanuel Kant and sometimes engaged diverse "Ancient Greek philosophers" in one sitting.[37] Mary Hall sat through "Objections to [Franz Joseph] Gall[']s and [Johann] Spurzheim[']s system of Phrenology."[38] The ecumenically capacious grab bag of titles reported by women is breathtaking: "The Huguenots," "Holy Week at Rome," "Mahomet," the "Jewish Commonwealth," "Hindoo Temples," and "Carlo Borromeo," whom Protestant Charlotte Forten dubbed "the saintly Italian cardinal."[39] Women sent doctrinaire notions packing.

Because New England women devoured European poetry, novels, and drama, they came out in droves for literature lectures.[40] Anything about Shakespeare was a draw, as were lecturers Henry N. Hudson, Francis C. Gray, George Vandenhoff, and William H. Simmons, who often read from the Bard's plays. Women delivered men's poetic lines as well. Shakespearean readings by English actress Fanny Kemble were phenomenally successful.[41] "Her face is wonderful—She can change it to almost any expression—& her voice is magnetic," one academy student reported.[42] Surprisingly, women seldom objected to one of their sex assuming male characters, as Kemble did when she "ventriloquized" Falstaff, Macbeth, or Richard II.[43] Courses on "English Literature," Milton's "Lycidas," Samuel Taylor Coleridge, Goethe, and Homer were more conventionally satisfying.[44] European poets could embody a nation. "Not only, may it be said of him that he represents Italy," Charlotte Forten wrote after hearing a James Russell Lowell lecture on Dante, "but almost that he *is* Italy."[45] Lectures on just about anything could slip in a litterateur. Martha Osborne Barrett was surprised to hear a favorite poet's verses in Edwin P. Whipple's 1855 lecture on "Cheerfulness": "Some of our noblest poets he affirmed expressed a spirit of equanimity and calm content, Wordsworth particularly—from whom he quoted largely to my great pleasure."[46] One wonders if it was glimpsing the English novelist William Makepeace Thackeray himself or hearing him that packed his lectures with women.[47]

For women came not only to listen but to see. It was through the many recent immigrant, expatriate, or foreign national speakers—regardless of their lecture topics—that women often explored the world in microcosm. We have already met Christopher Hatchik Oscanyan and Christophorus Plato Castanis. Women also flocked to lectures by Swiss-born naturalist Louis Agassiz, who spoke on "glaciers" and the "formation of animals."[48] Women eyed the big attraction when he opened a free lecture series for Worcester's Teachers' Institute.[49] A trip to Boston promised a glimpse of the Harvard professor. "I can probably hear Mr. Agassiz," an excited visitor from Philadelphia wrote home in 1860.[50] Women who heard Scottish phrenologist George Combe sometimes received a critique of U.S. party politics as well as a discourse on the "science" of human skull reading.[51] Wexford County, Ireland, native Henry Giles, equally at home with talks on "the English Government in Ireland" or "Extravagances of Public Speakers," could pack the house. "We did not get there till late," a schoolteacher complained after a Giles lecture, "so we had to sit back and we could not hear on acct of some young men who sat in the seats behind us who talked all the eve."[52] Bookings of the English-born "cold water warrior" John B. Gough guaranteed a flood of temperance-minded women who knew him as "one of the most eminent lecturers in the world."[53] Indeed, a Connecticut port collector sat through three of Gough's consecutive talks in May 1848 so that he could see "lots of ladies."[54] So much for men's vaunted "self culture."

A Feminine Lyceum Culture

The parade of cosmopolitan lectures and speakers was seemingly endless, as we have seen, and women clearly wanted to march to its beat. But what were the conditions under which they would join in? Women proceeded to the lecture hall through a distinctly feminine lyceum culture marked by engagement in courtship rituals, respites from domestic work rhythms, and triumph over limited mobility. But specially priced ticket offers also shaped this culture.

Well before lecture night, women's lecture-going was circumscribed by ticketing. They usually received a discount, but sometimes at a cost. One broadside, featuring talks on "Italy," the "Poetry of Mrs. [Felicia] Hemans," and "The progress of liberty in France" advertised "Tickets at two dollars each, to admit a gentleman and ladies."[55] To obtain the bargain, women depended on pooling with a man. No male bankrolling, no cheap ticket; and in this case, perhaps no ticket at all. These were sometimes called "family tickets," but they may have been used by single men who were dating. For going to the lyceum—and perhaps for some ice cream afterward—was a popular courtship activity.[56] The Jocelyn sisters, daughters of a New Haven engraver, were escorted during the 1840s by a steady supply of beaux to the "Young Men's Institute." Sometimes one young man named James Bradford Cleaveland took two of the siblings, evidently to impress his beloved with his gallantry but also to get his tickets' full value. "Mr Cleaveland called this evening to go to the institute Lecture with Cornelia and me," Elizabeth Jocelyn wrote in her diary in 1849. "Cornelia had been sick all day, and could not go, consequently Mr C . . . invited Miss Fuller to accompany us."[57] A few days later he took Elizabeth and her sister Frances to a talk by Thomas D'Arcy McGee, the Irish immigrant editor of the *American Celt*, which was titled "The Three Kingdoms" (i.e., England, Ireland, and Scotland).[58] Cleaveland's strategy paid off: three years later Elizabeth married her dashing escort.

Women could go alone, of course, and pay a higher individual rate. One broadside announced: "Tickets for a single person 50 cents—Lady and gentleman 75." However, gender conventions may have discouraged women's solo excursions.[59] Sometimes only single tickets, at 12½ cents, were available for popular lectures.[60] Worcester's John Park, a retired women's academy teacher, purchased separate season tickets for himself, his wife, and their daughter so they could go their own ways.[61] But cost was often no deterrent. "Hall was full at 25 cts [a] ticket," one stonemason's wife groused after a John Gough lecture.[62]

Although men laid out the cash, women often held the purse strings. Account books show that they bought family tickets, probably while shopping for other goods. For a ship chandler's wife, one day's expenses included "Turkey," "Vegetables," "Fish," a "Gas Bill," and "Tickets for Rev. T[homas] Stone's lectures on English literature" at "02.00."[63] Sponsors sold tickets at bookstores and other establishments where women shopped or mailed letters. Tickets for the Cambridge Lyceum's twelve-course season could "be had at the University Bookstore, and Mr. Munroe's Bookstore, next [to] the Post Office," or for the Salem Lyceum at "Mr. Buffam's bookstore."[64] Appealing to motherly instincts evidently boosted sales. One poster tugged at women's sympathies: "The proceeds of the tickets to be given for the benefit of the Infant school in this village."[65] Sponsors knew how to connect with female audiences.

Having tickets was one thing, but using them was another. Most lecture courses ran throughout the winter, when New England ice and snow alternately piled high and melted into slushy troughs. Either way, women's floor-length dresses and capes soaked it up like sponges. "Cousin William called & said it was so bad walking he advised us not to attempt going to the Hall," a minister's daughter lamented in March 1829. "I was quite disappointed, as I wish to hear Mr W[alker]."[66] Childcare also kept women at home, unless they could find babysitters. "I am housekeeper as it is Lyceum night," one young caretaker grumbled in 1852.[67] Tardy visitors were just as vexing. "I will not deny that I was a little disappointed that they stopped so late that I co'd not go to the last Shakespearian Lecture," complained Persis Andrews, a Maine lawyer's wife.[68] Flus and the sniffles also frustrated domestic nurses who cared for sick relatives.

Women fought the odds, however, because the worldly nurturing proffered by the lyceum was so vital to their intellectual well-being. Persis Andrews even left her children home asleep, unattended, in order to hear "Mr. [Rev. William A.] Drew's Lecture upon the 'World's Fair—in the glass Palace London.'"[69] Others risked frostbite and ruined garments. Mary Pierce, a minister's daughter living in Brookline, Massachusetts, grabbed winter by the horns to hear a travel lecture on Pompeii and Herculaneum: "Everybody here feels frightened out of their wits . . . & will not stir out of doors for fear of freezing. They do not know how much they lost."[70] Some dropped standards of feminine comportment and buffaloed through jam-packed crowds. Annie Lawrence and her two male escorts jostled for seats at a Shakespeare reading. "Notwithstanding the difficulty we had in getting in [we] were fully repaid," she declared.[71] To be sure, the cosmopolitan lyceum played hard to get, but it was worth the chase. The region's venerable institution was homey and, at the same time, exotic. One homesick Yankee woman sojourner in Macao summed it up best: "the ties that bind us to home, are very strong and not easily severed. The Lyceum lectures I miss beyond measure."[72] Even travel halfway around the globe could seem senseless when the world was at your doorstep.

Reception

Part of the lyceum's appeal for women was that it provoked thought and set new ideas in motion. Women may have ostensibly audited because they were dating, getting out of the house, or escaping into a fantasy. But no matter what their immediate reasons, they were invariably hungering for pieces of new information to fit into their cosmopolitan jigsaw. That Charlotte Forten thought Octavius Brooks Frothingham's 1857 lecture on Epicurus was "interesting and instructive" was the highest compliment.[73] To savor the orally delivered information at a future time, a few women stored it away in notes taken during the lectures; many more returned home to frantically scratch out synopses before memory faded.[74] Because fiddling with pencil and paper in the lecture hall could be distracting, and staying up late to write afterward could be exhausting, savvy suitors shared their scribblings with sweethearts. "Mr Peck called at noon and brought his notes on Dr Baird[']s Lecture," Frances Jocelyn noted in her diary.[75] Such was the value of studious record keeping. Only the most "poorly delivered" piece frustrated assiduous note takers.[76]

Where a native speaker's mumbling was unpardonable, a foreign visitor's fumbling was charming. Women often forgave accents even though they may have hindered note taking. So what if the pencils were tossed away? The information was still exciting. For female lecture-goers, such traces of national origins only enhanced the cosmopolitan sensibility, and so they commented favorably on them. For example, after Louis Agassiz delivered his first American lecture with heavy French overtones at Boston's Lowell Institute,[77] Charlotte Brooks Everett remarked that "his accent is very strong but the lecture was interesting."[78] A Boston editor's daughters went out the same evening and, according to their mother, "like[d] it exceedingly," even though their sewing circle "in general had not been able to understand him fully." But before pulling their science books back out, the seamstresses "lived in the hope that the next lecture would be more satisfactory."[79] Charlotte noted that after two months of practice, he was "very clear and interesting" about his glaciers.[80] Other lecturers spoke successfully in British English. Beneath George Combe's Scottish brogue, women detected clear-headed thinking on phrenology. Annie Lawrence admitted he was "not fluent but agreeable & distinct," and Sarah Jocelyn summed him up as a "thorough Scotchman," a compliment, evidently, to his national identity as well as his accent.[81] But visitors from England could confuse some auditors as well. While one woman "could hardly understand a word" of the rector of Welch Bicknor, classicist John Seager, her accompanying friend "could understand him without any difficulty." Although this minister's daughter had qualms with his "erroneous" ideas about the soul, she conceded that "Some of the passages were beautiful."[82] Cosmopolitan eloquence cut through the thickest accent and trumped religious differences.

Far more transgressive than speaking less-than-perfect English was speaking over auditors' heads. It seemed hypocritical to express cosmopolitanism in an exclusionary manner. Massachusetts' native son, historian George Bancroft, was the worst offender. Although one erudite woman enjoyed his "highly entertaining lecture upon Russian history" delivered at the local town hall, she regretted that "the language was not sufficiently simple for that portion of the audience, for whose instruction this course was established."[83] Women wanted cosmopolitanism to flourish. After hearing the first American biographer of the Prophet Mohammed, George Bush, lecture on Swedish philosopher Emanuel Swedenborg, a follower did "not think it was made *quite* so plain as it might have been, and as it ought to have been for those unacquainted with the doctrines"; she only hoped "it would at least . . . excite in them a desire to search and learn more."[84] Books might be the best antidote in such a case. Certainly, many women began to read up on a topic after hearing a lecture, regardless of the lucidity of the presentation. Conversely, lending books before lectures could broaden the cosmopolitan aura. For example, one of Elizabeth Jocelyn's suitors loaned her volumes by English historian Thomas Babington Macaulay and Romantic poet William Wordsworth before stepping out for a lecture on the Temple Periods in Jerusalem.[85] The mishmash of subjects made mental world-hopping all the more cosmopolitan.

Most women wanted something other than book knowledge from the cosmopolitan lyceum. They could read at home while sewing or nursing babies, between bouts of heavy lifting, or at the bedside of the ill. They could string beans while others read aloud to them. It was an appropriate activity for Sundays, when domestic chores were laid aside.[86] Lectures were different. For one, they got women out of the house. For another, they cemented social ties, whether they be romantic liaisons or neighborly bonds. However, the cosmopolitan lecture, as a window on the world, needed to deliver a unique product—a relativistic universe that seemed like no other. Charlotte Forten, for example, explained in 1854 that "I have read so much about the Holy Land I should have preferred hearing a lecture on some subject with which I was less familiar." The complaint was well taken by other women wanting something unusual.[87] But what made a lecture so special?

Surely hearing was part of it. Books talked only metaphorically. Although New Englanders were famous for reading aloud, they were not all professionals. Having Shakespeare's printed words come alive by experts like Fanny Kemble, who could read with the proper tone, understanding, and eloquence, was a transcendent experience for those used to the next-door neighbor's rendition. The same was true for other gems of English literature. "One enjoys the Faery Queene on hearing it well read, the ancient spelling preventing in a measure a person from enjoying it by themselves," Annie Lawrence remarked after hearing Francis Gray deliver excerpts from Edmund Spenser's epic poem.[88] In an age before recording technology, these performances were once-in-a-lifetime events that bridged past with present, the United States with the world. Not all sounds were so familiar. Christopher Hatchik Oscanyan at times "sang, chanted and prayed," to convey melodic strains of a mosque.[89] Refugee Christophorus Plato Castanis was known for his national airs and war songs of the Greek Revolution. These became selling points in letters of introduction written by lecture sponsors promoting his tours.[90] Frances Jocelyn found "his singing, recitations &c were very interesting."[91] Aurilla Moffitt, a Providence stablekeeper's wife, felt "well repaid for going" to his lecture because of "the lively Prof's description of oriental life &c."[92] What was this mysterious "etcetera" noted by both women? It could have been "the war-cries of Turk and Greek" or "the calls of the Islam Priests from the Minarets" that John Park heard resounding in Worcester's Brinley Hall.[93] Castanis's own vividly detailed books, which were advertised on lyceum posters, were no match for these echoes from afar.[94]

Besides sound, women often remarked on the visual elements distinguishing lectures from books. Castanis must have realized the audience appeal. The "curiosities and customs" he brought to lectures "fill a void which no reading can supply," one letter of introduction averred.[95] Broadsides announced he would "appear in his Martial costume" and that "Grecian and Turkish curiosities" would be exhibited, including "articles pertaining to the costumes of Grecian ladies . . . embroidered with gold" and the "identical Sword of Lord Byron," who joined the Greek revolutionaries—two bows to female readers of Byron. By some accounts, Castanis wore the sword at performances.[96] Christopher Hatchik Oscanyan also adorned himself in "the costumes of . . . the Sultan, and of a Bashi bozouk [Ottoman soldier]" while lecturing.[97] Cartes de visite show him in native dress, as does the frontispiece of his 1857 illustrated book, *The Sultan and His People.* Oscanyan also exhibited material artifacts, such as the tiny coffee cups Annie Lawrence recorded seeing, and sometimes dolls dressed in women's native garb.[98] He further capitalized on his "foreignness" by opening a New York gift shop and "Turkish saloon," or coffee shop, in 1855.[99] For many women, these props made all the difference; book illustrations, after all, paled before the real thing. Still, Oscanyan pitched some images at "it-getter" cosmopolitan women in his book, including the illustration entitled "What If a Turban!" (fig. 2.2). "The only occasion on which a foreigner might be permitted to appear in his own every-day clothes, would be at some fancy

FIGURE 2.2. Detail of illustration from Christopher Oscanyan, *The Sultan and His People* (1857). *Courtesy American Antiquarian Society.*

ball, as if in masquerade," he half jestingly wrote. "The fastidious ladies of upper-tendom show symptoms of nervous agitation, as you unwittingly mount their steps in your native head-gear, which may chance to be a sombrero, or a Turkish fess—what if a turban!"[100] The visual joke was not on Turks but on narrow-minded Boston Brahmins.

Sometimes props themselves stole the show, especially if manufactured abroad. European manikins used to illustrate anatomy introduced women to a global economy of medicine and health. One 1840 visitor to New York City from rural Maine, Mary Hoskins, marveled at an example of French anatomist Louis Thomas Jérôme Auzoux's models of the human body created, supposedly, "for popular lectures before mixed audiences"[101] but esteemed by contemporary surgeons, naturalists, and anatomists.[102] The papier-mâché manikin, mass produced in Auzoux's factory and replete with nerves, blood vessels, muscles, and organs, was ready and waiting as Hoskins entered the lecture hall.[103] It arguably outshined the lecturer, Gunning S. Bedford, who, as Hoskins was sure to note, "obtained [it] from Paris."[104] "It was a startling & thrilling, and unpleasant sight, which first met the eye . . . upon entering the room," she wrote to a friend, "but fear and terror, were quickly absorbed and overpowered by curiosity and interest, as the lecturer proceeded to show, and explain to us, the wonderful construction." Hoskins was fascinated that Bedford "operated" the body "by a knowledge of the screws and fastenings by which it was put together" and allowed her to further examine it.[105] Italian wax anatomical "venuses" were exhibited in Boston by émigrés Antonio Sarti and his wife, who addressed male and female audiences, respectively.[106] A Boston cooper's daughter who, with her normal school classmates, saw the model and heard Madame Sarti lecture in her home in 1851 was "very much interested."[107]

Larger-scale models interested women, too. Lectures on Jerusalem, intended as Christian instruction but offering histories of the city and its excavation, morphed into descriptions of models illustrating the spoken word. One rural Vermonter was so entranced by a replica of the city that she sat through two lectures about it in 1850.[108] If it was anything like Brunetti's famous model that took "nearly 20 years' study and labor" to construct, then it was the product of global economies of art, exploration, architecture, and exhibition. Based on early-nineteenth-century research by English artist Frederick Catherwood and American explorer Edward Robinson, the model was more than an evangelical tool; it embodied networks of international interventions into the history of an iconic urban center and left global footprints in its exhibition trail. The model was first displayed in Dublin in 1846, then in Liverpool and Manchester, before traveling through Europe and the United States.[109] When it finally landed in Paris, Maine, in 1849, it enthralled Persis Andrews. "The model—I think—is the result of great research,—but the lecturer is full of cant & twang."[110] Illustrative artifacts could speak for themselves and drown out even the most boring lecturer.

It is easy to think that women—bound to the home and domesticity—hungered for any exotic novelty to come their way, but their diaries and correspondence show they were discriminating about the quality of props and lecture content. Cosmopolitan women detected hoaxes, perhaps because they defiled the spirit of cultural and historical relativism. In 1838 Mary Pierce snickered at Sanborn's famous illuminated diagrams titled "History of Babylon." Although handbills ballyhooed his "40 splendid paintings, nearly eight feet in diameter" of the Temple of Memnon, Palmyra, and the Hanging Garden,[111] these were evidently recycled transparencies (paintings lit from behind) of contemporary Boston. Remnants of the old paintings peeked through the new in a bricolage of times and places. Poor detected Boston's Old South Church, popping up in the streets of ancient Babylon, and she noticed that King Belshazzar and his lords sat in contemporary chairs around a stylish dining table during the infamous "feast" documented in the Book of Daniel. She and her escorts "laughed the whole time" at the farce.[112] Mary's cosmopolitanism, like that of many women, reached deeper, beyond shallow facades of worldliness, into a search for knowledge.

That knowledge usually came in relativist wrappings. New information could break down stereotypes perpetrated by the unenlightened. One schoolteacher who deemed Bayard Taylor's lecture "The Arabs" to be "quite interesting" noted that he "thinks travellers misrepresent them."[113] Relativism could seemingly remedy national ills. Martha Osborne Barrett took from Edwin P. Whipple's lecture on cheerfulness the notion that "we are a nation of *grumblers*" who would benefit by reading the presumably more optimistic British poets.[114] But knowledge for its own sake, about cultural difference, was good enough. Annie Lawrence relished Christopher Oscanyan's descriptions of etiquette in two worlds: "He then described a grandee's mansion by fancying an American paying a visit to an Osmanlan gentleman; & the very different manner of receiving a stranger; saluting him &c. from the European or American fashion."[115] Cosmopolitanism encompassed the everyday.

In their quest for information, women also aspired to ethical and moral principles and fashioned an awareness of their "obligations" to others. They appreciated the "dramas of appraisal," as Tom Wright calls them, by which "performers brought reformist themes to the platform."[116] Because women took these international "dramas" so seriously, they held speakers of all nations to high standards of humanitarianism. "He is worthy of the glorious cause and that is a high compliment," Aurilla Moffitt wrote of temperance advocate John Gough. "I think him calculated to have a vast influence."[117] International stars could sometimes catalyze reform at home. We can also detect women's devotion to a worldly consciousness in their criticisms of lecturers who seemed to violate these sensibilities. Even Ralph Waldo Emerson was taken to task for his assessment of France. After hearing him for the first time in 1855, Charlotte Forten confessed to her diary that his lecture "was very interesting and entertaining though not particularly flattering does *his* estimate seem to be of the gay and fickle inhabitants of 'la belle France.' "[118] For Forten, reading about the country that had abolished the slave trade served as a critique of the U.S. government's sanction of slavery. After engaging a geography of France and longing to visit there, she sighed, "I wish that I could cast away some of these day-dreams—forget these vain hopes of the Future, which I fear too often prevent me from engaging earnestly enough in the actual labor of the Present," meaning, the abolition of slavery.[119] Any swipe at France was a swipe at her. She also took to task Benjamin C. Clark, described by one newspaper as "a Boston merchant of the conservative class,"[120] for his compromised antislavery message. "The lecturer spoke eloquently of the Haytians . . . and paid a well-deserved tribute to the brave and unfortunate Toussaint," she noted. "I was beginning to think him an earnest friend of freedom, when he proved to be a colonizationist." Quoting Byron, she wrote, "a very decided and unpleasant 'change came o'er the spirit of my dream.' "[121] Literature was enlisted to combat the misguided.

Reactionaries of all sorts rubbed cosmopolitan women the wrong way. The French social philosophy export of Fourierism was rigorously defended by Vermont native and former millworker Mary Paul against Unitarian minister Samuel K. Lothrop's condemnation. "Charles Fourier[']s doctrines . . . have enough of truth in them to keep them alive until the world shall be ready for them—and I am confident that it will take more than one lecture from Dr. Lothrop to annihilate" them, she fumed.[122] Mary Poor had it in for literary critic and High Church Episcopalian Henry Norman Hudson because of his elitist "Whig use of Shakespeare"[123] and for repeating in two lectures on Lear and Othello, respectively, some tired old interpretations: "On the whole I was disappointed, though interested. There was not much new light thrown on the characters, & he threw in episodes w'h showed him to be a bitter conservative & high-ch[urch] man. This behavior in company is anything but refined & gentlemanly."[124] Mary Poor herself identified with the more conservative American Whig Party,[125] but Hudson's recruitment of the Bard for unprogressive political agendas seemed out of place at the lecture hall. Other women read into Shakespeare's works a universalism that transcended class, and so expected the democratic spirit to guide those who purported to know him well. One, who was gearing up for Shakespeare readings by Fanny Kemble in 1857, could not let rest unsavory rumors about her snobbery.[126] The foreign born were not let off the hook.

So when Hungarian revolutionary and refugee Lajos Kossuth came to the United States in 1851 to raise money for his cause and to plead for aid against Russian and Austrian troops, many women questioned his positions despite his fiery speeches and grand tour. One woman went to the town lyceum debate in Vergennes, Vermont, to weigh in on intervention but left grumbling, "It was not as instructive as we expected."[127] Martha Osborne Barrett objected to the hoopla over Kossuth and his unwillingness to unite the cause of abolitionism to his own—in effect, to enlist the cosmopolitan ethic. After hearing Andrew Leete Stone deliver yet another laudatory lyceum lecture on the Magyar, she impugned him: "All are panygeric of the 'great Hungarian,' who our countrymen are making a *god* of just now and worshipping," she groaned. "The selfish Hungarian, who feels no oppression but that which is felt directly by his own nation, who dares not utter one word in disapproval of the tyrants of the United States, as one word of cheer to our own oppressed. O! Kossuth, how has thy glory departed thy brightness before our eyes."[128] Other women, like the Jocelyn sisters, instead saw international hand shaking in "the tricolored flag of Hungary [that] waved from the Liberty pole in company with our '*star spangled banner*' " at the New Haven state house.[129] Cosmopolitanism was a complex stance for women. They could divide over international issues, the global spread of reform, social movements, and class consciousness while still embracing cosmopolitanism at the lyceum. It was not a simple matter of cultural relativism, because cosmopolitanism was often a mirror on problems that were closer to home.

One of the problems was the withholding of full citizenship rights to women. Although only one or two of the women presented here pondered the issue of women's suffrage, most of them assumed a party affiliation and took definitive stances on legislation. Some, including Mary Pierce and Sarah Jocelyn, even campaigned for candidates during election season. New England women also commented on the global political arena and sometimes played instrumental roles as wives and daughters of politicians; most notable among these are Persis Sibley Andrews and Annie Lawrence. Yet these women endorsed an electoral system in which they were denied the right to participate fully. They developed a mainstream political consciousness equal to that of men but were marginalized because of their disfranchisement.[130]

Women's active and pervasive presence in lecture halls in antebellum New England and their interest in international topics discussed there prompts a reimagining of the cultural history from which these female auditors have been largely elided. As women responded to lectures in their diaries and letters they provide *prima facie* evidence of Woman Thinking, an intellection not solely based on private reading but on public listening, too. It is an important distinction. Lecture-goers of both sexes, whether in the halls themselves or in conversations and correspondence afterwards about what transpired there, thus witnessed firsthand actual women thinking. Writing women back into the picture of the American mind in this way expands the imaginary of what was *public*—traditionally, a masculinized term preconditioned upon formal civic participation—about the public lecture. Seen in a different light, when women are included in the specific public that lecturers addressed, it changes both how the lectures themselves should today be read and the manner in which the phenomenon of the lyceum can be understood. Insofar as the audience encompassed both men with full citizenship rights and women with limited ones, it becomes difficult to see that successful public lecturers could easily utter only an unalloyed expression of the muscular (read: male) "democratic" spirit. To some degree, then, speakers' dilemma of addressing a mixed-gender audience encouraged international topics and references from the podium, possibly with the intent of garnering attention from women who might find a boastful, androcentric nationalism unappealing or simply irrelevant.

Little wonder that disfranchised women naturally gravitated toward international lectures. After all, they could as easily imagine themselves citizens of the world as they could deem themselves citizens of their own country.[131] In a cosmopolitan world, national boundaries tumbled and, with them, local hierarchies of civic rights based on gender, race, ethnicity, and class. In the cosmopolitan lyceum, auditing took place on equal grounds with men; everyone could come away filled with the same knowledge, regardless of their education, property, or muscle at the polls. Perhaps women felt even more at home than men in the lecture hall when cosmopolitanism set the rules. As a truly democratic institution, then, the lyceum was at its best when it invited the world to stand at its podium and women, as well as other disfranchised Americans, to seat themselves at its table.

NOTES

1. Annie Lawrence, 11 December 1838, Diary, Lamb Family Papers, Massachusetts Historical Society (hereafter, MHS); "Miscellany," *Farmer's Cabinet,* 28 December 1838. On the Masonic Temple, see Helen R. Deese and Guy R. Woodall, "A Calendar of Lectures Presented by the Boston Society for the Diffusion of Useful Knowledge," *Studies in the American Renaissance* (1986), 24.

2. "A Turk," *Baltimore Sun,* 16 May 1838; "Lectures on Turkey," *New York American,* 26 December 1838. On Oscanyan, see Susan Nance, *How the Arabian Nights Inspired the American Dream, 1790–1935* (Chapel Hill: University of North Carolina Press, 2009), 55–64.

3. Fanny Kemble, "Lectures on Turkey," in *Journal of Frances Anne Kemble,* 2 vols. (Philadelphia: Carey, Lea and Blanchard, 1835); Frances M. Trollope, *Domestic Manners of the Americans* (London: Whittaker, Treacher, 1832); Basil Hall, *Travels in North America in the Years 1827 and 1828* (Edinburgh: Cadell, 1829).

4. Lawrence, 11 and 18 December 1838, Diary.

5. "A local proto-ethnographic ethic of enlightened relativism cultivated by culture consumers" (273) in the Boston area is discussed in Ronald J. Zboray and Mary Saracino Zboray, "Between 'Crockery-dom' and Barnum: Boston's Chinese Museum, 1845–1847," *American Quarterly* 56, no. 2 (June 2004): 271–307; on Lawrence as lecture-goer, see 288–89.

6. Lawrence, 20 December 1838; 3, 17, 18, and 24 January 1839; 1 and 8 February 1839; and 25 and 28 March 1839, Diary. On Gray's lecture, see Deese and Woodall, "Calendar of Lectures," 48.

7. On the address's audience, see Kenneth S. Sacks, *Understanding Emerson: "The American Scholar" and His Struggle for Self-Reliance* (Princeton: Princeton University Press, 2003), 2, 5, 12–13. On *Nature,* see Margaret Fuller to Ralph Waldo Emerson, 21 September 1836, and Ralph Waldo Emerson to Elizabeth Palmer Peabody, 15 November 1836, in *Letters of Ralph Waldo Emerson,* vol. 2, *1836–1841,* ed. Ralph L. Rusk and Eleanor M. Tilton (New York: Columbia University Press, 1939), 36, 46; Mary Pierce to John Pierce and Lucy Tappan Pierce, 16 November 1838, Poor Family Papers (hereafter, PFP), Schlesinger Library (hereafter, SL), Radcliffe Institute for Advanced Study, Harvard University. On lectures, see, for example, the diary entries of Laura Payson Hopkins from [n.d.] January and 31 January 1837, reprinted in *Life and Letters of Elizabeth Payson Prentiss,* ed. George Lewis Prentiss (New York: A. D. F. Randolph, 1882), 205; *Salem Gazette,* 19 and 22 April 1836; Mary Ann Laughton, 13 March 1838, Diary, Mary Ann Laughton Papers, Phillips Library, Peabody Essex Museum (hereafter, PL-PEM); Lucy Tappan Pierce to Lucy Pierce Hedge, 19 February [1840?], PFP, SL.

8. *Collected Works of Ralph Waldo Emerson: Nature, Addresses, Lectures,* ed. Robert E. Spiller and Alfred Riggs Ferguson (Cambridge: Belknap Press of Harvard University Press, 1971), 53. Others have similarly played on Emerson's term: Tiffany K. Wayne, *Woman Thinking: Feminism and Transcendentalism in Nineteenth-Century America* (Lanham, Md.: Lexington Books, 2005); and Mary Kelley, *Learning to Stand and Speak: Women, Education, and Public Life in America's Republic* (Chapel Hill: University of North Carolina Press, 2006), 153.

9. Martha Osborne Barrett to Moses Cartland, 27 April 1852, Cartland Family Papers, MS Am1752, Houghton Library, Harvard University. Barrett was unemployed at this time but occasionally taught school and did piecework until 1855, when she found steady factory employment; "Half of Our Citizens," *South Danvers Observer* 4, no. 3 (Spring 2010): 3, available at www.peabodylibrary.org/history/observer/South_Danvers_Observer_Spring_2010.pdf.

10. Donald M. Scott, "The Popular Lecture and the Creation of a Public in Mid-Nineteenth-Century America," *Journal of American History* 66, no. 4 (March 1980): 791–809; Carl Bode, *The American Lyceum: Town Meeting of the Mind* (New York: Oxford University Press, 1956); Mary Kupiec Cayton, "The Making of an American Prophet: Emerson, His Audiences, and the Rise of the Culture Industry in Nineteenth-Century America," *American Historical Review* 92, no. 3 (June 1987): 597–620. Cayton argues that Emerson's audience was male (604–7). Studies besides the above that touch on women include Richard D. Brown, *The Strength of a People: The*

Idea of an Informed Citizenry in America, 1650–1870 (Chapel Hill: University of North Carolina Press, 1996), 128; Cecil B. Hayes, *The American Lyceum: Its History and Contribution to Education* (Washington, DC: United States Office of Education, 1932); J. G. Holland, "The Popular Lecture," *Atlantic Monthly* 15 (March 1865): 365, 367, 369; and Carl David Mead, *Yankee Eloquence in the Middle West: The Ohio Lyceum, 1850–1870* (East Lansing: Michigan State College Press, 1951), 121. See also Thomas Wentworth Higginson, *Part of a Man's Life* (1905; repr., Port Washington, NY: Kennikat Press, 1971), 78; Kenneth Walter Cameron, ed., *The Massachusetts Lyceum during the American Renaissance* (Hartford, CT: Transcendental Books, 1969), esp. Henry K. Oliver, "Historical Sketch of the Salem Lyceum . . . ," 6; and Edward Everett Hale, "Lectures and Lecturers," in *Modern Eloquence,* 15 vols., ed. Thomas B. Reed et al. (Philadelphia: J. D. Morris, 1900) 4:xxi.

11. Angela G. Ray, "Frederick Douglass on the Lyceum Circuit: Social Assimilation, Social Transformation?" *Rhetoric and Public Affairs* 5, no. 4 (Winter 2002): 625–47; Angela G. Ray, *The Lyceum and Public Culture in the Nineteenth-Century United States* (East Lansing: Michigan State University Press, 2005), 57–62. According to Ray, women participated in and attended public debates as well; see Angela G. Ray, "The Permeable Public: Rituals of Citizenship in Antebellum Men's Debating Clubs," *Argumentation and Advocacy* 41, no. 1 (June 2004): 6–10. On the lyceum as a forum for advocating women's rights, see Angela G. Ray, "What Hath She Wrought? Woman's Rights and the Nineteenth-Century Lyceum," *Rhetoric and Public Affairs* 9, no. 2 (Summer 2006): 183–213.

12. Ronald J. Zboray and Mary Saracino Zboray, *Everyday Ideas: Socioliterary Experience among Antebellum New Englanders* (Knoxville: University of Tennessee Press, 2006), chap. 10.

13. On our method, see ibid., xx–xxv.

14. Thomas Fitzpatrick Wright, "Britain on the American Popular Lecture Circuit, 1844–1865" (PhD diss., University of Cambridge, 2010).

15. Ronald J. Zboray and Mary Saracino Zboray, *Literary Dollars and Social Sense: A People's History of the Mass Market Book* (New York: Routledge, 2005), 161.

16. Brown, *Strength of a People,* 130.

17. They informally acquired rhetorical skills that, as Nan Johnson reminds us, "were the undisputed province of the male professional classes"; Nan Johnson, *Gender and Rhetorical Space in American Life, 1866–1919* (Carbondale: Southern Illinois University Press, 2002), 3. Zboray and Zboray, *Everyday Ideas,* 206–14.

18. Nancy F. Cott, *The Bonds of Womanhood: "Woman's Sphere" in New England, 1780–1835* (New Haven: Yale University Press, 1977).

19. Kwame Anthony Appiah, *Cosmopolitanism: Ethics in a World of Strangers* (New York: Norton, 2006).

20. Anne K. Mellor, "Embodied Cosmopolitanism and the British Romantic Woman Writer," *European Romantic Review* 17, no. 3 (2006): 289–300; her definition also encompasses "a primary commitment to the interests of humanity as a whole [and] a desire to understand other cultures and customs" (289).

21. The phrase was perhaps most famously used in David Walker, *Walker's Appeal, in Four Articles Together with a Preamble, to the Coloured Citizens of the World. . . .* (Boston: By the author, 1829).

22. Heather Roberts, "'The Public Heart': Urban Life and the Politics of Sympathy in Lydia Maria Child's Letters from New York," *American Literature* 76, no. 4 (December 2004): 749–75; Barbara Pauk, "'The Parisian Beau Monde': Frances Trollope's Representations of France," *Women's Writing* 18, no. 2 (May 2011): 256–72; Richard Bonfiglio, "Proximate Cosmopolitanism: The Transnational Work of Victorian Domesticity, 1848–1875" (PhD diss., University of Chicago, 2010); Susan Toth Lord, "Extraordinary Women All: The Influence of Madame de Staël on Margaret Fuller and Lydia Maria Child" (PhD diss., Kent State University, 2004); Katy Brundan, "Cosmopolitan Complexities in Maria Edgeworth's *Ennui,*" *Studies in the Novel* 37, no. 2 (Summer 2005): 123–30; Philip Gould, "Catherine Sedgwick's Cosmopolitan Nation," *New England Quarterly* 78, no. 2 (June 2005): 232–58.

23. Ronald J. Zboray, *A Fictive People: Antebellum Economic Development and the American Reading Public* (New York: Oxford University Press, 1993), chap. 11; Ronald J. Zboray and Mary Saracino Zboray, "Political News and Female Readership in Antebellum Boston and Its Region," *Journalism History* 22, no. 1 (Spring 1996): 2–14.

24. Kristin L. Hoganson, "Cosmopolitan Domesticity: Importing the American Dream, 1865–1920," *American Historical Review* 107, no. 1 (February 2002): 55–84, quote on 83.

25. Zboray and Zboray, "Between 'Crockery-dom' and Barnum," 272; Jonathan Goldstein, "Cantonese Artifacts, Chinoiserie, and Early American Idealization of China," in *America Views China: American Images of China Then and Now,* ed. Jonathan Goldstein, Jerry Israel, and Hilary Conroy (Bethlehem, PA: Lehigh University Press, 1991), 43–55. Ping Chia Kuo, "Canton and Salem: The Impact of Chinese Culture upon New England during the Post-Revolutionary Era," *New England Quarterly* 3 (July 1930): 420–42.

26. Konstantin Dierks, "Letter Writing, Stationery Supplies, and Consumer Modernity in the Eighteenth-Century Atlantic World," *Early American Literature* 41, no. 3 (2006): 473–94.

27. Sarah Smith Cox Browne, Account Book, [n.d.] December and 9 July 1839; [n.d.] May 1840, Browne Family Papers (hereafter, BFP), SL.

28. Kristin L. Hoganson, *Consumers' Imperium: The Global Production of American Domesticity, 1865–1920* (Chapel Hill: University of North Carolina Press, 2007), 255.

29. Tom Genrich, *Authentic Fictions: Cosmopolitan Writing of the Troisième République, 1908–1940* (Oxford: Peter Lang, 2004), 25–28.

30. Lawrence, 20 November 1845, Diary; Frances Jocelyn, 22 June 1848, Diary, Jocelyn Family Papers (hereafter, JFP), Connecticut Historical Society (hereafter, CHS), Hartford; Forten, 28 February 1855, in *The Journals of Charlotte Forten Grimké,* ed. Brenda Stevenson (New York: Oxford University Press, 1988), 129; Frances Jocelyn, 23 June 1848; Eunice Hale Wait Cobb, 15 December 1853, Diary, New England Historic Genealogical Society (hereafter, NEHGS); Elizabeth Atwater Charnley, 8 May 1838, Diary, CHS; Elizabeth Jocelyn, 6 January 1848, Diary, JFP, CHS. Emmeline Augusta Ober, 31 January 1851, Diary, Beverly (MA) Historical Society.

31. See, for example, Forten, 8 November 1854, *Journals,* 109; Persis Sibley Andrews [Black], 11 March 1849, Diary, vol. 6, coll. 206, Collections of the Maine Historical Society, Portland; Susan Tucker, 12–14 March 1850, Diary, Vermont Historical Society, Barre (hereafter, VHS); Frederick Gleason, 15 and 22 December 1859, Diary, CHS; John Park, November 20 1845, Diary, Courtesy of the Trustees of the Boston Public Library / Rare Books (hereafter, BPL). We cite men's diaries when they reveal information about women attendees.

32. Tom F. Wright, "The Results of Locomotion: Bayard Taylor and the Travel Lecture in the Mid-Nineteenth-Century United States," *Studies in Travel Writing* 14, no. 2 (June 2010): 114.

33. Forten, 7 July 1854, *Journals,* 82. Zboray and Zboray, *Everyday Ideas,* 212.

34. Martha Osborne Barrett, 14 February 1855, Diary, PL-PEM.

35. Abigail M. N. Lummus, 19 December 1850, Diary, Abigail Makepeace (Newhall) Lummus Diaries, PL-PEM; Mary Hall, 30 December 1835, Diary, New Hampshire Historical Society, Concord.

36. Frances Jocelyn, 14 and 26 June, 6 July 1848, Diary; Elizabeth Jocelyn, 14 and 16 June 1848, Diary. One newspaper report criticized Baird's relativism regarding foreign governments; see *Berkshire County Whig,* 10 April 1845.

37. Lucy Tappan Pierce to Lucy Pierce Hedge, 19 February [1840?]. Ober, 1 November 1852, Diary; Cornelia Jocelyn, 9 January 1851, Diary, JFP, CHS. Forten, 14 January 1857, *Journals,* 182. Park, 20 January 1842, Diary. Lawrence, 27 December 1839, Diary.

38. Hall, 20 January 1836, Diary.

39. Elizabeth Jocelyn, 4 February 1852, Diary. Park, 15 March 1838, Diary. Martha Jane (Weston) Averill, 11 March 1857, Diary, Martha Jane (Weston) Averill Papers, PL-PEM. Tucker, 1 May 1850, Diary. Frances Jocelyn, 27 and 28 January 1852, Diary. Forten, 2 January 1856, *Journals,* 148.

40. For evidence of women reading international literature, see Ronald J. Zboray and Mary Saracino Zboray, "Books, Reading, and the World of Goods in Antebellum New England,"

American Quarterly 48, no. 4 (December 1996), 594, 602, 612–13, n. 24; Zboray, *A Fictive People*, 165–73; and Zboray and Zboray, *Everyday Ideas*, passim.

41. See, for example, Mary Crowninshield Mifflin, 1 March 1850, 6 April 1854, 5 March 1857, 7 December 1859, 18 February 1860, Diary, BPL; Sarah Preston Everett Hale, 9 December 1859, Diary, Hale Family Papers (hereafter, HFP), Sophia Smith Collection (hereafter, SSC), Smith College.

42. Ellen Wright to Martha Coffin Wright, 11 January 1861, Garrison Family Papers, SSC.

43. Marian Wilson Kimber, "Reading Shakespeare, Seeing Mendelssohn: Concert Reading of *A Midsummer Night's Dream*, ca. 1850–1920," *Music and Culture* 89, nos. 2–3 (2007): 199–236. On objections, see, for example, Mary Pierce Poor to Lucy Pierce Hedge, 17 January 1857, PFP, SL. For the gender politics of ventriloquy, see Elizabeth D. Harvey, *Ventriloquized Voices: Feminist Theory and English Renaissance Texts* (New York: Routledge, 1995).

44. Sarah Smith Cox Browne to Nellie Browne, [n.d., 1857?], BFP, SL. Mary Gardner Lowell, 9 March 1847, Diary, Francis Cabot Lowell Papers, MHS. Olive Gay Worcester, 9 February 1852, Diary, Swanton Family Papers (hereafter, SFP), SL. Park, 21 February 1846, Diary. Caroline Barrett White, 24 January 1850, Diary, octavo vol. 1, courtesy American Antiquarian Society (hereafter, AAS).

45. Forten, 25 February 1857, *Journals*, 196.

46. Martha Osborne Barrett, 9 January 1855, Diary.

47. Eyre Crow, *With Thackeray in America* (London: Cassell, 1893), 47, 111. Caroline Cary Curtis, 4 January 1853, Diary, Cary Family Papers III, MHS.

48. Mary Gardner Lowell, 20 December 1853, Diary; Forten, 6 December 1854, *Journals*, 115.

49. *Teachers' Institute in Worcester* (Worcester, MA: n.p., 1854), American Broadsides and Ephemera, Series 1 (hereafter, ABES1), no. 9045, AAS.

50. Edward Lurie, *Louis Agassiz: A Life in Science* (Chicago: University of Chicago Press, 1960), 144; Ellen Wright to Martha Coffin Wright, [n.d.] October 1860.

51. Lawrence, 24 November 1838; 23, 24, 25, 27, and 29 November 1839; 6 and 12 December 1839, Diary; Daniel F. and Mary D. Child, 29 November 1839, Diary, Daniel Franklin Child Papers, MHS; Browne, [n.d.] December 1839, Account Book. On his political commentary, see George Combe, *Notes on the United States of North America, During a Phrenological Visit in 1838–9–40* (Philadelphia: Carey and Hart, 1841), 2:179–83, 197–98, 211–12; and Lawrence, 27 November 1839, Diary.

52. Park, 18 November 1841, Diary; Mary Mudge, 19 January 1854, Diary, SL.

53. Phebe Beede Clark, 23 April 1857, Lynn (MA) Museum and Historical Society.

54. "Mr. John B. Gough," *Constitution* (Middletown, CT), 3 May 1848. Philip Sage, 9–11 May 1848, Diary, CHS. At an earlier temperance lecture (26 March 1848), he recorded, "Saw about three hundred ladies—what a good opportunity to select one for life."

55. *Boston Lyceum Programm* [*sic*] (Boston: n.p., 1834), ABES1, no., 4596, AAS.

56. Zboray and Zboray, *Everyday Ideas*, 200–205; Elizabeth Jocelyn, 14 June 1848, Diary.

57. Elizabeth Jocelyn, 20 December 1849, Diary.

58. Elizabeth Jocelyn, 27 December 1849, Diary. On courtship and lectures, see Thomas Augst, *The Clerk's Tale: Young Men and Moral Life in Nineteenth-Century America* (Chicago: University of Chicago Press, 2003), 193.

59. *Dorchester and Milton Lyceum* (Dedham, MA: Eben. Fish, 1833), ABES1, no. 4472, AAS. *Historical Sketch of the Salem Lyceum, with a List of the Officers and Lecturers since Its Formation in 1830* (Salem, MA: Press of the Salem Gazette, 1879), 6.

60. *Greece!!* (Concord: New Hampshire Patriot Office, [1848?]), ABES1, no. 7121, AAS.

61. John Park, 7 December 1837, Diary.

62. Clark, 23 April [1857?]; "Affairs in and about the City," *Boston Daily Atlas*, 9 April 1857.

63. Browne, [n.d.] 1857, Account Book.

64. *Historical Sketch of the Salem Lyceum*, 5. See also *Lyceum Lectures* (Cambridge, MA: n.p., 1846), ABES1 no. 6729, AAS; and *Boston Lyceum Programm*.

65. *Dorchester and Milton Lyceum.*

66. Zboray and Zboray, *Everyday Ideas,* 203; Elizabeth Pierce, 5 March 1829, Journal, PFP, SL.

67. Ober, 10 March 1852, Diary.

68. Andrews, 15 May 1846, Diary, vol. 5.

69. Idem., 29 February 1852, Diary, vol. 7.

70. Mary Pierce to Henry Varnum Poor, 19 January 1840, PFP, SL.

71. Lawrence, 25 December 1840, Diary.

72. Rebecca Chase Kinsman to Maria Chase, 7 March 1844, Peabody Family Papers, Series III, SSC.

73. Forten, 14 January 1857, *Journals,* 182. On the importance of new ideas at lectures, see Zboray and Zboray, *Everyday Ideas,* 212–13.

74. Zboray and Zboray, *Everyday Ideas,* 43–45.

75. Frances Jocelyn, 26 June 1848, Diary.

76. See, for example, Charlotte Henrietta Pettibone, 12 December 1842, Diary, CHS.

77. Jules Marcou, *Life, Letters, and Works of Louis Agassiz* (New York: Macmillan, 1895), 1:288–89; 2:230–37.

78. Charlotte Brooks Everett, 8 December 1846, Diary, Edward Everett Papers, MHS.

79. Sarah P. E. Hale to Edward Everett Hale, [n.d.] December [1846], HFP, SSC.

80. Everett, 17 February 1847, Diary.

81. Lawrence, 24 November 1838, Diary; Sarah Jocelyn, 21 February 1840, Diary, JFP, CHS. The young Combe enrolled in elocution lessons to "improve" his English; see David Stack, *Queen Victoria's Skull* (London: Continuum Books, 2008), 21.

82. Elizabeth Pierce, 21 and 28 May 1829, Journal; John Seager, "Observations on the Phaedo of Plato," *Classical Journal* 62 (June 1825): 209–17.

83. Elizabeth Pierce, 19 February 1829, Journal.

84. Agnes Paine to Mary A. Byram, 9 December 1845, SFP, SL.

85. Elizabeth Jocelyn, 27 January 1848, Diary.

86. On reading and work rhythms, see Zboray and Zboray, *Everyday Ideas,* chap. 9.

87. Forten, 8 November 1854, *Journals,* 109. Lawrence, 20 November 1845, Diary.

88. Lawrence, 1 March 1839, Diary. On reading aloud, see Zboray and Zboray, "Books, Reading."

89. "Oscanyan's Lecture," *New York Herald,* 14 December 1856.

90. See C. Tracy to [?], 19 January 1849, and C. L. Richmond to H. Orcott, 27 July 1850, Christophorus Plato Castanis, Letters (hereafter, CPCL), AAS.

91. Frances Jocelyn, 29 October 1848, Diary.

92. Moffitt, 22 April 1850, Diary, Old Colony Historical Society, Taunton, MA.

93. Park, 10 January 1844, Diary.

94. On advertisements, see *Oriental Entertainment* (Concord: New Hampshire Patriot Office, 1848[?]), ABES1, 7187; and *Greece!!* Castanis's books include *An Essay on the Ancient and Modern Greek Languages* (Andover, MA: Allen, Morill and Wardwell, 1844); *The Greek Captive: A Narrative of the Captivity and Escape of Christophorus Plato Castanis. . . .* (Worcester, MA: Henry Howland, 1845); *A Love Tale: The Jewish Maiden of Scio's Citadel* (n.p.: Philergomathia, 1845); and *Oriental, Amusing, Instructive, and Moral Literary Dialogues. . . .* (Boston: J. Putnam, 1849).

95. J. S. Pattingill to Messrs. Campbell, Prentiss & others, 9 November 1847, CPCL, AAS.

96. *Oriental Entertainment.* Park, 10 January 1844, Diary; Reb[ecca?] Nager to Laura Wild, 13 November 1841, CPCL, AAS. On readers of Byron, see Zboray and Zboray, *Literary Dollars and Social Sense,* 94–95.

97. Advertisement, *New York Herald,* 27 November 1856.

98. For his carte de visite, see www.picturehistory.com/product/id/18794; Christopher Oscanyan, *The Sultan and His People* (New York: Derby and Jackson, 1857); and Nance, *Arabian Nights,* 59.

99. Nance, *Arabian Nights,* 58; "Orientalism in New York," *Boston Daily Atlas,* 8 June 1855.

100. Oscanyan, *Sultan and His People*, 172.

101. Mary G. Hoskins to Mary A. Byram, 22 May 1840, SFP, SL. "Artificial Anatomy," *Boston Medical and Surgical Journal* 22, no. 15 (20 May 1840): 242–43.

102. Regis Olry, "Wax, Wooden, Ivory, Cardboard, Bronze, Fabric, Plaster, Rubber and Plastic Anatomical Models: Praiseworthy Precursors of Plastinated Specimens," *Journal of the International Society of Plastination* 15, no. 1 (2000): 32. According to Antonio G. Valdecasas et al., Auzoux "understood the level of anatomical detail necessary to teach medical students"; Antonio G. Valdecasas, Ana M. Correas, Carmen R. Guerrero, and Jesus Juez, "Understanding Complex Systems: Lessons from Auzoux's and von Hagens's Anatomical Models," *Journal of Bioscience* 34, no. 6 (December 2009): 837, 838.

103. Saroya de Chadarevian and Nick Hopwood, "Dimensions of Modeling," in *Models, the Third Dimension of Science*, ed. Saroya de Chadarevian and Nick Hopwood (Stanford: Stanford University Press, 2004), 9, 180.

104. Hoskins to Byram, 22 May 1840. Bedford founded the medical college at New York University and the country's first obstetric clinic; see J. J. Walsh, "Gunning S. Bedford," *Catholic Encyclopedia* from *New Advent*, www.newadvent.org/cathen/02386a.htm; and Joseph G. Ryan, "Doctor Gunning S. Bedford (1806–70) and the Search for Safe Obstetric Care, 1833–70," *Journal of Medical Biography* 16 (2008): 134–43, 140 n. 2.

105. Hoskins to Byram, 22 May 1840.

106. Francesco Paolo de Ceglia, "The Importance of Being Florentine," *Nuncius* 26 (2011): 100–103. "Signor Sarti," *Daily Atlas*, 17 May 1850.

107. Helen Warner, 22, 27, and 28 January 1851, Diary, NEHGS.

108. Tucker, 12, 13, and 14 March 1850, Diary.

109. Advertisement, *Weekly Eagle*, 6 August 1849; Brunetti, of Dublin, *Description of the Model of Ancient Jerusalem* (Dublin: John Fowler, 1846).

110. Andrews, 11 March 1849, Diary, vol. 6.

111. *History of Babylon* (Boston: n.p., 1842), Printed Ephemera Collection, portfolio 57, folder 37, Library of Congress, Washington, DC. *History of Egypt and Babylon* [Massachusetts: n.p., 1839?], ABES1 no. 5474, AAS.

112. Mary Pierce to her parents, 3 May 1838, PFP, SL.

113. Mudge, 1 December 1854, Diary.

114. Barrett, 9 January 1855, Diary.

115. Lawrence, 11 December 1838, Diary.

116. Wright, "Locomotion," 111.

117. Moffitt, 12 December 1843, Diary.

118. Forten, 14 March 1855, *Journals*, 130.

119. Forten, 27 January 1855, *Journals*, 124.

120. "Affairs in and about the City," *Boston Daily Atlas*, 15 March 1855.

121. Forten, 28 March 1855, *Journals*, 132.

122. Mary Paul to Bela Paul, 12 April 1855, Marion E. Blake and Tuttle Items, VHS.

123. John Stafford, "Henry Norman Hudson and the Whig Use of Shakespeare," *PMLA* 66 (September 1951): 649–61.

124. Mary Pierce Poor to her parents, 31 May 1846, PFP, SL.

125. Zboray and Zboray, *Voices without Votes: Women and Politics in Antebellum New England* (Durham, NH: University Press of New England, 2010), 88–91.

126. Sarah Smith Cox Browne to Nellie Browne, [1857?].

127. Tucker, 2 January 1852, Diary.

128. Barrett, 22 February 1852, Diary.

129. Frances Jocelyn, 23 April 1852, Diary.

130. Many of the actors presented here appear in Zboray and Zboray, *Voices without Votes*, about women's partisanship; on Pierce and Jocelyn as campaigners, see 88–91 and 95, and on Andrews and Lawrence as influential political kin, see chap. 6 and 91–96. Charlotte Forten and Ellen

Wright, for example, alluded to global issues and international figures; see Zboray and Zboray, "New England Women and World Politics, 1830–1861," paper presented at the annual Society for Historians of the Early American Republic conference, 17 July 2010.

131. Other marginalized groups pursued a similar strategy; see, for example, Carla L. Peterson, *Black Gotham: A Family History of African Americans in Nineteenth-Century New York City* (New Haven: Yale University Press, 2011), 16, 92, 30.

3

Bringing Music to the Lyceumites

The Bureaus and the Transformation of Lyceum Entertainment

SARA LAMPERT

THE SALE OF season tickets for the Worcester Lyceum Course was particularly lively the weekend of October 17, 1874. The first local residents began lining up outside the box office at Mechanics Hall at seven o'clock the evening before the sale began, and their numbers totaled twenty-five by midnight. The course for 1874–75 was slated to open with Camilla Urso's Concert Company. A French violinist and impresario, Urso was an "established favorite" in Worcester and sold out every seat in Mechanics Hall for her October concert.[1] The lyceum committee had discovered that the cost of bringing a concert combination in place of a lecturer more than paid for itself in ticket sales.

During the 1870s, both of Worcester's major lyceum courses, the Worcester County Mechanics Association Course and the Lyceum Course (formerly the Lyceum and National History Association Course), included at least one concert combination in a season of six to eight evening entertainments. Over the fall and winter months, patrons of the 1874 Lyceum Course would also enjoy dramatic celebrity impersonations by Helen Potter, including her portrayal of temperance lecturer John B. Gough, and then be able to compare Potter's version to Gough himself when he came to speak in January. Bayard Taylor promised an edifying lecture based on his travels in Egypt, and English dramatic reader Mrs. Scott-Siddons would provide a combination of "culture and instruction" with her selections from Shakespeare and popular novels of the day.[2] Although the lyceum remained a vital and thriving American institution in the decades after the Civil War, it was no longer a pure medium for lecturing—if it ever had been. The composition of its entertainment was shifting, featuring a more diverse array of spectacles in addition to lecturing. This brought European celebrities into the lyceum while also creating another market for American performers who aspired to global careers.

Dramatic readings and musical performances had occupied a small place in the lyceum since the 1830s. But by the 1870s, dramatic readers, musical combinations, and stereopticon and other entertainments occupied a growing segment of lyceum lists and were actively promoted by lyceum bureaus and their agents. In the late 1860s, the formation of these centralized bureaus, which represented lecturers and performers and marketed them to local lyceum committees, had the effect of standardizing the business of lecturing and expanding the capacity of the lyceum to accommodate new forms of entertainment. In 1872, the Redpath Lyceum Bureau introduced its Musical Department, which more than doubled the number of musical offerings on its lists. Many of the artists were European celebrities, such as Urso, who headlined concert combinations consisting of foreign and American-born musicians. The lyceum bureaus both accessed and contributed to the transatlantic circulation of performers, seeking out international musical celebrities, such as Urso and German prima donna soprano Ermina Rudersdorff, and organizing concert combinations of foreign and native-born performers designed to appeal to a broad popular audience. The first wave of continental stars entered American markets in the 1840s, having been preceded by British performers for at least thirty years.[3] Significantly, the increase in musical entertainment in the lyceum had the combined effect of expanding the market for foreign artists in America while creating new avenues for American musicians to develop regional and national touring careers, travel to Europe to study and perform, and obtain the foreign pedigree needed to facilitate claims to musical celebrity with the American public.[4]

Some contemporary critics such as Josiah Gilbert Holland, who had toured as a lecturer in the 1850s, accused the Redpath and other bureaus of contributing to the decline of lecturing in America, a sentiment echoed by early historians of the lyceum.[5] However, the story is far more complex. To understand it fully, we must move beyond a declension narrative, in which the rise of the bureaus and the influx of entertainments is viewed as contributing to the decline of lecturing, and examine the relationship between changing business and promotional models and the shifting popularity of different kinds of amusements relative to each other and to the public. When we place entertainments, and music in particular, at the center of the narrative, we can better situate the lyceum as a key historical example of the larger nineteenth-century process of the incorporation of culture.[6]

Business practices for managing and promoting diverse forms of entertainment within regional and national markets were changing drastically in many culture industries, from vaudeville to the circus, and lyceum bureaus were at the vanguard.[7] The introduction of concert combinations, touring virtuosos, and even English operetta, along with the proliferation of new styles of popular lecturing, enabled the post–Civil War lyceum to continue to thrive in an increasingly competitive market. Furthermore, by introducing musical entertainments, the bureaus redefined the role of the lyceum while constructing a vision of middle-class consumer identity built around the discerning consumption of lecturing, dramatic reading, and music performed by foreign and native artists. But the model of consumption promoted by the bureaus was not the only one found in postbellum America, as music became the object of mounting debates over the relationship between art, the public, and the marketplace.

In *Dwight's Journal of Music,* Boston intellectual John Sullivan Dwight promoted a vision of musical performance organized around a sacralized hierarchy that required it to be free from the "pressures of the market place."[8] Dwight's own ideals met the interests of other musicians and impresarios including Theodore Thomas, who explored different cultural and economic models for musical performance, striving to navigate competing pressures to appeal to popular tastes while introducing American audiences to European art music.[9] One solution came in the form of endowed cultural institutions, among them the Chicago Symphony Orchestra. The lyceum bureaus, by contrast, drew foreign artists and art music into a new centralized and corporatized system of entertainment management, one that emphasized cultural eclecticism rather than sacralization and embraced the marketplace as a legitimate way of organizing and promoting culture.[10] Lyceum bureaus encouraged lyceum committees to embrace new marketing strategies and models for organizing courses and to embrace new types of entertainments and categories of stars as well, with a roster of performers that included the finest musical talent in the nation and the world.

The bureaus encouraged American lyceumites to imagine themselves as contributing to a global musical marketplace both by patronizing "world-wide" celebrities like Camilla Urso, who had performed before audiences in

Europe, Australia, and South America, and by bringing out and supporting American talent (fig. 3.1).[11] Thus, in the context of musical entertainment, the lyceum participated in a longer history of not only marketing foreign celebrities to American audiences but also demonstrating that America produced and sustained a market for native talent.

The stance of the lyceum toward both foreign and American artists was fundamentally nationalistic. In the context of the long-standing preoccupation of American cultural critics with the degree to which American culture and art was derivative of, dependent upon, and ultimately inferior to that of Europe, the lyceum offered itself as a vital institution for constituting national identity and cultural achievement within an increasingly global cultural marketplace. By featuring both local and foreign talent, or as the Redpath advertised in 1872, arranging "engagements with Boston and foreign artists," lyceum bureaus also facilitated the careers and renown of American musicians in a genre of performance hitherto dominated by European artists.[12] While Dwight and the sacralizers bemoaned the popularity of the virtuoso and the prima donna, foreign or otherwise, fearing that a celebrity-driven music marketplace elevated the star above the symphony, the lyceum bureaus promoted foreign and national musical celebrities in a simultaneous appeal to edification and a consumer-based global citizenship.

Through the promotion of musical entertainment, as well as new modes of organizing and marketing such entertainment, the lyceum bureaus became a key corporate purveyor of middle-class culture in the post–Civil War period, implicitly encouraging audiences to connect their social and cultural aspirations with their engagement in a consumer marketplace. The bureaus presented themselves as the able mediator of an increasingly vast and international landscape of entertainment. They promoted a vision of middle-class culture that involved the consumption of foreign art music by foreign and national artists, but marketed music according to an eclectic rather than sacralized model. Ultimately, the lyceum's lecture-going audiences were encouraged to imagine themselves as the discerning patrons of an international musical world encompassing the lights of Europe and a rising generation of American aspirants to renown.

The Bureaus and the Transformation of Lyceum Entertainment

As James Redpath explained in his inaugural 1869 circular, the Boston Lyceum Bureau (later, Redpath Lyceum Bureau) was created to respond to a "need [that] has been felt for a long time" for a "common centre of

FIGURE 3.1. "Camilla Urso's Concerts," *Redpath's Lyceum*, 1875.
Courtesy American Antiquarian Society.

communication" between lecturers and lecture committees.[13] The Redpath, though often heralded as the first lyceum bureau, in fact followed similar experiments in managing the business of entertainment, in particular the Associated Western Literary Societies, which began managing lecturers in the mid-1860s before being absorbed into a commercial bureau in 1870. The Redpath became one of the most long-standing and successful of the lecture agencies established in the 1860s and 1870s, a group that included the American Literary Bureau (New York, 1868), Slayton Bureau (Chicago, 1874), and Williams' Lecture and Musical Bureau (Boston, 1869).[14] Their formation was a major watershed in managing popular entertainment, and similar strategies for centralized booking and management emerged later in the century to handle the circus and variety entertainments, later vaudeville. When *Werner's Directory of Elocutionists, Readers, Lecturers, and Other Public Instructors and Entertainments* was published in 1887, offering itself as a resource for those aspiring to the platform as well as for lecture committees and "others in search of talent," it included the Redpath in a list of over thirty "bureaus, agencies, and managers" devoted to handling platform speakers and musicians.[15]

Lyceum bureaus represented performers individually but drew them together under a corporate auspice that standardized marketing and contracting practices. In the 1800s, lecturing, theater, and music were basically itinerant careers, but by the 1860s the geographic scale of an itinerant performing career had changed significantly. Advances in transportation made it possible for performers of all varieties to travel farther faster, thus covering more venues in a wider geographic area within a shorter period and, increasingly, allowing them to develop transatlantic careers. In the first half of the century, the practice of relying on managers and agents to handle logistics had increased steadily among entertainers and venues alike. In the 1860s, lyceum bureaus like the Redpath established a central corporate bureaucracy and hired their own booking and advance agents to oversee the complex details of promoting and engaging performers. As an alternative to hiring an independent agent or advance man, performers could instead be represented and promoted by the bureau, which served as a middleman between them and the lyceum committees. In turn, lyceum bureaus became both gatekeepers and vehicles for celebrity on widening scales.

Bureaus further positioned themselves as authorities within the business of lyceum entertainment. Monthly circulars for the Redpath and the American Literary Bureau included articles advising local lyceum committees on best practices for arranging a profitable evening's entertainment or course.

The bureaus were able to establish themselves as the legitimate gatekeepers within the expanding market for lyceum entertainment in part by treating local lyceum committees as inexperienced with the market, susceptible to the puffery associated with new celebrity and lacking the knowledge of how to construct a profitable and popular course. Bureaus presented their cultural expertise and market savvy as being in sympathy with the needs and concerns of local auspices. It was a winning corporate strategy, key to the efforts of new entertainment agencies to insert themselves into a preexisting industry. By relying on bureaus, the *Lyceum Magazine* explained, lecture committees need not fear being taken in by the puffery of "new stars," those "rawest recruits" who nevertheless "succeed in beguiling lyceums into payment of the highest fees," thereby bankrupting committees and causing courses to lose their good reputations.[16]

Critics of the lyceum bureaus, like J. G. Holland, accused them of doing precisely that: saturating the market with unworthy applicants to public renown just to make money off both parties: the committees and the aspiring talent. Holland waxed nostalgic for a time when the "really acceptable lecturers" were drawn from a handful of "men who made the platform popular and useful" and whose speeches "shaped opinion, developed sentiment, [and] agitated great public questions."[17] Holland contended that the platform of 1871 drew together these former lights "in a common column with literary jesters and mountebanks, readers, singers," and "men who, outside of a lecture-course, would not draw auditors enough to pay for the rent of their audience-rooms." The lyceum system had "degenerated into a string of entertainments" lacking in civic, educational, or cultural value. Holland was particularly distressed by the growing affinity between the lecture system and celebrity culture. The lecture system had long served as a celebrity vehicle for men aspiring to careers in literature, law, and the church; in the early decades of the lyceum's history, lecturing played a key role in constituting these kinds of careers.[18] Holland, however, identified changing categories of lyceum lecturing and the emergence of new classes of lecturers with degeneration. Likewise, an unspoken gender politics lay behind Holland's remarks, for these "literary jesters and mountebanks, readers, [and] singers" increasingly included women.

The question of the relationship between celebrity and cultural merit was an ongoing preoccupation of nineteenth-century cultural critics. Holland built on these critiques, arguing that the rise of "star-lecturing" had caused the "lecture-room" to become a "show-room of fresh notorieties, at high prices." He advocated a return to the days of long courses, featuring men "called to lecture for the simple reason that they have something to say."[19] Of course, as lecture committees had discovered at least a decade earlier, long courses of long lecturers did not generate ticket sales. Holland's critique of the lyceum system of the 1870s equated new economic systems of organizing public amusement with the deterioration of content. More generally, nineteenth-century critiques of the star system reflected an ongoing negotiation of the relationship between the market and the question of literary and cultural value. Increasingly, in the second half of the nineteenth century, new economic systems for organizing the promotion, distribution, and content of popular culture were met by efforts of social and cultural elites (like Holland) to define the terms according to which culture should be consumed *regardless* of the demands of the market.

Lyceum bureaus, in contrast, urged lyceum committees to shape entertainment according to the demands of the market, balancing celebrity with variety, and to advertise liberally. Redpath circulars repeatedly warned lyceum committees, "Do not attempt to give individual lectures; but in every case have a course, opening it with the most popular, or one of the most popular, lecturers you can secure." They advised committees to schedule the entertainments "at regular intervals" and make sure to "have your season-tickets for sale a month before the opening night."[20] Season tickets helped protect the sponsors from a bad night, perhaps a snowstorm or stiff competition from the theater or church services, and ensured the financial viability of the season as a whole. The American Literary Bureau advised committees to advertise "liberally and judiciously," noting ruefully that, lest some balk at an unseemly degree of puffery, "there is no reason why a lecture should have less publicity than a minstrel show."[21] To sustain the profitability of the lecture business and ensure that edifying entertainment persisted alongside the ascendance of burlesque troupes and minstrel shows, lyceum committees needed to learn how to apply the same promotional techniques and scheduling savvy as those used by theater managers. Lyceum bureaus offered such expertise.

Bureaus encouraged committees to design courses around a new organizational principle: variety. Lyceum courses failed when committees arranged them as an endless repetition of the same type of lecturer or content, or if they leaned too heavily on an established star to carry the profits for a season. Celebrity was not a silver bullet for financial success. The appeal to variety also helped lyceum committees expand their conception of an audience by responding to the popularity of concert music, emerging literary celebrity of Western humorists like Mark Twain, popular fascination with science and travel, and the continued vogue for dramatic reading as an alternative to the theater. Both the Redpath and the American Literary Bureau advised that in addition to being "varied" in subject, all courses should contain "a Reading, a Humorous Lecture, a Scientific Lecture and a Concert."[22] They promoted this model through "contract courses," a special package structured around a range of entertainments. Such courses enabled bureaus to maximize business from a single committee by arranging bookings for as many of its entertainers as possible. This strategy managed the bureaus' dual interests in promoting celebrity performers as well as lesser-known personalities and types of acts while also encouraging local committees to transform their model of lyceum entertainment.

The bureaus promoted musical concerts by noting the overlap between lyceum audiences and the "music-loving public," which justified the relatively higher cost: $100 to $300 for a concert troupe, compared to an individual lecturer at $75 to $150.[23] Musical entertainment had been a feature of lyceum culture since the 1830s. Many lyceums presented organ concerts or amateur recitals before a visiting lecture, which also afforded audiences an opportunity to socialize.[24] As the American Literary Bureau noted in its advice to committees on sustaining a popular course, opening a lecture with a concert by "home talent" was another way of generating popular interest and investment in the course. It followed that those "who would patronize a course just to hear some good music" before a lecture would be as glad to patronize concerts within a lecture course.[25] Bureaus aligned music with the larger educational project of the lyceum while also invoking community social practice, leisure culture, and the broader popularity of concert music to assure organizers that lyceum concerts could be a profitable venture. For "as long as pianos are to be found in nearly everybody's parlor, and the cultivation of a better taste for music so universal," concerts would continue to appeal to and draw in a more diverse public. Committees would discover that popularity offset the higher cost, making concerts "as profitable to associations as lectures."[26] And in many cases they were.

In 1872, when the Redpath announced the formation of its Musical Department, the scale and implications of its management of musical combinations had shifted significantly. As the *Lyceum Magazine* explained, demand for musical entertainment extended beyond the desire of lyceums for sundry concerts. Both the Redpath and the American Literary Bureau continued to encourage lyceums to incorporate concerts into their courses while positioning themselves more broadly as agents for music entertainment. In addition to furnishing entertainment for courses, the American Literary Bureau announced that it was "prepared to supply parties desiring first-class music for special occasions, such as balls, parties, sociables, weddings, private theatricals, watering-places, Sunday-school celebrations, pic-nics, etc." as well as to arrange vocal ensembles or soloists for church choirs.[27] This move to market entertainment beyond the auspices of lyceum committees should not be taken as evidence of the decline of the lyceum, despite the recurring swan songs by the likes of Holland. As lyceum bureaus created new organizational systems to mediate between lecture committees and lecturers, they consequently found themselves in a position to represent and market entertainment associated more broadly with edification and middle-class respectability, even beyond the lyceum courses to which they already appealed.

In his memoirs, James Redpath's partner James Pond presented the introduction of musical entertainments as a strategy to save the institution from decline, even obsolescence. As the old "warhorses" Ralph Waldo Emerson, John Gough, and Anna Dickinson left the platform or declined in popularity in the mid-1870s, the survival of the lyceum depended on its ability to gather new forms of entertainment under its umbrella. Pond's memoirs also demonstrate that the "desire" of local lyceums for musical concerts could also be stimulated by the promotional strategies of bureau agents. In 1896, James B. Pond recalled a strategy that he and Redpath used in the 1870s—probably in the wake of the Panic of 1873—to keep lyceum courses from "go[ing] under." Pond describes how he paid the Italian impresario Max Strakosch $10,000 to hold ten "grand" concerts to open the "principal courses" in the major cities of the Northeast. The concerts were a success and Pond more than recouped his investment: the Strakosch combination "sold to each of the other courses for two hundred dollars more than we paid Strakosch."[28] Clearly the continued viability—let alone profitability—of the Redpath agency depended on its success in convincing lyceum committees to book new types of entertainments, those that Redpath and Pond were convinced could make a profit for both the committees and the agency and bring committees back to the Redpath agency the next season. Ultimately, marketing new entertainments such as concerts sustained bureaus and committees alike, in turn transforming the contours of lyceum entertainment.

Music in the Lyceum

In November 1872, the Worcester Lyceum Course brought out the Grand Rudersdorff Combination at an expense that, the local paper noted, "would maintain an ordinary lecture course," but the committee felt "confident that their venture would be rewarded by an appreciative public" (fig. 3.2).[29] This confidence—or solicitous gesture to public patronage and good taste—was not misplaced, and the next morning the paper "congratulated" audience members for "hearing the concert in place of one of the so-called popular lectures of the day."[30] In major eastern cities like Worcester, which boasted several lyceum courses, musical entertainments in lyceum courses consistently drew large crowds. For this local critic, music had more merit in a lyceum course than some of the celebrity lecturers—or lecturing celebrities—promoted and brought out under lyceum auspices. The snide allusion to the "so-called popular lectures" underscores the complex array of attitudes toward the cultural and literary merit of different forms of lyceum entertainment in an ongoing debate over which entertainments were in fact worthy of the middle-class publics that lyceum committees were hoping to draw.

Worcester's lecture courses began to offer concerts and other "novel and popular attractions" in 1869 and continued to feature a range of entertainments and lecturers through the 1870s.[31] The popularity of foreign musical celebrities and novel entertainments helped offset the cost to committees, even and particularly during the economic depression of the mid-1870s. The depression seems not to have discouraged the bureaus from promoting the more expensive musical entertainments, but rather created an incentive for experimentation with inexpensive but novel entertainments that continued to be profitable.

Erminia Rudersdorff appealed to Worcester audiences as an international celebrity who "has held the highest position in the musical world of Europe." Attending her concerts provided lyceumites with the opportunity to see a great musical star and imagine themselves as constituting part of a transnational public. Their patronage revealed the capacity of Americans to appreciate the greatest that Europe could produce while simultaneously affording lyceum-goers the opportunity to evaluate this European prima donna according to their tastes and standards. Rudersdorff and her managers in America understood the tastes of this market. For although Rudersdorff had become known in London for her oratorio, her lyceum combination performed pieces from a familiar repertoire of French and Italian bel canto opera by Meyerbeer and Donizetti as well as the English ballad music that American audiences expected from their prima donnas.

Lyceum advertisements assured audiences that Rudersdorff excelled "not only in Oratorio and classic music, but also in Home Ballads." The performance of "Home Ballads" like Henry Bishop's "Last Rose of Summer" remained the gold standard by which American audiences preferred to judge, and enjoy, celebrated vocalists. Even in 1872, Jenny Lind's lyrical and sentimental repertoire from her 1850 American tour and her celebrated

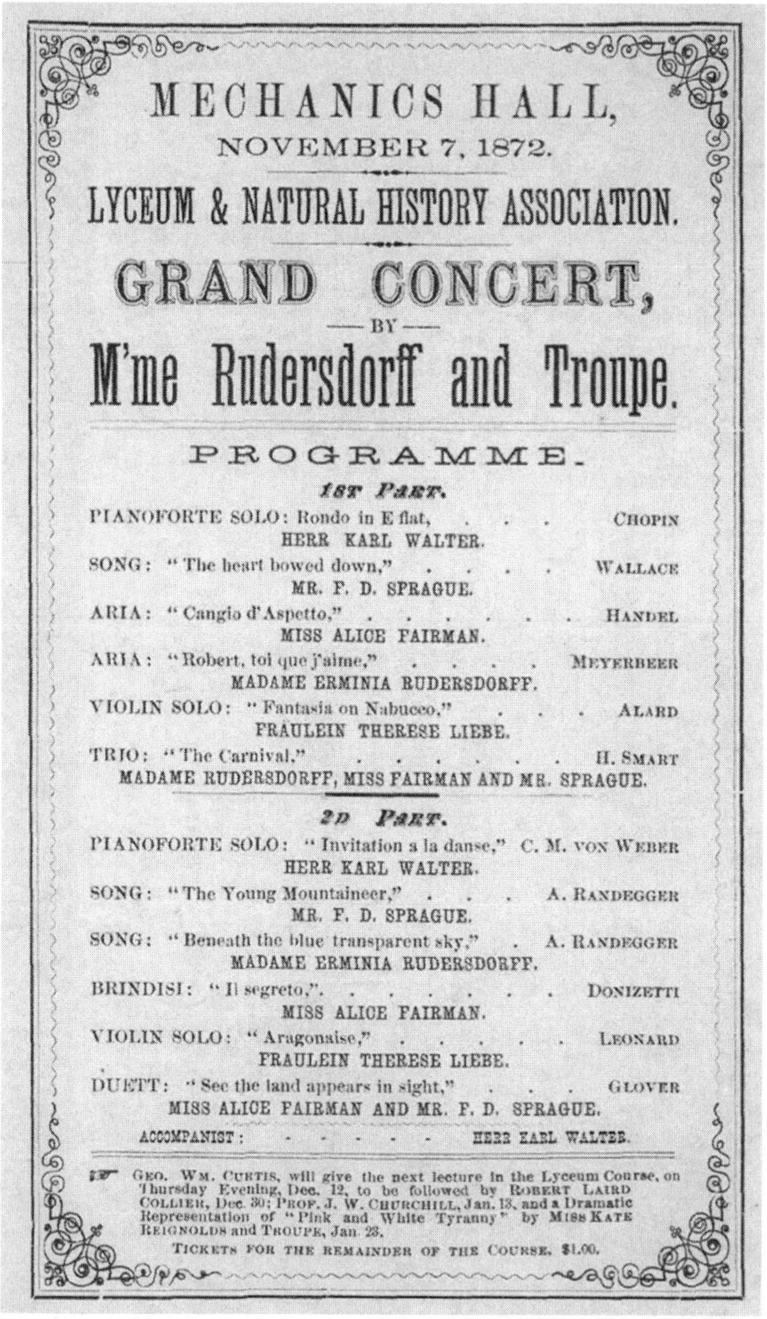

MECHANICS HALL,

NOVEMBER 7, 1872.

LYCEUM & NATURAL HISTORY ASSOCIATION.

GRAND CONCERT,

— BY —

M'me Rudersdorff and Troupe.

PROGRAMME.

1st Part.

PIANOFORTE SOLO: Rondo in E flat, . . . CHOPIN
HERR KARL WALTER.

SONG: "The heart bowed down," . . . . . WALLACE
MR. F. D. SPRAGUE.

ARIA: "Cangio d'Aspetto," . . . . HANDEL
MISS ALICE FAIRMAN.

ARIA: "Robert, toi que j'aime," . . . . . MEYERBEER
MADAME ERMINIA RUDERSDORFF.

VIOLIN SOLO: "Fantasia on Nabucco," . . . . ALARD
FRAULEIN THERESE LIEBE.

TRIO: "The Carnival," . . . . H. SMART
MADAME RUDERSDORFF, MISS FAIRMAN AND MR. SPRAGUE.

2d Part.

PIANOFORTE SOLO: "Invitation a la danse," C. M. VON WEBER
HERR KARL WALTER.

SONG: "The Young Mountaineer," . . . A. RANDEGGER
MR. F. D. SPRAGUE.

SONG: "Beneath the blue transparent sky," . A. RANDEGGER
MADAME ERMINIA RUDERSDORFF.

BRINDISI: "Il segreto,". . . . . DONIZETTI
MISS ALICE FAIRMAN.

VIOLIN SOLO: "Aragonaise," . . . . . . LEONARD
FRAULEIN THERESE LIEBE.

DUETT: "See the land appears in sight," . . . GLOVER
MISS ALICE FAIRMAN AND MR. F. D. SPRAGUE.

ACCOMPANIST: - - - - - HERR KARL WALTER.

☞ GEO. WM. CURTIS, will give the next lecture in the Lyceum Course, on Thursday Evening, Dec. 12, to be followed by ROBERT LAIRD COLLIER, Dec. 30; PROF. J. W. CHURCHILL, Jan. 13, and a Dramatic Representation of "Pink and White Tyranny" by MISS KATE REIGNOLDS and TROUPE, Jan. 23.

TICKETS FOR THE REMAINDER OF THE COURSE, $1.00.

FIGURE 3.2. "Grand Concert, by M'me Rudersdorff and Troupe" at Mechanics Hall, November 7, 1872. *Courtesy American Antiquarian Society.*

style of emotive simplicity continued to provide the terms of vocal celebrity for a broad popular audience. Worcester did not miss the opportunity to judge Rudersdorff's accomplishments in oratorio but instead celebrated her appeal as a "quite jolly" entertainer and accomplished vocalist in the popular mode.[32] Indeed, for her 1872 troupe Rudersdorff calculated that the current vogue for female violinists would appeal more than oratorio, and she secured German violinist Therese Liebe rather than assemble a vocal quartet.[33]

The second quarter of the nineteenth century was a period in which musicians and impresarios explored different cultural and economic models for musical performance while attempting to introduce American audiences to new forms of European art music, including oratorio and symphonies. Theodore Thomas, a German musician who came to America with the Germania Musical Society in 1848, attempted to introduce symphonic works to American audiences in his orchestral concerts but was consistently frustrated by poor response, which made it more difficult to sustain the cost of a larger orchestra. The discourse of popular uplift promoted in *Dwight's Journal of Music,* and by such musical associations as the New York Philharmonic Society, retained a strong undercurrent of ambivalence toward the public and the popular and their ability to serve as a viable market for European art and orchestral music or even to sustain an orchestra as a profitable venture.

With the Theodore Thomas Orchestra, which began touring in 1869, Thomas developed a concert strategy of combining movements from different symphonies to educate audiences about classical music while appealing to a prevailing preference for variety and familiarity. But audiences and critics less disposed to symphonic works complained when Thomas began to "drop" the "lighter music," offering programs in 1875 and 1876 that were "entirely too heavy." A writer for *Dexter Smith's Paper* urged, "Give us all the Wagner you please, but don't ignore Strauss!"[34] The style of music and standards of symphonic performance advocated by Dwight, and to which Thomas aspired, would lead to the formation of endowed professional orchestras. Among these was the Chicago Symphony Orchestra, established in 1891, where Thomas made his home after a stint as music director of the New York Philharmonic Society, which had been run as a cooperative since its founding in 1857.[35]

Though the Redpath managed large outfits like Gilmore's Band and the Theodore Thomas Orchestra, these entertainments proved too expensive for lyceums outside major cities. The Rudersdorff concert troupe, in contrast, followed the model of lyceum musical entertainment advanced by the bureaus, which emphasized celebrity soloists performing in ensembles of three to five musicians—in the case of the Rudersdorff troupe, three vocalists and a female violinist. Concerts featured well-known songs, both ballad music and opera, as well as classical excerpts. James Redpath's biographer Charles Horner credits Redpath with achieving a winning balance between the promotion of celebrity soloists and emphasis on the ensemble as a model for musical entertainment. Doing so allowed Redpath to "uphold high musical standards and yet so dramatize musical programs so that their appeal became more general."[36]

While the 1872 Musical Department prominently featured its services as "sole agent" for Erminia Rudersdorff and Adelaide Phillips, the names of these celebrities were accompanied by a list of close to forty vocalists, four accompanists, and nine instrumentalists available for grand concerts and from which the Redpath was prepared to "make up any trios or quartettes" or "concerts partly vocal and instrumental." This, in addition to the "regularly-organized combinations": the Highland Quartette and Temple Quartette, both all-male ensembles "assisted by a lady vocalist"; Kempton Double Quartette Club, under the direction of Mrs. Jennie Kempton, contralto; and the Hyers Sisters, "colored singers" from San Francisco who had secured the Redpath to arrange a series of concerts for these "musical wonders" in New England.[37]

The number of its musical acts and profile of musicians had increased steadily since the founding of the Redpath bureau. In 1869, the Boston Lyceum Bureau included 126 lecturers in its roster of talent and seventeen different acts categorized as "Readings and Other Entertainments." These "entertainments" included dramatic readers, combined "Literary and Musical Entertainments" featuring a dramatic reader supported by a musical ensemble, and three musical acts: the Hutchinson Family Singers, Washington Band (composed of students from the "Institutions for the Blind"), and Madame Nina Pizzotti, a young pianist recently arrived from Dublin.[38] Within two years, this category had splintered, and the Redpath advertised its new roster of lecturers, readers, entertainments, and concerts. This last category included P. S. Gilmore's Band, the Mendelssohn Quintette Club, and an assortment of vocal quartets drawn from musicians in Boston.

Some of these musicians no doubt began their concert careers at the National Peace Jubilee, a cultural watershed that would serve as a touchstone for debates about the role of music in American public life and the status of music as a sacralized art. Organized by bandmaster Patrick Gilmore in Boston in July 1869, the jubilee was one of the largest musical events to date; it introduced international musical celebrities and compositions to the greater public while also drawing together musicians from throughout the nation in a nationalistic celebration of peace and America's musical culture. Early that year, Gilmore's agents had advertised widely in schools, musical societies, and church choirs for ensembles and singers to include in his mammoth chorus of 10,000 voices, as well as for local soloists.[39] Both the National Peace Jubilee and the 1872 World Peace Jubilee afforded the opportunity for local musical amateurs to perform alongside such international celebrities as Erminia Rudersdorff, Adelaide Phillips, and Camilla Urso and imagine advancing the trajectory of their own careers beyond local music societies, parlor recitals with the family, or even the enviable salaried position with a local church. In some respects, the Redpath picked up where Gilmore's National Peace Jubilee left off, establishing a longstanding corporate structure to solicit and facilitate the professional careers of rising native talent alongside those of established celebrities. Its 1872 Musical Department featured a growing cohort of local vocalists whom Gilmore had featured in the 1869 and 1872 jubilees, including Annie Granger (Dow), Addie Ryan, Mrs. Charles A. Barry and Mrs. H. M. Smith. Significantly, the Redpath emphasized "Boston and foreign talent." This explicit pairing is telling, suggesting the dual interests of the Redpath as an agent of musical celebrity and as facilitator of a local professional performance culture.

Camilla Urso's own career arc, and the composition and content of her company, is an effective example of the role the bureaus played in facilitating a popular market for concert music in the lyceum while drawing on an expanding group of American musicians in which female soloists figured prominently. Urso began performing as a child prodigy violinist around 1850 in Europe, where she caught the attention of an American agent who hoped to present her to American audiences in a series of concerts. Urso arrived in New York with her father in 1852 only to discover that the financial backing for the venture—if it had ever existed—had fallen through. These kinds of speculations and arrangements were the most common ways that European artists, including Swedish opera singer Jenny Lind, came to America to perform.

Urso's American career was salvaged by Marietta Alboni, an Italian contralto who, like Lind, developed a transatlantic renown for her performances in Paris and London before arriving in America. In 1852, Alboni featured Urso in a series of concerts during which New York audiences could compare Urso with another foreign child prodigy and violinist, Paul Julian. The next year, Urso began touring as a featured soloist with the Germania Band. She retired briefly from performing at the age of thirteen, when it became difficult to appeal as a child star, but returned to the concert stage in 1862, at the age of twenty. She toured the United States and Canada through the 1860s with a range of different concert outfits, including Gilmore's Band; in the 1870s, with her own concert company, she secured bookings through agencies such as the Redpath and the American Literary Bureau, embarking on tours that took her beyond Europe to Australia and Central and South America.[40]

Throughout her fifty-year career in America, Urso was known for introducing the violin as a suitable instrument for women to play and perform. Audiences and critics praised her for the sweetness of her playing and what they identified as a uniquely feminine quality of tone and expression. Thus Urso's popularity as a violinist was connected with her feminization of the instrument. She was a curiosity, a "lady violinist," but through this instrument she epitomized midcentury ideals of female musicianship that were more readily associated with vocalists like Lind. Reviews of Urso from the 1870s suggest that audiences' fascination also grew from the combination of her emotional expression—identified as feminine—and the undeniable physicality of her playing. A review from *Watson's Art Journal* used in Urso's Redpath circular described her style as "broad and large, tinctured by a woman's tenderness and sympathy" and combining a "woman's grace and tenderness" with the "breadth and largeness of manner of a man."[41] Urso's sustained popularity as a performer can be attributed to both her musicianship and the fascination she elicited by successfully complicating gender boundaries around genres and styles of performance. But she also was savvy as a director, arranging concerts and concert combinations with broad popular appeal.

Like Theodore Thomas, Urso saw herself in a unique position to introduce American audiences to new compositions of classical music. In an 1874 interview with *Dexter Smith's,* she explained that although "it would be rash . . . to give programs composed purely of classical music to audiences untutored in it," she considered it the "*duty* of artists to set before the public a good order of music." Urso believed her audiences expected this of her, and she followed a policy of introducing a "few choice '*morceaux*' of the masters" into each of her programs. Yet Urso found that most of her audiences preferred a "marked melody" to the new "classical music," and she tended to approach the latter as more of a "duty than a pleasure."[42]

In her lyceum concerts, Urso performed only two or three selections, excluding encores, in a program of nine to twelve pieces that featured different members of the company. For her 1875 program, printed in her lyceum circular, Urso performed a solo polonaise by Louise Spohr and the Rondo Papageno by Heinrich Wilhelm Ernst, both short, playful compositions designed to show off virtuoso technique. This in contrast to the series of concerts Urso performed in Boston in 1874, which featured a classical chamber music repertoire by Wolfgang Amadeus Mozart, Franz Schubert, and Joachim Raff that would have been less familiar and less popular with lyceum audiences. In 1873 Urso, with orchestra accompaniment, successfully introduced Worcester to Mendelssohn's Violin Concerto in E Minor at the Sixteenth Annual Festival of the Worcester County Musical Association. The following season, she performed only a single movement from the Mendelssohn for the November 1874 Lyceum Course concert, this time with piano accompaniment. Clearly, Urso understood the varying expectations of her audiences and regarded the concert company and the lyceum as a different kind of cultural space suited to the "morceau" but not the concerto or symphony.[43]

This approach hardly met the approval of critics like J. S. Dwight, who ignored the Redpath Lyceum Bureau for a decade before finally delivering a stern sentence against its role within the field of popular and classical music. By 1879, fresh from a series of Lyceum Bureau Concerts in Boston, Dwight took up the torch that Holland had once wielded so determinedly. The concert had been so unpleasant that the critic left early, unable to endure the "long, miscellaneous series of unconnected solo pieces" performed by a succession of prima donnas, who epitomized Dwight's enduring frustration with American popular concert culture for placing the virtuoso or celebrity soloist above the music itself. After Marie Litta's performance of Bellini's "Qui la voce"—a piece from soprano repertoire already familiar to American audiences when Jenny Lind earned raptures for her rendition in 1850—Dwight whined, "one such prima donna was enough, one would think, for any concert." And yet Litta was followed by an American soprano, Mrs. Abbie Carrington, recently returned from study in Italy and eager to display her new accomplishments, and then by an Italian female "tenor" who "sang in English" and, "in spite of the Italian name, seemed like an English-woman."[44]

Dwight took out his frustration with the Redpath in another page, declaring that the lyceum, once a "sober, useful, New England Institution," had since "fallen into the hands of the showmen, who, under the name of Bureaux, have for some years made it a field for speculation." Like Holland, Dwight accused the bureaus of entering the lecture field only to make money from lecturers, with the effect of replacing "amusement for instruction, personal exhibition for intrinsic worth [and] sensational 'attraction' for wholesome mental food." Here again the lyceum's embrace of celebrity culture called into question its claims about the value of its content. Dwight was particularly frustrated with the "certain nondescript style of concert-giving" practiced by the bureaus, in which music was presented not as "music for its own sake" but rather to service the "array of bright galaxies of star performers, virtuosos, famous singers, violinists, or pianists." The lyceum, Dwight lamented, had become about "the artists, not the art."[45] Of course, what Dwight missed was the degree to which the "bright galaxies of star performers" also served an expanding field of popular musical culture that, while not arranged around the values of "music for its own sake" that Dwight envisioned, nevertheless broadened American audiences' engagement with music culture on both sides of the footlights.

Significantly, the emphasis of the lyceum bureau combinations on vocal music had the added effect of facilitating the careers of female vocalists and creating opportunities for aspiring impresarios. The Camilla Urso Concert Company was drawn not only from the "galaxies" of celebrity, but also from an expanding cohort of native-born musicians. Each season, the Camilla Urso Concerts featured a different company of vocalists. Some were foreign, such as Clara Doria, an English soprano who had come to America with Maurice Strakosh's Italian opera troupe. But Urso also selected local artists, including Louise Oliver, the lead soprano of New York's Grace Church until hired to tour with Urso in 1875, or Edith Abell, who debuted with the Caroline Richings English Opera Troupe in 1868 as an "amateur" from Springfield, Massachusetts.[46] Abell toured with Richings's company for two seasons, then traveled to Italy to study and try herself before a Milanese audience. Newly credentialed, Abell returned to the United States and secured an engagement through the Redpath Lyceum Bureau as the soprano assisting the Mendelssohn Quintette Club in 1872, and in 1873 she toured with Urso.

By 1870, popular periodicals were commenting on the growing number of aspiring female vocalists. The *Girl of the Period Miscellany* complained that so-called lady amateurs were entirely "too ambitious" and that any "girl who has a good voice, which is really effective in a small room thinks—and herein deceives herself—that it will be equally effective in a large concert room or theatre."[47] Although many middle-class families considered the opera too much like the theater for a respectable girl, growing numbers of young women who aspired to careers as professional singers sought training and performance opportunities with the Italian opera. The wave of American women seeking vocal instruction in Italy became a matter of discussion in music and literary periodicals. According to a "Cincinnati Girl," who covered the topic of a foreign musical education for *Dexter Smith's*, Milan in 1874 was swarming with Americans—"mostly girls"—eager to train for opera or concert singing, and "for every one who is here there are probably twenty more at home looking with longing eyes towards Italy and expecting with more or less definiteness of purpose to come."[48] English soprano Clara Louise Kellogg cautioned readers that Milan masters "do their biggest business now swindling American girls," telling them "lies about their voices" and filling them with "great ideas as to their future." Kellogg admitted to being "fairly disgusted" with the slavish attention American audiences lavished on foreign singers, which fed the obsession with obtaining foreign training to establish legitimacy back home. Kellogg wished that Americans would make more effort to "bring out our home talent" rather than foreign stars.[49]

When viewed through the perspective of the lyceum bureaus, Americans did "bring out our home talent," creating a range of new opportunities for aspiring local musicians and introducing concert music into the lyceum. Likewise, a growing chorus of voices from such periodicals as *Dexter Smith's* and *The Folio* actively championed "native talent," arguing that America was quickly advancing to rival Europe, especially in musical achievements.[50] In 1873, *The Folio* triumphantly announced that although "vocal artists of continental Europe" retained their "glamour" for American audiences, the "musical firmament is [now] indebted to America for some of its brightest stars," such as long-standing lyceum favorites Mrs. H. M. Smith and Annie Granger Dow. All this was made possible by expanding musical education, which extended from the middle-class home, where the piano had become a fixture and focus of domestic leisure, to churches, amateur musical societies, and public school curricula. The graduating classes of the first musical conservatories established in the late 1860s had increasingly made it possible to sustain a choral society and music hall in "every town and village" based solely on "native talent." And so, *The Folio* proclaimed, the "American citizen" could finally show "just pride" before the "merit-roll of nations" in matters aesthetic and artistic.[51]

Foreign celebrities remained a crucial part of lyceum lists, but were increasingly joined by an expanding cohort of native-born musicians, the majority from New England, who booked through entertainment bureaus, performed in lyceum courses, and sought instruction abroad. In most cases their musical careers extended far outside the boundaries of lyceum entertainment; but in drawing music into the lyceum, the bureaus broadened the market for American musicians and created new trajectories that allowed them to imagine not just national but global careers. Significantly, lyceum bureaus created an alternative avenue for professionalism and renown that is less visible within the history of the professional orchestra and similar institutions or in histories organized around the careers of major celebrities. The story of music in the lyceum epitomizes the ways in which the emergence, in the mid- to late nineteenth century, of corporate structures for managing the entertainment business created new professional paths for aspiring performers, in turn transforming the content of popular entertainment. Even as the lyceum became more tied into the global circulation of entertainment, it continued to serve a vital function as a celebrity vehicle on a regional and national scale for emerging American musicians. Likewise, Americans who attended a lyceum concert in the 1870s might have connected the purchase of a lyceum concert or season ticket with a vision of middle-class status tied to their ability to patronize and evaluate the great celebrities from Europe and rising American talent.

From the perspective of the bureaus, encouraging lyceum committees to bring musical entertainments into their courses connected the institution with an expanding site of middle-class leisure, thereby sustaining the lyceum while transforming its role within American culture and the entertainment marketplace. In the post–Civil War period, America continued to serve as a lucrative market for foreign artists, while the growth of musical education, the continued popularity of local musical associations and the expansion of industries selling sheet music and instruments to middle-class homes broadened the market for both musical entertainment and musical entertainers. The lyceum bureaus intercepted these shifts and, by marketing an eclectic mélange of foreign art music and foreign and national musical stars, constituted a new role for the lyceum as a key corporate purveyor of middle-class entertainment.

NOTES

I would like to thank Allison Abra, Sara Babcox First, Laura Hilburn, Matt Largo, Diana Mankowski, and Tom Wright for providing feedback on earlier drafts of this essay, as well as the participants in the Cosmopolitan Lyceum Conference and James Cook, all of whom shaped my engagement with these questions through conversations and feedback. And thank you to the American Antiquarian Society for funding this research with a Kate B. and Hall J. Peterson Fellowship.

1. *Worcester (MA) Daily Spy*, 17 October 1874.
2. Ibid., 30 October 1874.
3. Simon Williams dates the influx of continental performers to midcentury, but musicians and dancers were making inroads with American audiences by the late 1830s and early 1840s. See R. Allen Lott, *From Paris to Peoria: How European Piano Virtuosos Brought Classical Music to the American Heartland* (New York: Oxford University Press, 2003); and Simon Williams, "European Actors and the Star System in the American theatre, 1742–1870," in *The Cambridge History of American Theatre*, ed. Don B. Wilmeth and Christopher Bigsby (Cambridge: Cambridge University Press, 1998), 1:303–37.

4. This expansion also made women performers far more prominent because of the association of vocal music as a feminine form of performance. Many of the major international female celebrities of midcentury—Marietta Alboni, Henrietta Sontag, Jenny Lind—were vocalists. Lind's celebrity in the 1850s helped popularize the concert stage as an acceptable form of public femininity, a reputable alternative to the dramatic theater or even the opera. Lyceum musical combinations featured women as vocal soloists and occasionally as piano accompanists or violin soloists. No male vocal ensemble was complete without a prima donna. On Lind's celebrity, see Bluford Adams, *E Pluribus Barnum: The Great Showman and the Making of U.S. Popular Culture* (Minneapolis: University of Minnesota Press, 1997); Peter Buckley, "To the Opera House: Culture and Society in New York: 1820–1880" (PhD diss., State University of New York at Stony Brook, 1984); and Neil Harris, *Humbug: The Art of P. T. Barnum* (Chicago: University of Chicago Press, 1981). On women in the lyceum and women's rights, see Angela Ray, "What Hath She Wrought? Woman's Rights and the Nineteenth-Century Lyceum," *Rhetoric & Public Affairs* 9, no. 2 (2006): 183–214; and Lisa Strange, "Dress Reform and the Feminine Ideal: Elizabeth Cady Stanton and the 'Coming Girl,'" *Southern Communication Journal* 68, no. 1 (Fall 2002): 1–13.

5. For a discussion of Holland and contemporary critics of the post–Civil War lyceum, see Paul Cherches, "Star Course: Popular Lectures and the Marketing of Celebrity in Nineteenth-Century America" (PhD diss., New York University, 1997). On the decline of the lyceum, see Angela Ray, *The Lyceum and Public Culture in the Nineteenth-Century United States* (East Lansing: Michigan State University Press, 2005); and Carl Bode, *The American Lyceum: Town Meeting of the Mind* (Carbondale: Southern Illinois University Press, 1968).

6. Alan Trachtenberg, *The Incorporation of America: Culture and Society in the Gilded Age* (New York: Hill and Wang, 1982).

7. On the lyceum bureaus, see Cherches, "Star Course"; and Marjorie Eubank, "The Redpath Lyceum Bureau from 1868 to 1901" (PhD diss., University of Michigan, 1968). Other scholarship that examines the incorporation of culture: in vaudeville, Alison Kibler, *Rank Ladies: Gender and Cultural Hierarchy in American Vaudeville* (Chapel Hill: University of North Carolina Press, 1999), and Robert Snyder, *The Voice of the City: Vaudeville and Popular Culture in New York* (New York: Oxford University Press, 1989); in the circus, Janet Davis, *The Circus Age: Culture and Society Under the American Big Top* (Chapel Hill: University of North Caroline Press, 2002); in theater, Douglas McDermott, "Structure and Management in the American Theatre from the Beginning to 1870," in *The Cambridge History of American Theatre,* ed. Don B. Wilmeth and Christopher Bigsby (Cambridge: Cambridge University Press, 1998), 1:182–215; in print, Richard Ohmann, *Selling Culture: Magazines, Markets, and Class at the Turn of the Century* (New York: Verso, 1996); and on the centralization of American media, Paul Starr, *The Creation of the Media: Politics Origins of Modern Communications* (New York: Basic Books, 2005).

8. Lawrence Levine, *Highbrow/Lowbrow: The Emergence of Cultural Hierarchy in America* (Cambridge: Harvard University Press, 1988), 132. See also Paul DiMaggio, "Cultural Entrepreneurship in Nineteenth-Century Boston: The Creation of an Organizational Base for High Culture in America," *Media, Culture and Society* 4 (1982): 33–50.

9. Key works on classical music in nineteenth-century America also include John Ogaspian and N. Lee Orr, *Music of the Gilded Age* (Westport, CT: Greenwood Press, 2007); Joseph Horowitz, *Classic Music in America: A History of Its Rise and Fall* (New York: W. W. Norton, 2005); Derek Vaillant, *Sounds of Reform: Progressivism and Music in Chicago, 1873–1935* (Chapel Hill: University of North Carolina Press, 2003); Richard Crawford, *America's Musical Life: A History* (New York: W. W. Norton, 2001); and Nicholas Tawa, *From Psalm to Symphony: A History of Music in New England* (Boston: Northeastern University Press, 2001).

10. The endowed symphony orchestras that, as Levine and DiMaggio both argue, were part of the creation of the highbrow and the process of sacralization are also an example of ongoing experimentation in the late nineteenth century with economic models for funding, promoting, and presenting musical entertainment. A closer attention to different models for marketing musical

entertainment contributes to our understanding of the larger context within which sacralization occurred; the sacralization of culture was in part a reaction to the growth of entertainment capitalism. But not all methods of marketing European art music accepted the same premise as the sacralizers. Levine's work has mainly been critiqued for overemphasizing the social motivations of the sacralizers at the expense of a serious consideration of the aesthetics of concertgoing and music appreciation. Although my arguments are in sympathy with Ralph Locke's call to scholars to examine countervailing efforts to make music accessible and popular, my main interest here is how different economic models for entertainment promoted competing social, moral, national, and aesthetic visions. The lyceum bureaus promoted music through a strongly nationalistic celebration of the tastes of American publics and the significance of rising American artists. Ultimately, this nationalistic vision embraced a more expansive vision of the popular and a more eclectic model of musical entertainment than the sacralizers would allow. For recent critiques and modifications of Levine, see Daniel Cavicchi, *Listening and Longing: Music Lovers in the Age of Barnum* (Middleport, CT: Wesleyan University Press, 2011); Horowitz, *Classic Music in America;* Steven Baur, "Music, Morals, and Social Management: Mendelssohn in Post–Civil War America," *American Music* 19, no. 1 (Spring 2001): 64–130; and Ralph Locke, "Music Lovers, Patrons, and the 'Sacralization' of Culture in America," *19th-Century Music* 17, no. 2 (Autumn 1993): 149–73, esp. 154–55.

11. "Camilla Urso's Concerts," *Redpath's Lyceum,* August 1875, 47.

12. "Musical Department," *Lyceum Magazine,* June 1873, 11.

13. "Lyceums and Their Wants," *The Lyceum,* August 1869, 1.

14. Ray, *Lyceum and Public Culture;* Cherches, "Star Course"; and Eubank, "Redpath Lyceum Bureau."

15. These included the New England Musical Bureau, Roberts' Lecture and Musical Agency, the Chickering Musical Bureau, and Williams' Musical Bureau. Elsie M. Wilbor, ed., *Werner's Directory of Elocutionists, Readers, Lecturers, and Other Public Instructors and Entertainments* (New York: Edgar S. Werner, 1887).

16. "Hints for Lyceums," *Lyceum Magazine,* July 1871, 1.

17. "Star-Lecturing," *Scribner's Monthly* 8 (May 1874): 110–11.

18. Donald Scott, "The Popular Lecture and the Creation of a Public in Mid-Nineteenth-Century America," *Journal of American History* 66. no. 4 (March 1980): 791–809.

19. The same effect, Holland noted, had long been observed in theater and opera. Audiences attended theater "not to witness a play, but to see Booth, or Joe Jefferson." Likewise the opera "is nothing without Kellogg, or Patti, or Nilsson, or some miraculous tenor who to-day is, and to-morrow is not." In contrast, those "trained, laborious, patient, admirable" orchestras "pass for nothing." Choruses and supporting singers therefore earn next to nothing compared to the stars "who shine brighter in the sky of mediocrity." "Star-Lecturing," 110–11.

20. "Hints for Lyceums," *Lyceum Magazine,* July 1871, 2.

21. "Some Words of Advice to New Committees," *American Literary Magazine and Lecture Season,* August 1872, 6.

22. "Why Lyceums Fail," *The Lyceum,* August 1869, 4.

23. "Musical Department," *American Literary Magazine and Lecture Season,* August 1872, 32.

24. For examples, see Eubank, "Redpath Lyceum Bureau," 207–8. On social practices around public lecture culture, see Ronald J. Zboray and Mary Saracino Zboray, *Everyday Ideas: Socioliterary Experience among Antebellum New Englanders* (Knoxville: University of Tennessee Press, 2006).

25. "Some Words of Advice to New Committees," *American Literary Magazine and Lecture Season,* August 1872, 7.

26. "Music in the Lyceum," *American Literary Bureau,* July 1874, 4.

27. "Musical and Other Entertainments," *American Literary Bureau,* July 1874, 11.

28. James Pond, "The Lyceum," *Cosmopolitan: A Monthly Illustrated Magazine,* April 1896, 598.

29. *Worcester (MA) Daily Spy,* 7 November 1872.

30. Ibid., 8 November 1872.

31. Ibid., 7 October 1869.

32. Ibid., 8 November 1872.

33. *Dexter Smith's Music, Literary, Dramatic and Art Paper,* September 1872, 210–11.

34. Ibid., October 1875, 102.

35. Discussions of the social and cultural significance of Thomas's career appear in Vaillant, *Sounds of Reform;* Levine, *Highbrow/Lowbrow;* and Crawford, *America's Musical Life.*

36. Charles Horner, *The Life of James Redpath and the Development of the Modern Lyceum* (New York: Barse & Hopkins, 1926), 213.

37. "Musical Department," *Lyceum Magazine,* July 1872, 6–7.

38. "Readings and Other Entertainments," *The Lyceum,* August 1869, 4.

39. Jon Seymour Nicholson, "Patrick Gilmore's Boston Peace Jubilees" (PhD diss., University of Michigan, 1971).

40. Details of Urso's life and career are in Christine Ammer, *Unsung: A History of Women in American Music,* 2nd ed. (Montclair, NJ: Amadeus Press, 2001); Susan Kagan, "Camilla Urso: A Nineteenth-Century Violinist's View," *Signs* 2, no. 3 (1977): 727–34; and Charles Barnard, *Camilla: A Tale of a Violin* (Boston: Loring, 1874)

41. "Camilla Urso's Concerts," *Redpath's Lyceum,* 1875, 48.

42. "Chat with Camilla Urso," *Dexter Smith's,* September 1874, 72.

43. Urso also participated in the culture of music festivals, and in 1870 she organized the Grand Musical Festival in San Francisco to raise money for the Mercantile Library Association. Urso's festival followed Gilmore's model in appealing to audiences with feats of scale and flights of popular song while also introducing them to oratorio and classical music; *Dwight's Journal of Music,* 9 April 1870, 220. See also Betsy G. Miller, "A Lady Gives a Monster Concert," *Society for American Music Bulletin* 26, no. 1 (Spring 2000), available at www.american-music.org/publicantions/bullarchive/Miller.html.

44. "Concerts. Redpath Lyceum Bureau." *Dwight's Journal of Music,* 11 October 1879, 166.

45. "Lyceum Bureau Concerts," *Dwight's Journal of Music,* 11 October 1879, 159–60.

46. *Cleveland Plain Dealer,* 24 April 1868.

47. Reprinted in *Dwight's Journal of Music,* 20 November 1869, 137.

48. "Getting a Musical Education," *Dexter Smith's,* December 1874.

49. "American Opera Singers Abroad," *Dexter Smith's,* January 1875.

50. *Folio* was far more subscribed than *Dwight's Journal of Music* and may be more representative of popular tastes and attitudes toward musical culture in America in the 1870s. Dexter Smith edited *Folio* from 1869 to 1871 before starting his own paper. H. Earle Johnson, "*The Folio* of White, Smith and Company," *American Music* 2, no. 1 (Spring 1984): 88–104.

51. "Aesthetic Advancement," *Folio,* March 1873, 72.

PART II

COSMOPOLITAN AUTHORSHIP

4

Mr. Emerson's Playful Lyceum

Polyvocal Promotion on the Lecture Circuit

Robert Arbour

On a bitterly cold January evening in DeWitt, Iowa, in 1866, Ralph Waldo Emerson, a veteran lecturer on the lyceum circuit with some thirty-three years of experience under his belt, stood at the rostrum and began skipping wildly over the pages of his manuscript, glancing every so often at his watch. The reason was simple: he had double-booked himself. Emerson's tight schedule did not allow him to finish the full lecture. He had to catch an 8:50 train to give another lecture in Dubuque the next night, and the audience of tiny DeWitt suddenly became dispensable. "Mr. Emerson treated his audience in a most indifferent and insulting manner," the *DeWitt Observer* fumed. It was a blow made all the more offensive by his "world-wide" reputation as a scholar and orator, the cosmopolitan intellectual hurrying away without the decency to give his listeners their money's worth. "Now we look at it in this way," the reporter went on, "Mr. Emerson had received his price from the Association for his lecture, and the citizens had paid the Association the fee of admission to hear it delivered, and for Mr. Emerson to then withhold half of it, is not a very genteel way of swindling people."[1]

If there was a genteel way of swindling people, Emerson would seem to have found it in his career as a lyceum lecturer. Of the almost 1,500 lectures he delivered over forty-eight years, few were considered rhetorical gems.[2] Some charitable scholars have called their reception inconsistent, but most concede that listeners thought of him less as a font of wisdom and more as an oratorical curiosity. For every mediocre review praising his lucidity on the sentence level, bundles more lambasted him for everything from the incomprehensible structure of his lectures to the awkward posture of his person. He was usually stooped over, leafing through manuscript pages seemingly at random, often appearing to lose his place and speaking in a low voice just above a whisper, with nary a gesture except the occasional twitch of his left hand at his side. To audiences, his lectures often appeared unprepared, disconnected, and convoluted. The *Milwaukee Sentinel* complained of his "nervousness of expression, now rapid in motion, now impressively—almost painfully—slow" and the "interruptions to his lecture, caused by omissions which he saw fit to make." The *Western Reserve Chronicle* of Warren, Ohio, noted that he was "more attractive on the printed page than on the rostrum." After one lecture, a reporter for the *Cleveland Plain Dealer* grew tired of this "rather sleepy affair." "We had quite as lief see a perpendicular coffin behind a lecture-desk as Emerson," he quipped.[3]

Yet for all his shortcomings, Emerson enjoyed success as a lecturer. During the 1850s, when he began to tour the Midwest and used lyceum bureaus and booking agents to schedule his events, he gave between seventy and eighty lectures each year. As William Charvat remarks, Emerson was "not only the most popular of all 'literary' lecturers, but one of the most popular of all lecturers" in nineteenth-century America, even though his listeners rarely understood what he said.[4] His books and investments brought in little money, and the bulk of his income came from lectures.[5] He treated lecturing as his occupation, sometimes dismissively, as when he wrote to Samuel Gray Ward in 1843: "Whenever I get into debt, which usually happens once a year, I must make the plunge into this great odious river of travellers, into these cold eddies of hotels & boarding houses,—farther, into these dangerous precincts of charlatanism, namely Lectures, that out of all the evil I may draw a little good in the correction which every journey makes to my exaggerations." But often he wrote enthusiastically about lecturing as a gratifying profession, not least because it provided a respite from the strictures of writing. "I hate the details," he wrote in the same letter to Ward, "but the whole foray into a city teaches me much." In an 1839 journal entry he praised the "convertible audience" that the lyceum afforded him: "here are no stiff conventions that prescribe a method, a style, a limited quotation of books, & an exact respect to certain books, persons, or opinions. No, here everything is admissible."[6]

Emerson prepared methodically for lectures, crafting anecdotes specifically for his audiences and later removing them from published versions.

So amused was he by these stories that he had to practice reading them at home as many as twenty times before making it through them without giggling.[7] As odious as the details of lecturing may have been, he devoted himself to reaching his listeners, heartened by the hope that his ideas, and to a great extent his persona, would become accessible to them. After he gave the lecture "The Anglo-American" to the Concord lyceum on December 12, 1853, Emerson recounted in his journal a conversation with Thoreau, who complained that "whatever succeeded with the audience was bad," praising instead "the better lectures which only reached a few persons." Emerson took the opposite position: "I am ambitious to write something," he responded, "which all can read, like Robinson Crusoe. And when I have written a paper or a book, I see with regret that it is not solid, with a right materialistic treatment, which delights everybody."[8] Note Emerson's simultaneous concerns with the publication of the lectures and with solidity. At a time when his writing, associated as it was with transcendentalism, struck readers as increasingly abstruse and ethereal, he wishes to make it concrete and material, approachable in a way that his public lectures rarely were. It is no coincidence that in this conversation on lecturing, Emerson's thoughts turn immediately to published works. As the excerpts from his letter to Ward indicate, the lecture hall is for Emerson a space of revision. The journey along the lecture circuit corrects his exaggerations, and the foray into the city teaches him lessons. The lyceum itself may have had "no stiff conventions," but Emerson envisions the loose lectures he delivers as springboards for firming up his ideas in print, arriving at a stable persona that he wants to make as substantive as the books his readers hold in their hands.

In this essay, I wish to address this paradox of Emerson as the inept lecturer who dedicated himself so carefully and so successfully to a craft he took seriously. I will argue that not only may Emerson have been more willing to fail on the lecture circuit than scholars typically acknowledge, but that in his willingness to fail he negotiated a complex sense of identity, as he fashioned in his print essays a promotional persona designed to change his listeners' expectations of him. This promotional strategy makes Emerson a cosmopolite, if he hasn't seemed to be one already. Rather than concentrate on the transatlantic Emerson, I want to explore ways in which he illustrates another modality of cosmopolitanism. By virtue of the fluid form of the lyceum lecture and his own frustration with his affiliation with transcendentalism, Emerson put forth a theoretical cosmopolitanism that is based on the free play of identity. The bulk of this essay discusses a relatively inward-oriented cosmopolitanism. The cosmopolitan posture of openness I describe is inward-oriented for three reasons: it stems from

Emerson's idiosyncratic motives and compositional strategies; it invites introspection and even confusion in individual listeners; and it is confined by the imagined boundaries of the mid-nineteenth-century nation-state of America. Although this sense of *cosmopolitanism* might seem peculiarly insular, it nevertheless furnishes the structural framework for an outward-oriented American cosmopolitanism that takes into account a multiplicity of unfamiliar perspectives, domestic and international, a cosmopolitanism that is consonant with an understanding of the purposes of the midcentury lyceum lecture. As Emerson forces himself and his audience to renegotiate his public persona, which he locates finally in the interstices between his oral and printed works, he encourages listeners to interrogate and refine their own cosmopolitan attitudes.

In contemporary scholarship the term *cosmopolitan* tends to evoke the accumulation of multiple perspectives and identities. However, the original term coined by the Stoics, notes Kwame Anthony Appiah, was grounded in negation, a skeptical "rejection of the conventional view that every civilized person belonged to a community among communities." Central to cosmopolitanism, he explains, is the notion that recognition of responsibility to an inclusive human community supersedes all local attachments and loyalties. But for Appiah cosmopolitanism is not synonymous with globalism or universalism; cosmopolitanism does not promote any "single mode of life" for all humans but is instead attuned to differences and particularities. Detached from their nations, classes, or other affiliations, particular individuals must enter into "conversation," both in the traditional sense of coexistence and in the contemporary sense of exchange.[9] Sparked by a "cosmopolitan curiosity," this conversation between strangers produces a "shared identity," suggesting at least momentarily a rejection of those constitutive aspects of the self that are not shared; this shared identity creates the possibility "that we will be able to enjoy discovering things we do not yet share."[10] The cosmopolite, then, enjoys a multiplicity of identities that change or reshuffle according either to contact with different individuals or to the rejection or creation of particular affiliations. Cosmopolitanism in this formulation describes a conversation across any and all local boundaries and among individuals who negotiate and renegotiate their own identities in a fluid and entertaining process of discovery.

Appiah's useful definition might not have seemed so foreign to lyceum-goers in mid-nineteenth-century America. Although the lyceum system comprised localized organizations throughout the country, each with its own operating procedures, these organizations had in common a patriotic emphasis on democratic appeal and, increasingly, a mission to introduce local listeners to lecturers of national and international renown, speakers the listeners would never ordinarily encounter. As Angela Ray has shown in her seminal study *The Lyceum and Public Culture in the Nineteenth-Century United States,* many local lyceums evolved from debating societies, and though controversial lecture topics were discouraged, the lyceum never lost its association with the open discussion of differing perspectives.[11] The schedules of some lyceums featured debaters one week and lecturers the next,[12] blurring lines between the two genres and encouraging audience members to consider the lecture a conversational debate of sorts. "It is, of course, a great thing to be said for the lecture system in America," explains an 1872 London *Daily News* article, reprinted proudly in the Boston *Daily Advertiser,* "that it gives people an opportunity of hearing opinions to which they are not accustomed, and therefore trains them in the discipline of listening with patience." As prominent lecturers transcend cultural boundaries and challenge assumptions in these American city-states, "we cannot doubt that good must result from these interminglings of opinion, and consequent comparison of views."[13] Those "interminglings of opinion" suggest precisely how fluid and contingent identities could be in the contact zone of the lyceum.

Though the lyceum lecture was promoted ostensibly as an educational event, those who attended understood it also to be an opportunity for the exchange of points of view, a time for the negotiation of individual identity based on what listener and lecturer did and did not share. "A lyceum audience has apparently no prejudices," the article muses. "It will listen to anybody's views on anything, provided only the speaker has information to give or entertainment to provide."[14] And the proximity here of "information" and "entertainment" points us to the sine qua non of lyceum culture. A trip to the lyceum, as Ray puts it, "became a chief means of acceptable diversion and social interaction in many towns and villages." Participants in the lyceum expected to have fun, albeit "serious fun."[15] Consequently, Emerson was whispering from the rostrum into no silent space. Sidebar conversations abounded in the lecture hall, from the sweet nothings traded between lovers and the excited chatter among children sitting beside their parents to the rounds of applause from the speaker's supporters and the taunts and jeers of hecklers.[16] In many senses, the lyceum lecture was a large-scale conversation in which multiple identities collided or coalesced, inviting immediate responses from listeners who delighted in what they discovered about both the lecturer and themselves. Built to entertain, the lecture hall offered the audience a space of free play wherein ideas and identities became fluid and negotiable. Although listeners certainly didn't accept all the ideas they heard, what brought them to this space to hear famous strangers speak could be described in the words of Appiah as a cosmopolitan curiosity.

By 1865 Emerson had come to be seen as a figurehead for cosmopolitan conversation in the United States. A report in the *National Aegis* on his lecture "Table Talk," given in Worcester, Massachusetts, paraphrases in terms appropriate for the lyceum his discussion of conversation "as an art which all mankind play at." While conversation flows freely in cultured Paris, "America in common with other nations is narrowed by its intense egotism." "Nationality is babyish," this mediated version of Emerson chides, "and the hope is that our widely increasing arrangements for travel will make us more cosmopolitan." The friend of Thomas Carlyle and William Wordsworth, the writer of essays on Montaigne and Swedenborg among other European figures, and the student of Indian philosophy, Emerson had long been known for his international travel and worldliness. As we shall see, however, early in his career this worldliness was subsumed under the heading of an abstruse transcendentalism strongly associated with his unintelligibility. In this report, his globalism comes to the fore to characterize him as a master of cosmopolitan conversation who instructs his listeners that the "triumph of culture is to import the flower of each nation's genius into our own hospitable courtesy."[17] Emerson's cosmopolitanism describes a tapestry of ideas from different nations woven together, paradoxically, to elevate the cultural status of America by broadening its horizons beyond the frontiers of nationality. As in his 1844 lecture "The Young American," when he called for a "more catholic and cosmopolitan" American legislation reflective of the country's "most expansive and humane spirit," Emerson frames cosmopolitanism as a rather nationalistic transformation.[18] The implication seems clear: by coming into conversation with international perspectives different from their own, Americans will construct stronger and wiser versions of themselves, leaving their identities open through a cosmopolitan curiosity, one that complements nicely the listening posture that the lyceum audience has been trained to assume.

I have begun here with the end of the story I would like to tell, when Emerson embraces cosmopolitanism and when his audience (of listeners and readers) embraces him as an American cosmopolite. In the early 1840s and before, he was known strictly as a transcendentalist, a label that would eventually make him uncomfortable. I aim to fill in some of the gaps between these two personas by sketching out a cosmopolitan Emerson who offered to readers and listeners alike multiple versions of himself as he used the relationship between his spoken and written works to reconfigure his public identity, in essence modeling the fluidity of identity through conversation that resists affiliation. I first look briefly at Emerson's general approaches to the lyceum to suggest that, like his audience, he conceived of the lecture hall as a relaxed space of free play; I then turn to a particular crisis in identity that Emerson experienced during his 1841–42 lecture series, "The Times." As Emerson began to question the affiliation of both his oratorical and literary voices with transcendentalism, he used his print essays as a promotional vehicle to leave his voice fluid, responding directly to his own concerns about his voice in the lecture hall. My analytical focus for this theory is "The Transcendentalist," Emerson's 1843 essay based on one of the lectures in "The Times." It is a polyvocal essay in which different personas, all aligned with Emerson, serve to leave open and ambivalent his public identity, encouraging readers to approach this unfamiliar Emerson with a cosmopolitan curiosity.

Emerson's impressive lecturing career, which spanned four decades, has not escaped the notice of critics.[19] Focusing particularly on Emerson's listeners, scholars such as Mary Kupiec Cayton and Bonnie Carr O'Neill have explained Emerson's success by suggesting that his primarily working-class listeners were encouraged by the lyceum system to interpret his messages for their own purposes.[20] Few critics, however, have posited reasons for what appear to be Emerson's consistently terrible performances in the lecture hall. For some, such as Vern Wagner, the explanation is that in his rhetorical style, Emerson never completely left the pulpit. He is the preacher, always trying to convert the audience and never willing to adapt to his listeners, fulfilling his own doctrine of self-reliance, intransigent in his devotion to a high, intellectual style devoid of oratorical flourishes.[21] For others, he is simply hopelessly untalented as a speaker, propelled along fortunately from town to town on the lecture circuit, as O'Neill suggests, by the strength of his burgeoning celebrity both in the United States and abroad.[22] But where the first view tends to disregard Emerson's assiduous attentiveness to his audience, the latter tends to downplay the importance of the lectures themselves, separating them entirely from Emerson's written oeuvre.

I want to reconsider the significance of Emerson's lectures by suggesting that his celebrity afforded him a certain latitude in the lecture hall. Structurally and financially, the lyceum lecture hall was for Emerson a safe space that invited play. In studies of both his reception as a speaker and his attempts at speaking, we tend to assume that when Emerson gave a lecture, he strove above all to be understood and that his lectures were often incomprehensible because he lacked poise and ability. Breaking from this tradition, I wish to place more weight on Emerson's own compositional strategies, and even control, in his approach to lecturing. I argue for a cannier Emerson, who spoke with an eye toward the essays he would write and for whom lucidity in his public speech was a secondary concern. Stylistically in his essays, Emerson constructs a flexible, promotional persona that establishes the expectations of his prospective audiences. He then plays with those expectations in his lyceum lectures, revising his public persona and estranging his audiences from him. As his body, written over and against his printed words, moves from town to town across the United States, deracinated from any particular locus, he projects to his audience the image of the cosmopolite, settled neither in identity nor in place.

It was not uncommon for Emerson to resist the rather procrustean stamps his listeners wanted to place on his public identity. During a course of six lectures in Philadelphia in January and February 1843, for instance, he complains in a letter to Margaret Fuller about the "streams" of people he meets: "Yet this seems very plain that one should never allow himself to stand sponsor for an opinion, it spoils your relation to men so quickly. It is assumed in all companies that you think so & so, you who at that very moment wish to fly in the face of just *that* way of thinking."[23] The assumptions that bother Emerson are those of his readers, who approximate Emerson's transcendentalist persona in print and his voice at the rostrum. With the lecture, Emerson aims to convert his readers into listeners, flying in the face of their expectations and forcing them to reconcile a different man with the one they have read about in print. And the public lecture, as Emerson knew, may have been the perfect tool for altering audience expectations. Pliable, lacking the strict and stultifying conventions of the published page, the lecture liberated Emerson, giving him a new freedom in demeanor and expression, allowing him to present to his audiences multiple versions of himself, no one version necessarily consistent with any other. On the lecture circuit, Emerson could, to a large extent, revise himself and his works anew by playing with his audiences. If we consider the lyceum lecture hall a form of *ludus*, a structured, calculated play with emphasis on subordination to rules, we might consider Emerson's lectures a form of *paidia*, or active, spontaneous, and unstructured play.[24] Emerson acts spontaneously within and despite the rules constructed both by the lyceum system, framed often as a forum for the moral and intellectual improvement of the citizens of the United States, and by the expectations of his readers. Emerson, I suggest, experiments in his lectures, editing and revising *while* he speaks, in anticipation of his essays, which will help to promote his name to prospective audiences, constructing a literary imprimatur that is consistently revisable.

Indeed, Emerson's gaffe in that Iowa lecture hall may not have been that anomalous after all. Although he probably skipped more pages than usual, his shuffling of manuscript pages that night is nothing that isn't found in several other reports of Emerson's lectures. As in many towns, it was Emerson's "world-wide reputation" that drew the people of DeWitt to the lecture. And perhaps the worst repercussion Emerson could expect from swindling the town's audience was simply not being asked to return. I don't mean to suggest that Emerson was apathetic about lecturing or that he deliberately underperformed. He prepared meticulously for lectures and wrote about them frequently in his journals and correspondence. But he was also practical, thinking about lectures in terms of dollars and cents, as well as experimental, often frustrated with the ready-made opinions his readers had formed about him before he arrived to speak. I want to suggest that Emerson could fail as a lecturer with virtually no penalty, particularly if that failure resulted in stronger essays, which helped promote his reputation to prospective audiences.

The lyceum, Emerson wrote to Thomas Carlyle in 1836, was "the most flexible of all organs of opinion; from its popularity & from its newness permitting you to say what you think, without any shackles of prescription." Unlike in the pulpit, he continued, "in the Lyceum, nothing is presupposed. The orator is only responsible for what his lips articulate. Then what scope it allows!"[25] As Gay Wilson Allen has argued, as he loosed the shackles from his lips on lyceum tours, Emerson adjusted his literary style, often revising his lectures stylistically based on audience reaction, adding epigrams, for instance, and deleting repetitious passages.[26] These adjustments, made by Emerson in the lecture hall, then directly informed the production of his essays, which in turn served to market a particular persona to readers. The importance of a speaker's persona was not lost on Emerson, popular orator that he was. "The audience is of all classes," he explained to Carlyle, "and its character will be determined always by the name of the lecturer."[27] More than the actual lecturer, the lecturer's *name* constructs the listeners and their horizon of expectations. More stable than his flexible, paidiac lectures, Emerson's persona, crystallized by his published works, governs the rules of the hall. And as that persona changes before their eyes, his listeners must reconcile for themselves a polyvocal Emerson, a cosmopolitan speaker who challenges their preconceptions about identity.

Emerson's imprimatur held such great sway with audiences because it extended even beyond his readership to those who had neither seen his written works nor heard him speak a word. His promotional persona, that is, ran ahead of him, generating interest in both his lecture tours and his essays. It was not until the 1850 publication of *English Traits* that one of Emerson's books turned a profit; but his books did indirect financial work, becoming vehicles for the promotion of Emerson as a literary and intellectual celebrity of sorts. Emerson was first invited to Cincinnati, for example, by Ainsworth P. Spofford of the Cincinnati Literary Club, whose members had read his early essays. Indeed, the man who would become his publicist in that city, Moncure Daniel Conway, learned about Emerson when, while in Warrenton, Virginia, he read an article in the Scottish literary review *Blackwood's,* which printed excerpts from Emerson's essays in 1847, prompting Conway to order a copy of *Essays: Second Series.*[28] On the lyceum circuit, Emerson was billed consistently as an "Essayist and Poet," titles familiar even to those like Conway who had caught only glimpses of Emerson's work in magazines or reviews of his essays in newspapers.[29]

A significant contributing factor to the popularity of Emerson's 1841–42 lecture series "The Times" was a review of his *Essays: First Series* in the Boston *Daily Advertiser* of December 16, 1841, the day that Emerson gave the third talk in a course of six lectures at that city's Masonic Temple. Although the review was not particularly complimentary of Emerson as an author, questioning his method and his "originality," it did have the effect of associating him with the luminary Carlyle, who wrote a preface for Emerson's book, thus advancing his reputation as a man of letters to people who had not read the book of essays. The review makes clear that Emerson should be hailed as a man of intellectual depth, but it also caricatures him as a man who is far too deep. Emerson is cast as a thinker lost forever in the abstract and thus doomed to error: "An enthusiast and a recluse, he is so shut out from all external influences, that he is wholly unconscious of the startling contradictions which daily experience offers to his abstractions." "So far from being 'above' a system," the reviewer laments, "Mr. Emerson, we repeat, is the veritable slave of the theories he has adopted."[30] Before Emerson's name, the reviewer implies, comes the name of transcendentalism. His persona in *Essays: First Series,* a book that includes several essays converted from lectures,[31] promotes him to the residents of Boston as a thinker without solidity who does not venture outside the confines of his own mind to see the physical, even corporeal, applications of his transcendental theories in the world. Although this review and Emerson's literary imprimatur were enough to drum up interest in Emerson as a lecturer as he embarked on "The Times," he came to resent precisely this representation and saw the lectures as an opportunity to reconstruct his promotional persona in order to distance himself from transcendentalism and abstraction at once.

As Emerson learned to his dismay, the voice his audience was expecting when he delivered "The Times" was decidedly that of a transcendentalist. It was the voice Emerson had used even in earlier essays such as *Nature* (1836) and "The American Scholar" (1837), his Phi Beta Kappa oration at Harvard, and it was the voice that characterizes "Self-Reliance" (1841) with a persona who universalizes his own experience even as he distances himself from readers to maintain a sense of authority. Lawrence Buell has called this persona of Emerson's early essays a confident and universal "exemplary persona."[32] Inflexible and authoritative, he presents his injunctions as universal laws, speaking often in the third-person plural. The exemplary persona opens *Nature,* for instance, with the definitive diagnosis of "Our age is retrospective" before suggesting reform with a prophetic proposal to readers: "Let us demand our own works and laws and worship."[33] The mention of "worship" and the anaphora of "Let us" in the introduction mark the confident voice of the preacher who speaks for his congregants. The persona begins the first chapter alone, in apparent "solitude," but the concluding paragraph starts with a prophecy containing the pronoun *we,* tacitly indicating a shift to universality: "So shall we come to look at the world with new eyes."[34]

Emerson began to grow uncomfortable with this voice and to turn away from it during the "Times" lecture series. The remainder of this essay will focus on this shift because it represents a significant transitional period in Emerson's literary career, providing him with a particular motive to experiment with his audience in the lecture hall. For, by this point in his career, Emerson had grown disenchanted with the label of transcendentalist despite remaining aligned with the movement. His own thoughts now took him away from the abstract ideals he had praised in *Nature* and "The American Scholar" and rooted him more firmly in the value of experience. He was no longer sure, moreover, whether the pursuit of ideals and self-fulfillment he had discussed in his early works could be universalized, whether these were in fact available to everyone. In short, Emerson entered into a crisis of voice, and his correspondence indicates that he began to search for a new voice, and a new persona, in the lectures he gave at the end of 1841 and the beginning of 1842. This search, I argue, had the effect of encouraging Emerson, along with his listeners, to renegotiate his public identity, favoring a cosmopolitan, polyvocal persona.

As early as March 1840, when he was delivering lectures in Providence,

Rhode Island, Emerson began to have misgivings about the specter of transcendentalism that followed him wherever he lectured. He wrote to his mother: "You must know I am reckoned here a Transcendentalist, and what that beast is, all persons in Providence have a great appetite to know." He has become a "dissipated villager" in Providence, he tells his mother, shuttled from house to house and interrogated about transcendentalism, his public identity misty and without substance, scattered over the city by virtue of his affiliation with transcendentalism. "I have read here," reports Emerson, "my essay on the Age, the one on Home, one on Love, & one on Politics,—These seem all to be regarded as mere screens & subterfuges while this dread Transcendentalism is still kept back." By August 1841, the beast Emerson used to describe his transcendentalist identity has dissolved into a formless, and contradictory, entity. "I have no barrier," he tells Margaret Fuller, "but am all boundless conceding & willowy." He explains to Fuller: "I detect twenty contradictions which hedge me round where I saw nothing but white walls in all my previous good easy days." And according to Emerson in a letter to his wife, Lidian, it is this persona who gives a speech on August 11, 1841, at Waterville College in Maine, a very abstract lecture titled "The Method of Nature" that notoriously left his audience puzzled, giving rise to his fear that all of his "speech public or trivial will betray my spectral life, & seem bodiless."[35]

Becoming increasingly aware and concerned that his listeners envision him as a transcendentalist with his head in the clouds, completely aloof from the common man, Emerson senses a division from them, and he attributes it to the ideals of transcendentalism. Moreover, he describes that division consistently in terms of corporeality. He feels the bodilessness of his exemplary persona, recognizing that without some accessibility, some substance and concrete reality, his public identity will fast become a cipher. In March 1842, indeed, he complains to Lidian that Horace Greeley and his friends "fasten me in their thought to 'Transcendentalism,' whereof you know I am wholly guiltless, and which is spoken of as a known & fixed element like salt or meal." He must issue "endless disclaimers & explanations—'I am not the man you take me for.'"[36] His own public identity virtually indecipherable, Emerson falls victim to the easy fixity of the category of transcendentalist as his listeners try to contain him within one concrete identity.

Greeley was meeting with Emerson while the latter was in New York City to read six of the eight lectures that make up "The Times," in which Emerson aimed to sketch different types of people emblematic of contemporary times.[37] Basing the concept for the series on photographic sketches, Emerson referred to the lectures as a "portrait gallery,"[38] presenting his audience with talks devoted to such figures as "The Conservative," "The Poet," and "The Transcendentalist." He gave eight of the lectures at the Masonic Temple in Boston from December 2, 1841, to January 20, 1842, and then shortened the course to five lectures, which he gave in Providence in February 1842, finishing the series in March with the six lectures in New York. It was in a letter to his brother William, who would arrange the appearances in New York, that Emerson first broached the idea of this series. After he asks William about distributing copies of the spectral "Waterville Speech" to readers in New York, Emerson mentions his plan to speak in Boston: "I think these 'lectures' capable of a variety of style & matter which no other form of composition admits. We can laugh & cry, curse & pray, tell stories & crack jokes, spin a web of transcendentalism a thousand times finer than spiderthread . . . do all this in one discourse." Juxtaposing his plan for a new kind of lecture and, as he puts it, "an eloquence that is still possible" against the "Waterville Speech," which he has associated with his bodiless and ineffective lecturing persona, Emerson sees in "The Times" an opportunity to reinvent himself as a speaker. Here, transcendentalism is so gossamer thin, like a spider's web, that it is barely visible or present and is completely subordinated to the substance of the lectures, yet perhaps also indicative of Emerson's desire to capture his audience.

On December 4, 1841, two days after he gave his introductory lecture in Boston, Emerson reports proudly to William that "they told me in town this time that I was grown more direct & intelligible than in former years."[39] In the midst of a crisis of rhetorical identity, Emerson seizes on "The Times" as an opportunity to refashion his persona, experimenting and playing with his audience to dispel their beliefs about his identity as a transcendentalist. He works actively against listeners like Greeley and those in Providence who seek to pin him down and concentrates instead on a valence of identity, locating himself and his identity *between* the types that he describes. Emerson always gauged audience reaction in order to revise and refine his essays, but here the free play afforded by the lecture hall allows him to play out his personal anxieties about his voice as he aims to explode the assumptions his audiences have about him.

Moreover, as an extension of his concern with voice, Emerson often makes use of dialogic format in "The Times," portraying conversations between pairs of characters, such as Saturn and Uranus or Youth and Property in "The Conservative," to represent at once two different points of view. With their frequent shifts of voice and viewpoint in a conversational format, these lectures serve as metacommentaries on the power of voice in the lecture hall as Emerson tests different personas in front of his listeners. Rather than one authoritative voice, Emerson's focus on conversation decenters the authority of the lecturer, estranging him from his listeners, who have been awaiting the appearance of the familiar exemplary persona. When the lectures are later converted to essays for publication, they become crucial to the formation of a new promotional persona, preparing readers and future listeners for the voice of a different Emerson, one more cautious and circumspect, one hesitant, even, to make the declarations that his exemplary persona embraced as a matter of course. Perhaps the most revealing example is "The Transcendentalist," which was published as an essay in *The Dial* in 1843 and later in the book *Nature: Addresses and Lectures* of 1849, a year before Emerson would embark on his lecture tours to the Midwest. I will conclude this essay with an examination of "The Transcendentalist" to demonstrate how it gives readers the contradictory voices of a bifurcated narrator in order to qualify Emerson's enthusiasm for transcendentalism through a self-ironical play of perspectives, thus encouraging audiences to cultivate a cosmopolitan attitude of openness to multiple identities.

A lyceum-lecture-turned-essay, "The Transcendentalist" reflects a polyvocalic tension even formally. As he experiments with form, Emerson designs a persona reflective of the transitional period of his career, interrogating his own literary identity while setting out to define the transcendentalists. Although the essay purports to provide such a definition, Emerson caricatures transcendentalists as inactive thinkers saddled with a heightened "double consciousness," or an awareness of the temporal and earthly life of "the understanding" and the permanent and spiritual life of the soul.[40] Their double consciousness prompts them to withdraw from society and await the inspiration that will enable them to achieve "universal aims" (198). The essay includes debates between Kantian idealists and Lockean materialists, a transcendentalist man of genius and the world at large, and several different incarnations of transcendentalists who speak in the first person. Of particular interest, though, is the objective distance that Emerson maintains from the transcendentalists he describes in spite of his apparent alignment with their beliefs.

From the start, Emerson throws his audience into a state of confusion by shifting pronouns. In an essay whose ostensible purpose is to classify and characterize the transcendentalists, Emerson has his subjects occupy every possible pronominal position (they appear as "I," "you," "he," "we," and "they"), suggesting the fluidity and relativity of identity. On multiple occasions, the transcendentalists question the nature of identity. A transcendentalist states cryptically: "if you ask me, Whence am I? I feel like other men my relation to that Fact which cannot be spoken, or defined, nor even thought, but which exists, and will exist" (196). They hold, the narrator explains, that everything has a "subjective or relative existence" (195), and the essay performs this very characteristic. "What am I?" one transcendentalist asks. "What but a thought of serenity and independence, an abode in the deep blue sky?" (206), underscoring their ethereal and mercurial sense of identity and recalling, too, Emerson's own misgivings about his dangerously spectral nature as a thinker and lecturer. For Emerson's transcendentalists, identity becomes ineffable and either an integral part of nature ("that Fact" and "the deep blue sky") or a subjectively constructed "thought." Emerson seeks to rehabilitate his own public persona through this parody of the transcendentalists, grounding himself by contrast in concrete, corporeal experience.

Sometimes Emerson indicates passages of dialogue with quotation marks. More frequently, he provides no transition whatsoever to dialogue that he represents in free indirect discourse. In these cases, he briefly removes his promotional persona entirely from the essay by modulating into the first-person voice, as when, for instance, a transcendentalist suddenly states: "I do not wish to do one thing but once. I do not love routine" (204). Statements such as this disrupt the objectivity and critical distance that Emerson's persona attempts to maintain by momentarily plunging the reader into uncertainty. Here, the narratorial "I" is confused with the transcendentalist's "I," forcing the reader to identify with the transcendentalist as the voice of authority before retracting that identification when the narratorial voice returns. Often in the text, Emerson refers to the reader as "you" just before using "you" to denote the transcendentalists, and the frequent shifts of the pronoun "I" displace the speaker's voice of authority. No longer does the exemplary persona command the essay with his pontification; his voice is now one among many, as the transcendentalists and the narrator seem to grapple for control of the text. Even as he estranges himself from the reader, then, Emerson makes the reader confront the transcendental Other, now aligning them, now distancing them, encouraging a cosmopolitan ambivalence of identity.

But neither is the exemplary persona entirely absent from "The Transcendentalist." It appears as the enthusiastic voice of the preacher, a confident scholar, learned and poetic, with a philosophical and often prophetic bent. The preacher delivers sweeping statements surveying history and definitive pronouncements diagnosing societal ills. Imitating some representations of Emerson as a distanced, abstract lyceum lecturer, the preacher often sets himself apart from "my audience" (198) by speaking in the first person to establish authority and suggest his exemplarity. As his exemplary predecessor did, he uses the language of the pulpit. He calls transcendentalism "this heresy" which "cannot pass away without leaving its mark" (200) and says of the transcendentalists: "Their heart is the ark in which the fire is concealed, which shall burn in a broader and universal flame. Let them obey the Genius then most when his impulse is wildest" (208). The authoritative tone and cadence of "Let them," a phrase he repeats anaphorically, the images of the flame and the ark, and the injunction to obey the godlike "Genius" all echo biblical sermons. With this voice, Emerson makes himself familiar to readers, writing in tones they recognize and giving them the transcendentalist that they expect.

As this passage suggests, the preacher embraces transcendentalism unhesitatingly while also claiming that the transcendentalism he embraces remains unrealized. By apotheosizing a pure transcendental ideal, Emerson maintains both a critical distance from and an allegiance to transcendentalism. His adherence to this ideal gives the preacher occasion to launch into optimistic prophecy and fervent social critique:

> Although, as we have said, there is no pure Transcendentalist, yet the tendency to respect the intuitions, and to give them, at least in our creed, all authority over our experience, has deeply colored the conversation and poetry of the present day; and the history of genius and of religion in these times, though impure, and as yet not incarnated in any powerful individual, will be the history of this tendency. (199)

Emphasizing the universality of his prophecy with "our experience," the preacher assures his congregants that the pure transcendental intuitions "as yet not incarnated" will inevitably arise, with Emerson cleverly keeping transcendentalism at arm's length.

But now Emerson does not let this voice stand alone. If the preacher's voice is the voice of the overt and exemplary transcendental advocate, Emerson tempers that voice in "The Transcendentalist" by introducing a detached observational voice, a documentarian (to borrow another term from Buell),[41] who seeks to give the reader a biographical sketch in a reportorial tone. The documentarian rarely speaks in the first person, addressing the reader instead as "we" or "you," and maintains, in an understated manner, at least the pretense of objectivity as he attempts to describe and classify the transcendentalists: "They are lonely; the spirit of their writing and conversation is lonely; they repel influences; they shun general society; they incline . . . to find their tasks and amusements in solitude" (200). Speaking in typically sedate sentences, with the anaphora of "they," the documentary voice distances himself from the transcendentalists, refusing the preacher's embrace of the movement, as he isolates them, relegating them to solitude. This voice, indeed, evokes Emerson's 1842 letter to his aunt, Mary Moody Emerson, in which he says of the lecture, "I only write biographically, —describing a class of young persons whom I have seen—I hope it is not confession and that, past all hope, I am confounded with my compassionated heroes & heroines."[42] By inventing a new voice, Emerson nuances his public and literary identity, suggesting to readers that just as they are made to identify occasionally with transcendentalists in the course of the essay, so has Emerson been identified with the transcendentalists. But, importantly, just as his readers draw distinctions between themselves and the transcendentalists, so does Emerson have sharp differences with transcendentalism.

Emerson thus gives listeners and readers glimpses of the voice they expect, the full-throated transcendentalist, even as he test-drives a new persona, exposing the instability of his own identity while destabilizing his readers stylistically through the text. Significantly, however, this is not Emerson's farewell letter to the transcendentalists. Although these two personas differ in tone and tendency, Emerson aligns both with the transcendentalists even as he distances both from that movement through his experiments with polyvocality. Emerson alternates and juxtaposes these personas while treating them as one unified authorial voice, reconfiguring his promotional persona to alter audience expectations, a project he began when he revised himself in lecture halls while delivering "The Times" series in Boston, Providence, and New York City. By placing emphasis on the relativity of identity, and by interrogating his own authorial identity, he follows the methods of the transcendentalists, who with their double consciousness constantly interrogate themselves; paradoxically, he also reinforces central tenets of transcendentalism. As a promotional vehicle for Emerson, the essay subtly modifies his stance on transcendentalism, leaving him room for irony, critique, and free play as well as more concrete and direct language than he once used on the lecture circuit. He implicates his listeners and readers in the same struggle for identity that he enters into, inviting them to negotiate multiple versions of themselves while keeping in mind that he embodies multiple versions of himself, not all of them transcendentalists. By layering his own identity, Emerson asks his future listeners to see in him not simply a transcendentalist but a cosmopolite who negotiates several identities and voices at once and who cannot be contained by one label or another.

As "The Transcendentalist" shows us, Emerson's published works interacted with his spoken works in ways that have heretofore gone unrecognized.

The rostrum may have been the place where Emerson appeared to be at his least comprehensible, but public lecturing was arguably his forte for more than four decades. Scholarship has traditionally preferred to treat his lectures and essays as if they were blocked off completely from each other, implying that Emerson's struggles with lucidity on the lecture circuit were all more or less genuine failures. An examination of his approach to lecturing vis-à-vis his printed works, however, suggests that Emerson began to see the lyceum as a space of free, spontaneous play, ideal for the revision of his own public identity, particularly when he longed to change the public's perception of him. I argue not that Emerson wanted to fail when he delivered a lecture, but that he *could* fail without having to fear dire consequences to his livelihood, precisely because he understood the lyceum as a testing ground for his future essays and his new personas. As he presented "The Times," in particular, Emerson worked through his own anxieties about his voice as a lecturer and his affiliation with transcendentalism. When the label of transcendentalist weighed on him, he turned to the lyceum lecture as an escape hatch, making use of its unstructured play to refashion his own identity and securing that identity by promoting his new persona with the more rigid and permanent form of the published essay. In a very real way, he aimed to reconstruct his public body by playing his new lectures off his previously written work, responding to his listeners' ideas, caricatures, and stereotypes of him as he tried to reinvent himself.

Finally, as seen in "The Transcendentalist," Emerson did not give his readers and listeners one specific identity to latch on to. He preferred instead a multiplicity of identities, which allowed him at times to affiliate with transcendentalism but also to draw away. Emerson set out to make himself less abstract and more approachable, identifying himself not only with the transcendentalists but with his readers and listeners as well, exposing stylistically their multivalent identities. He was later able to use a similar theoretical formula to great effect when he constructed himself not as a transcendentalist but as a patriotic yet transnational cosmopolite juggling multiple identities and affiliations while turning his curiosity to international sources and ideas. By creating particular conversations among his various personas and his audience, thus engendering a cosmopolitan curiosity, Emerson deployed cosmopolitanism rather strategically in the lyceum, locating his public identity between his written and oral works to make it imminently renewable and revisable.

NOTES

1. *DeWitt Observer,* 26 January 1866.

2. Emerson gave lectures from 1833 to 1881. These included both public lectures, which were arranged for him by organizations that paid him a flat sum, and private lectures, which Emerson or a friend organized independently.

3. "Emerson," *Milwaukee Sentinel,* 24 January 1865, [1]; *Western Reserve Chronicle,* 25 January 1865, quoted in David Mead, *Yankee Eloquence in the Middle West* (1951; repr., Westport, CT: Greenwood Press, 1977), 53; "Emerson's Lecture," *Cleveland Plain Dealer,* 21 January 1859, 3.

4. William Charvat, *Emerson's American Lecture Engagements: A Chronological List* (New York: New York Public Library, 1961), 5.

5. See William Charvat, *The Profession of Authorship in America, 1800–1870* (1968; repr., New York: Columbia University Press, 1992), 299. Charvat notes that Emerson once earned as much as $2,000 in one season of lecturing (306).

6. Ralph Waldo Emerson to Samuel Gray Ward, 26 January 1843, in *The Letters of Ralph Waldo Emerson,* vol. 7, *1807–1844,* ed. Eleanor M. Tilton (New York: Columbia University Press, 1990), 523; "Lyceum," 1839, in *The Journals and Miscellaneous Notebooks of Ralph Waldo Emerson,* vol. 7, *1838–1842,* ed. William H. Gilman et al. (Cambridge: Belknap Press of Harvard University Press, 1969), 265. The latter quotation comes from a loose, undated sheet inserted in the beginning of Emerson's 1839–1842 journal.

7. On this point, see Robert D. Richardson, *Emerson: The Mind on Fire* (Berkeley: University of California Press, 1995), 422.

8. December 1853, reprinted in *Emerson in His Journals,* ed. Joel Porte (Cambridge: Harvard University Press, 1982), 449.

9. Kwame Anthony Appiah, *Cosmopolitanism: Ethics in a World of Strangers* (New York: W. W. Norton, 2006), xiv, xv, xxix.

10. Ibid., 97, 98, 97.

11. Angela Ray, *The Lyceum and Public Culture in the Nineteenth-Century United States* (East Lansing: Michigan State University Press, 2005), 33.

12. Ibid., 26.

13. "Lecturing in the United States," *Boston Daily Advertiser,* 9 November 1872.

14. Ibid.

15. Ray, *Lyceum and Public Culture,* 25, 6.

16. Ibid., 25.

17. "Mr. Emerson on Table Talk," *National Aegis,* 18 March 1865.

18. Ralph Waldo Emerson, "The Young American," in *Ralph Waldo Emerson: Essays and Lectures,* ed. Joel Porte (New York: Library of America, 1983), 217.

19. For notable discussions, see Charvat, *Emerson's American Lecture Engagements,* 5–11; Mary Kupiec Cayton, "The Making of an American Prophet: Emerson, His Audiences, and the Rise of the Culture Industry in Nineteenth-Century America," *American Historical Review* 92, no. 3 (June 1987): 597–620; Richardson, *Emerson,* 418–22; Sallee Fox Engstrom, *The Infinitude of the Private Man: Emerson's Presence in Western New York, 1851–1861* (New York: Peter Lang, 1997); R. Jackson Wilson, "Emerson as Lecturer: Man Thinking, Man Saying," in *The Cambridge Companion to Ralph Waldo Emerson,* ed. Joel Porte and Saundra Morris (Cambridge: Cambridge University Press, 1999), 76–96; Thomas Augst, *The Clerk's Tale: Young Men and Moral Life in Nineteenth-Century America* (Chicago: University of Chicago Press, 2003), 114–57; Bonnie Carr O'Neill, "'The Best of Me Is There': Emerson as Lecturer and Celebrity," *American Literature* 80, no. 4 (December 2008): 739–67; and Tom F. Wright, "Listening to Emerson's 'England' at Clinton Hall, 22 January 1850," *Journal of American Studies* 46, no. 3 (August 2012): 641–62.

20. See Cayton, "The Making of an American Prophet"; and O'Neill, "'The Best of Me Is There,'" esp. 598–600, 741. For earlier, helpful studies of Emerson's reception as a lecturer, see particularly Hubert H. Hoeltje, "Ralph Waldo Emerson in Minnesota," *Minnesota History* 11, no.

2 (June 1930): 145–59; Willard Thorp, "Emerson on Tour," *Quarterly Journal of Speech* 16, no. 1 (1930): 19–34; Louise Hastings, "Emerson in Cincinnati," *New England Quarterly* 11, no. 3 (September 1938): 443–69; Vern Wagner, "No Tumult of Response: Emerson's Reception as a Lyceum Lecturer," *Western Humanities Review* 6, no. 2 (Spring 1952): 129–35; Mead, *Yankee Eloquence in the Middle West,* 24–61; John H. Sloan, "'The Miraculous Uplifting': Emerson's Relationship with His Audience," *Quarterly Journal of Speech* 52, no. 1 (1966): 10–15; and Gay Wilson Allen, "Emerson's Audiences: American and British," *Ariel: A Review of International English Literature* 7, no. 3 (1976): 87–108.

21. Wagner, "No Tumult of Response," 134.

22. O'Neill, "'The Best of Me Is There,'" 748.

23. Ralph Waldo Emerson to Margaret Fuller, 31 January 1843, in *The Letters of Ralph Waldo Emerson,* vol. 3, *1842–1847,* ed. Ralph L. Rusk (New York: Columbia University Press, 1966), 137.

24. I take the terms *ludus* and *paidia* from Roger Caillois, *Man, Play, and Games,* trans. Meyer Barash (1961; repr., Urbana: University of Illinois Press, 2001), x, 13. Caillois builds on Johan Huizinga's discussion of *ludus* in *Homo Ludens: A Study of the Play-Element in Culture* (1949; repr., London: Routledge, 2000), 35.

25. Ralph Waldo Emerson to Thomas Carlyle, 8 April 1836, in *The Correspondence of Emerson and Carlyle,* ed. Joseph Slater (New York: Columbia University Press, 1964), 143.

26. See Allen, "Emerson's Audiences," 87, 96.

27. Ralph Waldo Emerson to Thomas Carlyle, 8 April 1836, in *Correspondence of Emerson and Carlyle,* 143.

28. For a discussion of Emerson's lecturing in Cincinnati, see Cayton, "Making of an American Prophet," 603.

29. See Wagner, "No Tumult of Response," 130.

30. *Boston Daily Advertiser,* 16 December 1841. See Cayton's analysis of this review, "Making of an American Prophet," 602.

31. Nine of the twelve essays in *Essays: First Series* originated from lectures Emerson gave. They are "History," "Self-Reliance," "Compensation," "Spiritual Laws," "Love," "Prudence," "Heroism," "Intellect," and "Art."

32. Lawrence Buell, *Literary Transcendentalism: Style and Vision in the American Renaissance* (Ithaca, NY: Cornell University Press, 1973), 289.

33. Ralph Waldo Emerson, *Nature,* in Porte, *Ralph Waldo Emerson,* 7.

34. Ibid., 9, 48.

35. Ralph Waldo Emerson to Ruth Haskins Emerson, 28 March 1840; Emerson to Margaret Fuller, 31 July 1841, and 2 August 1841; Emerson to Lidian Emerson, 2 August 1841, in *The Letters of Ralph Waldo Emerson,* vol. 2, ed. Ralph L. Rusk (New York: Columbia University Press, 1966), 266; 438; 439–40.

36. Ralph Waldo Emerson to Lidian Emerson, 1 March 1842, in *The Letters of Ralph Waldo Emerson,* vol. 3, ed. Ralph L. Rusk (New York: Columbia University Press, 1941) 18.

37. The eight lectures of "The Times" are titled "Introduction," "The Conservative," "The Poet," "The Transcendentalist," "Manners," "Character," "Relation of Man," and "Prospects." Emerson delivered the full course of eight only in Boston. The six lectures he gave in New York are "Introduction," "The Poet," "The Conservative," "The Transcendentalist," "Manners," and "Prospects."

38. Ralph Waldo Emerson to William Emerson, 4 December 1841, in *Letters of Ralph Waldo Emerson,* 2:469.

39. Ralph Waldo Emerson to William Emerson, 17 October 1841; Emerson to William Emerson, 4 December 1841, in *Letters of Ralph Waldo Emerson,* 2:460, 469.

40. Ralph Waldo Emerson, "The Transcendentalist" in Porte, *Ralph Waldo Emerson,* 205. Cited parenthetically hereafter.

41. Buell, *Literary Transcendentalism,* 294.

42. Ralph Waldo Emerson to Mary Moody Emerson, 20 and 22 June 1842, in *Letters of Ralph Waldo Emerson,* 3:65.

5

With Press and Paddle

William H. H. Murray's "Adirondack" Lectures and the Making of a Wilderness Guide

Virginia Garnett

On May 10, 1870, standing before a thousand of Boston's curiosity seekers, learned men, and armchair travelers, renowned pastor, gamesman, writer, and soon-to-be popular lecturer William Henry Harrison Murray offered himself as a guide to the Adirondacks, a wild mountainous region still foreign to many but only a day trip away. His lecture drew from his sporting experiences on and around Raquette Lake and included practical advice regarding when and how to travel as well as Emersonian descriptions of the woods.[1] The wilderness should be open to all, regardless of class, he argued, for it offered spiritual fulfillment and wisdom to those who traveled there. Black flies, the swarming, biting antagonists of campers, were but a small price to pay for a "Sabbath in the Woods." For over an hour, Murray entranced listeners with descriptions of "autumnal scenery" and stories of "careening down a flight of rapids" and asked them to forsake "the brain smiting sound of flinty streets" for the "silence of profound solitude."[2] All accounts of Murray's lecture were favorable, and journalists noted that audiences remained engaged, laughing and applauding throughout.

Murray's Adirondack lectures appealed to an increasingly cosmopolitan-minded audience who had the means to travel. The antebellum lyceum fostered an appreciation of exotic locales through its promotion of such travel lecturers as Bayard Taylor, who offered regular talks on his trips to Africa, Japan, and Moscow.[3] These lectures allowed audience members to live vicariously through the speaker's "oral renditions of first-hand experience."[4] Murray's lectures on the Adirondacks tapped into this growing interest in the exotic and benefited especially from the region's close proximity to his audience's home. A steadily expanding railroad and the resulting cheapening of railway tickets in postbellum America allowed Murray's Boston audience easy access to the Adirondacks. For $9, travelers could take the Rutland, Ogdensburg, and Montreal Railway from Boston to Plattsburgh, New York.[5] For another $2 they could continue on to Ausable River Station, where they would be met by stagecoaches that could transport them to the various lodges and "other forest resorts."[6]

Murray depicted a region vastly different from his listeners' urban setting, and his lectures offered a primer for Americans seeking to explore the foreign as mediated by a knowledgeable kinsman. Staring up at the man who, the previous year, had "launched a thousand guide boats" with the publication of his *Adventures in the Wilderness; or, Camp-life in the Adirondacks*, audience members could feel part of a larger world, essentially living and learning vicariously through his experience.[7] For the next five years Murray lectured for the Redpath Lyceum Bureau while continuing his ministerial duties at Park Street Church. According to his friend and biographer Harry V. Radford, Murray delivered at least one of his Adirondack lectures to over 500 different audiences: "At thirty [Murray] was considered one of the intellectual giants of America; and within the next few years was receiving a salary and perquisites of $15,000 to $20,000, besides earning $10,000 additional annually upon the lecture platform."[8]

On the platform as on the page, Murray sought to initiate the uninitiated, to open the wilderness to those who desired rest, recreation, and a little adventure. He accomplished this goal by shrewdly using print and oral technologies, relying on his written work to create a market for his lectures and for himself as a wilderness guide. Murray's books, manuscript lectures, correspondence, reviews, and other printed ephemera assert the limitations of book learning and encourage readers to view his lectures as supplements, if not substitutes, for their own experience. Books like *Adventures in the Wilderness* served to whet the reader's appetite but would, as Murray argued, inevitably fall short of offering a true guiding experience. Murray's public lectures could then fill the void left by the book while also promoting that very written work. For those who could not attend, newspapers published transcripts of his lectures and reviews of varying lengths that served as advertisements for Murray's upcoming talks and published texts.[9]

Murray's career helps us understand the nineteenth-century platform as a site where Americans worked through ideas of authority and knowledge transmission, education, and culture. Throughout his career Murray insisted on the importance of his lectures, often placing them above print in terms of influence: "I have often been asked to which I attributed the greater influence in advertising these woods and sending people into them, the Adirondack volume or the Adirondack lecture. There has never been the least doubt in my mind. It was the lecture on the Adirondacks that won the fight."[10] For Murray, print gave him an audience, but oratory gave him authority.

Murray's insistence on the importance of oratory taps into contemporary conversations about the relative merits of oratory and print. Author Thomas Wentworth Higginson, for example, argued in "The American Lecture-System" (1868):

> Oratory and literature still remain two distinct methods of utterance, as distinct as sculpture and painting, and as difficult to unite. Their methods, their results, and their rewards, are wholly different. It is the general testimony of those who have tried both, that they put poorer work into their speeches than into their writings; but that, on the other hand, the very act of speech sometimes yields such moments of inspiration as make all writing seem cold.[11]

In 1878 Frederick Jackson Turner commented on this perceived binary, discussing the reason for what he saw as the end of an oratorical era:

> But the former measure of power and influence held by the orator, has been irrevocably consigned to a new power, which unites to all his greatness the ability to speak to an audience of such magnitude as the orator of the past never dreamed—to the audience of the whole civilized world—and to place its utterances in a form that can last forever. This is the glorious province of the Newspaper.[12]

Now faced with the potential decline of the printed newspaper in light of new technologies, we may find Turner's belief in the immortality of the newspaper somewhat naive. Turner's statement regarding the perceived dominance of print is consistent with contemporary popular opinion, however. In 1872 Dorsey Gardner of the *North American Review* claimed that "the orator has abdicated his power in favor of the journalist"[13] and that this trend would continue throughout the nineteenth century, as Carl F. Kaestle and Janice A. Radway assert in the introduction to their 2009 book, *A History of the Book in America:* "Across the six decades of this watershed period beginning in 1880, the printed word became the sine qua non of influence and organization. In a culture of print, the printed word acted as both an instrument and an expression of change, whether directed toward more orderliness or toward new assertions."[14] Despite such assertions, however, print did not completely subsume oratory, nor did it squelch the public's enthusiasm for popular lecturing. By the time of Murray's first platform appearance in 1870, lectures had become standard fare for Americans seeking entertainment. What had begun in the 1820s as primarily educational lectures inspired by Josiah Holbrook's New England Lyceum became international forms of entertainment, managed by national booking agencies whose sole purpose was to schedule foreign and domestic talent across the United States.[15] For Murray the platform was a forum that allowed him to take on the role of guide and provided a space for testing the relationships between private study and lived experience, print and oratory.[16]

A Misguided Guide to the Adirondacks

Just one year before Murray's popular lecture debut, his first secular book, *Adventures in the Wilderness; or, Camp-life in the Adirondacks,* had introduced a wider public to the Boston preacher as an Adirondack authority and wilderness guide. Part guidebook, part collection of tall tales, Murray's *Adventures* offered readers a practical guide to travel as well as the motivation to undertake it, with its wild stories about ghosts, trout fishing, and deer hunting by lamplight. Almost the first third of the book is dedicated to the estimated costs of travel—Murray states that one could spend a month in the wilderness for $125—the required provisions for both men and women, information about hotels and guides, and suggested routes into the region, among other equally practical topics.[17] Of guns, for example, he states that he "prefers the 'Ballard' or 'Maynard' among breech-loaders. No shot-guns should be taken."[18] The latter two-thirds of the book is made up of embellished sportsman tales that readers might now expect to hear bandied about the campfire, including one story about chasing a ghost down a waterfall and another in which the narrator shares a boxcar with a mad horse. This combination of the practical and the fantastic appealed to the period's interest in combining education and entertainment.

Murray's book and subsequent Adirondack lectures were written at a time when, as David Strauss has noted, Americans were increasingly interested in and had the time to pursue leisure activities: "The escape from the office for eastern urbanites was a way to test their manhood and to simulate the demands and excitement of the frontier or the war which had passed them by. In this sense, the wilderness vacation was a useful institution because it met the need for a more healthful as well as a more exciting lifestyle for professional men in the cities."[19] Indeed, Murray's writings reveal this very sentiment. In an address delivered before the Magnetic Fish and Game Club in 1900, Murray states, "The great war did much to give to us as a people the right ideas touching outdoor life. When the vast army disbanded, the veterans that returned—knew the value and joy of outdoor life, and they contributed directly and beyond estimate to the movement already inaugurated which had for its object the introduction and establishment of new ideas, habits and a fashion in the social life of the American people."[20] One new fashion Murray hoped to foster was that of American tourism, and he argued that Americans should forego travel abroad to visit the Adirondacks. In "The Adirondacks," Murray pleads, "If you are a tourist, do not, lest you forfeit your claim to both patriotism and common sense, go to Europe, when a region whose mountains are as wild and lakes as beautiful as any Scotland can show you, remains unvisited within twenty-four hours ride of the house where you were born."[21] Travel to the Adirondacks could, in Murray's estimate, satiate Americans' desire for new experiences and new perspectives without sacrificing their duties to the nation.

In less than four months' time, *Adventures in the Wilderness* had gone into its tenth printing, a testament to the broad appeal of Murray's tales and perspective. According to the historian Warder H. Cadbury, "The book's impact on the Adirondacks . . . was enormous. Unprecedented crowds pushed for the Adirondacks, a stampede that ever since has been called 'Murray's Rush.'"[22] In the summer after publication, an estimated 3,000 tourists (many from Boston and New York City) crowded into the Adirondacks in search of the recreation and sporting opportunities depicted in Murray's book.[23] Jane Eblen Keller estimates that this increase was up from a mere "few hundred" tourists the previous year and that, "within six years of 1869, the number of hotels had grown four-fold" and "include[d] elegant inns, big hotels with wide porches and sweeping lawns, efficient staffs, and plentiful food."[24] Murray's fools, as these tourists came to be called, entered the Adirondacks wide-eyed and in desperate need of reliable guides but found few to meet the demand. With only 26 vetted guides listed by the Independent Guides Club in 1868, these tourists had to take whoever was available, often hiring unofficial guides with poor reputations and a general lack of skills.[25] Adirondack historian Charles Brumley offers one such example: "The would-be guides included 'a beardless youth in faultless sailor attire,' in actuality an amateur yachtsman from Narragansett who evidently thought guiding for a summer would be quite the lark."[26] With so few reliable escorts available, eager tourists were left with the only "guide" they could secure: Murray's *Adventures in the Wilderness.*[27]

In response to this increased demand for guidance, Murray's publishers released a tourist's edition of *Adventures in the Wilderness* in the summer of 1869. This edition sported an orange cover and included an introduction by George F. Field, general agent of the Montreal Railway, that described important locations along the routes and listed railway timetables and fares. The book, which was included in the price of a railway ticket, contained two folded maps: one of the railway line and the other a copy of the 1867 William Watson Ely map. The edition contained everything a tourist might need—except common sense. Likely confused by the seriousness of the prefatory material, Murray's readers entered the wilderness with unrealistic expectations. Armed with their copy of "Murray" and all recommended provisions, Murray's disciples marched into the Adirondacks only to be greeted by marked disappointment. Though a few, like fellow traveler and actress Kate Field, found the landscape and sport exhilarating, most complained of the hardship of travel, the lack of game, and poor accommodations.[28] Murray himself was blamed for the prevalence of black flies and even for the death of a few consumptives. Unable to differentiate between fact and fiction, recommendations and commands, many would-be sportsmen accused Murray of gross misrepresentation and denounced him as a liar and "quack":[29] "Your imaginative man, led on by [the book's] descriptions uses language too strong to print, while speaking of it. Your matter-of-fact man expresses his surprise that a minister should tell such 'whoppers,' and your true sportsman laughs at it all, as a huge joke."[30] Murray was thus regarded as either a fool or a charlatan.

Murray suffered initially, to some extent, from his readers' misunderstanding of the genre, which made them interpret *Adventures in the Wilderness* as a work of nonfiction. Although both editions share the same title, the cover of the tourist's edition reads, "Murray's Adventures in the Adirondacks," as opposed to the original *Adventures in the Wilderness; or, Camp-life in the Adirondacks,* a subtle change that suggests Murray the author is also the hero of the tall tales. The Murray who chased a ghost down the fictional Phantom Falls was confused, for example, with the one who wrote for "mental recreation" to "prove a source of pleasure to many who, pent up in narrow offices and narrower studies, weary of the city's din, long for a breath of mountain air."[31] A writer for the New York–based *Circular* reinforces this conflation, pronouncing, "Denunciations of 'Murray' are heard everywhere, and many think there is danger of his being assassinated."[32] Even Charles Hallock's parody "The Raquette Club," published in 1870, obscures the man with his text by referring to *Adventures in the Wilderness* as Murray: "Take 'Murray' for your guide, and be happy."[33] Murray's book proves as insufficient in the parody as in real life, however, and the club members—a lawyer, a printer, a sexton, a geologist, and a "gravel scratcher"—are ill-prepared for the trip. After a series of mishaps involving exploding beer bottles, broken fishing rods, and aggressive black flies, they agree to return home with the realization that they have "no taste for these things."[34]

Adventures in the Wilderness and the critical apparatus surrounding its reception gave Murray a reputation as an unreliable guide, and his own statements about the importance of guides worked against him. In his lengthy preface to *Adventures,* Murray insists that the matter of hiring a guide is "the most important of all considerations to one about to visit the wilderness." He continues: "An ignorant, lazy, low-bred guide is a nuisance in camp and useless everywhere else. A skilful, active, well mannered guide, on the other hand, is a joy and consolation, a source of constant pleasure to the whole party. . . . A good guide, like a good wife, is indispensable to one's success, pleasure, and peace."[35] The ideal guide is at once master and servant: his intimate knowledge of the region makes him superior to those he leads, but his social position makes him personally responsible for providing for his clients' wants and needs. Murray's book had capitalized on readers' interest in the foreign but failed, in their minds, to offer them the knowledge, comfort, and security expected of a guide. If a guide failed to do his job on the trails, the client (or "sport") could demand a refund and disparage him to future travelers. Those who purchased Murray's book and had already invested in travel, however, were left with little recourse but to complain and condemn the author in print.

Murray initially attempted to quell critics in the same medium as his troublesome book. In October 1869, six months after the book's publication and in the height of anti-Murray rhetoric, he published "The Adirondacks: Murray on Murray's Fools; Reply to His Calumniators" in the *New York Tribune* as a way of addressing criticisms and regaining the trust of his readers. This lengthy treatise addressed all charges laid against him in sprawling sections titled "The Wilderness," "Mr. Murray's Book," "The Fools," "Correspondents," "Guides," "Game," "Ignorant Sportsmen," "The Black Fly," "Hardships of Camp-life," "The Wilderness Health," and "The Wilderness Free." Detailed though his response was, criticisms did not abate. Murray's rebuttal was drowned in a sea of print, merely another letter in an ongoing debate about Murray's fools.

Print forced Murray to struggle to appease those who felt personally slighted through a medium that necessarily negated personal relationships. Commercial and technological advancements proved both a blessing and a curse, as widespread publication gave national readers an ostensibly personal knowledge of Murray while exposing him to a broader range of criticisms. In his article "Antebellum Reading and the Ironies of Technological Innovation," Ronald J. Zboray explores this tension by pointing to what he deems "the ultimate irony of antebellum technological innovation": that technological and economic advancements allowed publishers to create a sense of national community by disrupting local ones.[36] The lecture, by contrast, provided a means by which to reconnect Murray with his audience, to assert his side of the argument with his physical person rather than the printed representation already in circulation.

Motivated by a desire to appear more staid than his books and the subsequent reviews suggested, Murray took up popular lecturing in the fall of 1870. As he tells it in his "Reminiscences of My Literary and Outdoor Life" (1904), "If I write a lecture to kill off these charges of sensationalism I had better take a subject that is sensational, something that gives me every opportunity to be a sensationalist and an oratorical mountebank, and that subject is certainly the Adirondack life and experience in the woods."[37] Murray's platform persona succeeded in dispelling rumors of sensationalism, for his ease of manner stood in contrast to the fantastical stories he told. A journalist for *Every Saturday* praised Murray's style, stating that his "elocution is exceeding simple and unassuming. He gesticulates moderately, and every gesture seems demanded and impelled by thought."[38] Another article from the same newspaper described his "public manner" as "simplicity's own self,—quiet and unstudied even to homeliness, but a homeliness full of dignity."[39] This simplicity extended beyond his vocal styling, however, and manifested in his attire as well. Donning a cap in lieu of the more fashionable bowler and a colorful "cardigan jacket under his coat," Murray adopted the "whole breezy, bright exterior of a man of the mountains."[40] His appearance, like his lecture style, allowed him to straddle two worlds. He looked rugged enough to project authority, but kempt enough for a Boston audience. The advertisements for his lectures highlighted his approachable demeanor, and Amherst's *Farmer's Cabinet* offered audience members a chance to "take a stroll with the rare genius of a Murray, thro' the Adirondacks" in his lecture at the 1870 Milford Lyceum.[41] Murray's decision to use the popular lecture to address his perceived weaknesses in print indicates the degree to which nineteenth-century authors understood print and oratory as interrelated and interdependent technologies.

The Lecturer as Guide

Murray's lectures had succeeded in rebuilding his reputation where his printed "Reply" had failed, but his ongoing platform success did not hinge on his manner alone. Murray's writings served to reinforce his authority as a speaker by promoting oratory over print as a more authoritative means of communication. His subsequent stories demonstrated the importance of oratory as a means of driving people to action. "The Story That the Keg Told Me," originally serialized in the *Golden Rule* in 1876 and published in his 1877 volume *Adirondack Tales,* recounts a series of tales from the perspective of different people (and objects) to arrive at a fuller understanding of the vices of greed. His tale begins with Thoreauvian exhortations on the beauty and value of a solitary communion with Nature, echoing sentiments from *Adventures in the Wilderness,* before narrating the story of how a talking keg came to live in the Adirondacks. Broken into short chapters, the story becomes a series of tales within tales, as the keg's narrative gives way to the miser's, whose, in turn, gives way to that of John Norton, the trapper and Murray's self-identified "mouthpiece."[42]

These narrative shifts are punctuated by Murray's frequent references to the orator–auditor relationship. The keg, for example "propose[s] to tell [his story] if you will only sit still and hear me, and not go clean off to sleep as you seem inclined to do," a clear articulation of the anxiety felt by many speakers and a sentiment Murray repeated throughout his fiction. Murray's descriptions attend to the delivery style of his speakers as well. He describes the keg, for example, as he "lifted one of its little thin hands, and placed it with great emphasis upon its heart," and asserts the moral import of his story of greed, loss, and death. Murray's narrator is likewise attuned to the power of oratory and is "profoundly interested in his [John Norton's] recital," describing the "natural eloquence of tone, feature and gesture which only those have whose experiences have been narrow but intense, and who speak from the simple earnestness of untutored and therefore unfettered power."[43] These descriptions of John Norton's rhetorical prowess remind readers of Murray's own oratorical style and his attention to content, tone, and physical manner.

The narrator continues his description with focused attention on the relationship between voice and body:

> His narrative had been told from the beginning in two languages; one verbal and the other pantomimic, and he carried me along with his story as it advanced as much by that which addressed the eye as by that which entered the ear. He had gathered warmth and energy of expression as he had gone on, until I found myself moving in sympathy with the visible action of his features,

> body and hands; and when he reached the climax of his discovery, I shared to the full in the excitement of his pantomimic action, and doubt if the shock of surprise which he had experienced eleven years before in his boat under the bank, on the point which lay in the moonlight full in view, was much greater at the startling discovery he had made, than was mine.[44]

In Murray's estimate, Norton is at his best as an orator when the narrator finds himself "moving in sympathy with the visible action of his features, body and hands."[45] Norton moves more than sympathies; he drives people to act.

In "The Man Who Didn't Know Much" (1877), a tale of a young boy slow in most things but quick in the art of paddling, shooting, and—in a surprising turn—violin playing, Norton transfers his strength to the lad through an act of speech:

> The old man had risen and was standing erect in his boat, still holding the oars in his mighty hands. His eyes flamed; his face was bloodless in the whiteness of an unutterable rage; he shook the heavy oars in the air as if they had been reeds, and shouted with a voice that sounded awful in its intensity:—'Lad, now pull for the sake of John Norton and save his grey hairs from shame! Pull with every ounce of strength the Almighty has given ye, or my curse shall follow ye to yer grave!' . . . It seemed as if the strength of the Trapper, by the medium of the awful appeal, had actually been imparted to the Lad and put at the disposal of his skill.[46]

Norton's power over the boy underscores Murray's insistence that oratory is a superior form of communication to print, for oratory is akin to action.

Murray's fiction also asserts the importance of experiential knowledge over traditional book learning. In "The Man Who Didn't Know Much," Norton, the trapper, and Henry Herbert, the respected city man, discuss the relative value of books and experience:

> It isn't what folks tells us that makes us knowin'; but it's what we find out for ourselves. It's the blaze on the tree that the hunter sarches for and finds with his own eyes, that he never forgits; and I have never seed a city man yit that knowed anything, of his own self; for his edication was what he had been larnt by others, or had read in books. And ye know Henry, that the raal wisdom of Natur' has never been printed in books yit.[47]

Murray uses almost identical language in his nonfiction book *Lake Champlain and Its Shores* (1890): "The best wisdom of the world has never been printed. . . . Knowledge can be obtained out of books. But knowledge is only the gross, fleshly body of wisdom; and the soul of wisdom, the fine spirit of intelligence, the divinity of fact, and law, and life expressive of persons, and force, and things, abhors the crash of the printing-press."[48] Murray's fiction is interspersed with many such conversations that serve as challenges to readers, placing the book-reading cosmopolitan in competition with the well-spoken John Norton. Exchanges like those between Norton and Henry encourage readers to rank sources of knowledge and, by extension, to view Murray the speaker as more authoritative than Murray the writer.

By embracing Norton as a mouthpiece, Murray takes advantage of the very conflation that had caused him so much trouble in the publication of *Adventures in the Wilderness* ten years before. In his subsequent fiction, Murray used print to reflect his oratorical message rather than let his message be dictated by print. Likewise, he understood the important role that print played in the promotion of lectures, and he experimented with both forms in creating a market for himself and his speaking engagements. He considered his lectures ready for delivery only when they were printed, for example; he also promoted his works in his self-edited newspaper, the *Golden Rule,* and corresponded on specialty stationary designed for each of his works.[49] Murray's interest in controlling the narrative, both on the stage and on the page, extended to the creation of the Murray Lyceum Bureau (sometimes called the Murray Literary Bureau) in 1888.[50] This bureau, headed by his second wife, Fanny Mary Rivers of Montreal, handled Murray's Canadian Lecture tour, a two-day series that marked the culmination of his efforts to promote himself as a wilderness guide.

Adventures in Another Wilderness: Murray's Canadian Lectures

Having found success on the platform in the 1870s, Murray embraced a similar approach in 1885 when he proposed returning to the platform with a series of lectures on Canada. Learning his lesson from the mixed reception of *Adventures,* Murray began by marketing himself and his lectures, rather than a book. *Daylight Land,* a novel loosely based on his experiences traveling the Canadian Pacific Railway, would not be published until 1888, and *Doom of the Mamelons,* a novel about the mythic history of the Lake St. John and Saguenay regions in Canada, would not appear until later that same year. By 1885 Murray had lived in Canada for only two years but, acting as he had almost thirty years before, claimed an intimate knowledge of the country. In pitching "Canada: Its Past, Present and Future," Murray emphasized the singularity of his subject and his unique perspective ("no native or foreign scholar has had the patience or inspiration to do as I have"), and he cites his "study, residence and contact with [Canada's] humble men" as the source of his insights.[51] Murray presents himself as lying somewhere between resident and tourist, insider and outsider, as he discusses everything from the "beauty and sublimity of its scenery" to the opportunities for diverse sport, including lacrosse and tobogganing. Murray's lectures also served to encourage Canadians to work toward national progress, particularly in their pursuit of independence. He advised them, for example, to bolster their economy and, in turn, the country's international standing by cultivating a wheat belt in the west.

Murray derived his authority from the guise of unstudied experience. The precirculated program to his "Illustrated Canadian Lectures" downplayed his lengthy preparation to encourage audience members to view him (and his subject) more favorably: "we beg leave to state that these lectures are extemporaneous rather than manuscript orations."[52] Despite such assertions, Murray did not lecture extempore. He wrote multiple drafts and printed many copies of each lecture, which he then cut and pasted into old notebooks for greater ease of handling. Murray's lectures, the physical item as well as the spoken address, were carefully crafted in the service of presenting himself as an authority on the platform and, in turn, as an insider and guide. Within the manuscript lectures, we can see evidence of Murray's conscious and skillful crafting of his insider persona. In multiple places in the document, he changes pronouns to reposition himself in relation to his Canadian audience. For example, discussing Canada's history, Murray's lecture reads, "he named the Island of Bachus, but which ~~you~~ call the Ile of Orleans."[53] He has struck the word "you," originally printed in the typescript, and added "we," a subtle change that suggests a commonality between him and his Canadian audience. Murray furthers this claim of insider status at the beginning of the section "Memories of Your Woods," when he strikes through a reference to "your woods" and changes it to "our woods."[54] Murray may not be Canadian, but, as a woodsman, he claims insider status that transcends national borders. He echoes this sentiment in the later-published *Daylight Land*, a fictionalized account of a trip into the Canadian wilderness punctuated by facts and anecdotes given in the 1885 lectures:

> 'The fact is Canada knows less of herself than she did a century and a half ago. She is absolutely engaged in rediscovering her own geography. The same thing is happening in Canada, touching her great rivers, lakes, and fertile plains, as happened in Italy in respect to Pompeii and Herculaneum. . . . They have lain buried under a huge deposit of ignorance, and are now being exhumed. There are a dozen sportsmen who I could mention who know more about Canada than the Geographical Department at Ottawa.'[55]

In keeping with his role as guide, Murray promotes Canada as a tourist destination much in the same way as he did the Adirondacks, and he encourages Americans to take advantage of their proximity to the bourgeoning nation: "I wish our [American] countrymen would learn the facts about this huge empire of opportunity to the north of them, or that the Canadians had knowledge of it themselves, faith in it, and the right connections with us. Then you would see this western land jump to the front of continental observation."[56] Hoping to increase Canadian tourism, Murray even marketed his subsequent publication of *Doom of the Mamelons* (1888) to "anglers and tourists" by including a map of the Lake St. John and Saguenay regions.[57]

Despite his efforts, however, Murray's Canadian lectures did not have the same impact as his Adirondack lectures—there was no "Murray Rush" into western Canada—but what little was said about them was generally positive. Vermont-based newspapers forwarded a report that Murray was "successful with his illustrated lectures in Canada," and one Canadian newspaper complimented the stereopticon images that accompanied the entertainment.[58] Likewise the *Montreal Gazette* praised the lecture for Murray's accounts of the wilderness: "His descriptions of forest scenery—for which he is deservedly famous—held his audience spellbound."[59] The *Gazette* also excerpted a portion of the second night's lecture about the importance of infrastructure to Canada's future success. That Murray "was received with much applause," according to the *Boston Evening Journal*, is testament to his ability to impart knowledge in a nonthreatening manner and to speak of the foreign as both exotic and accessible.[60] Murray was never going to be convincing to the "old Adirondackers" or to western Canadians, but for those urbanites in search of adventures in exotic locales, he proved an attractive model.

Murray's platform career, through its reaction to printed criticism and its reliance on a carefully crafted printed persona, encourages us to think about the complex relationship between print and oratory during the late nineteenth century. Though discrete art forms, Murray's lectures and printed fiction worked in tandem to create a market for the lecture as a substitute for personal experience. In the lecture hall and on the printed page, Murray offered himself as an intermediary between metropolitan lecture-goers and the wilds of the North Woods and western Canada, and his lectures encouraged audience members to experience these seemingly foreign locales through his firsthand accounts. He was successful because he learned to intersperse his "word paintings" with pointed advice for travel, thereby providing his audience with the semblance of a guiding experience.[61] For those listeners with the means and inclination to travel, Murray's lectures afforded the motivation and confidence to undertake their own excursions.

They could embrace their roles as "citizens of the world" by traversing its more exotic locations without traveling outside their comfort zones.

The eagerness with which Murray's followers sought to tame these regions, however—providing more regular transportation to Canada and increasing the amenities of the Adirondacks' great camps, for example—indicates a contradiction inherent to the nineteenth-century platform. An hour in the lecture hall could expose listeners to new perspectives, new cultures, and new locales, but thc audience's desire for difference was often overshadowed by its need to experience that difference through a process of control and assimilation. The platform of Murray's making was not, then, purely cosmopolitan, nor were his followers' subsequent trips to the Adirondacks and western Canada acts of cosmopolitanism. They were, more accurately, acts of nationalism fueled by cosmopolitan interests. By promoting the foreign element within our national borders as beautiful, exotic, and, most appealingly, accessible, Murray encouraged listeners and readers to view themselves as part of an ever-expanding nation, one whose intellectual and geographic borders remained permeable in the pursuit of recreation and adventure.

NOTES

For so generously lending their time and expertise at various stages of this project, I am indebted to the following people: Halina Adams, Joshua Calhoun, Marcy Dinius, Karen Glass, Susan Goodman, and Jerold Pepper, as well as the participants at the 2011 "Cosmopolitan Lyceum" Research Symposium.

1. "Lecture in Music Hall by Rev. W. H. H. Murray," *Boston Daily Journal,* 11 May 1870.

2. Ibid.

3. Tom F. Wright, "The Results of Locomotion: Bayard Taylor and the Travel Lecture in the Mid-Nineteenth-Century United States," *Studies in Travel Writing* 14, no. 2 (June 2010): 113.

4. Ibid.

5. By 1870 tourists could travel from Boston to Plattsburgh, NY, via the Rutland, Ogdensburg, and Montreal Railway in just under 12 hours. Travel from New York City took about twice as long—the Harlem Railway Line could take travelers from New York City to Plattsburgh in just under 24 hours. This timeline reflects the June 1, 1869, timetable reproduced in the 1869 tourist's edition of *Adventures in the Wilderness;* William Henry Harrison Murray, *Adventures in the Wilderness; or, Camp-life in the Adirondacks* (Boston: Fields, Osgood, 1869), 10–12. General agent George F. Field claims, "This is the most direct and quickest route into the Adirondacks," but he also acknowledges that "there are other delightful routes" for those with "leisure" (7).

6. Ibid., 12.

7. Warder H. Cadbury, introduction to *Adventures in the Wilderness; or, Camp-life in the Adirondacks,* by William Henry Harrison Murray (New York: Syracuse University Press, 1989), 32.

8. Harry V. Radford, *Adirondack Murray: A Biographical Appreciation* (New York: Broadway Publishing, 1905), 56.

9. For a more in-depth discussion of the relationship between oratory and print on the nineteenth-century platform, see Donald M. Scott, "Print and the Public Lecture System, 1840–60,"

Printing and Society in Early America, ed. William L. Joyce et al. (Worcester, MA: American Antiquarian Society, 1983), 278–99.

10. William Henry Harrison Murray, "Reminiscences of My Literary and Outdoor Life," *The Independent* 57 (28 July 1904), 278.

11. Thomas Wentworth Higginson, "The American Lecture-System," *Macmillan's Magazine* 18 (May 1868), 56.

12. Frederick Jackson Turner, "The Power of the Press," 28 June 1878, reprinted in Ronald H. Carpenter, *The Eloquence of Frederick Jackson Turner* (San Marino, CA: Huntington Library, 1983), 119.

13. Quoted in Barnet Baskerville, *The People's Voice: The Orator in American Society* (Lexington: University Press of Kentucky, 1979), 122.

14. Carl F. Kaestle and Janice A. Radway, *A History of the Book in America: Print in Motion; The Expansion of Publishing and Reading in the United States, 1880–1940* (Worcester, MA: American Antiquarian Society, 2009), 4:8.

15. On the rise of the lyceum, see Carl Bode, *The American Lyceum: Town Meeting of the Mind* (New York: Oxford University Press, 1956), and Angela G. Ray, *The Lyceum and Public Culture in the Nineteenth-Century United States* (East Lansing: Michigan State University Press, 2005).

16. Murray's audiences took advantage of their time with the sportsman and often stayed to ask questions. The *Boston Evening Journal* describes how "some two-hundred" remained after the lecture and that, "in response to queries, Mr. Murray talked for nearly another hour in a free, conversational manner, on the routes to and through the Adirondacks" ("Maude's Assonances," 14 May 1873).

17. Murray, *Adventures in the Wilderness,* 25.

18. Ibid., 28.

19. David Strauss, "Toward a Consumer Culture: 'Adirondack Murray' and the Wilderness Vacation," *American Quarterly* 39, no. 2 (Summer 1987): 272.

20. William Henry Harrison Murray, "The Changes in the Thought and Habit of the American People in Respect to Outdoor Life Which Have Occurred During the Last Thirty Years," typescript, William Henry Harrison Papers, Adirondack Museum Library, Blue Mountain Lake, NY.

21. William Henry Harrison Murray, "The Adirondacks," 6, Loomis Collection, Keene Valley Library, Keene Valley, NY.

22. Cadbury, introduction to *Adventures in the Wilderness,* 40. Alfred L. Donaldson posits that the book's popularity stemmed from its unique specificity; Donaldson, *A History of the Adirondacks,* 2 vols. (1921; New York: Harbor Hill Books, 1977), 1:196. Jane Eblen Keller suggests that it likewise benefited from having been published during the "post-Civil War boom," which provided people with the money and "opportunity to love nature"; Keller, *Adirondack Wilderness: A Story of Man and Nature* (New York: Syracuse University Press, 1980), 123.

23. Murray's works coincided with a resurgence of interest in the American landscape that would lead to the parks movement of the 1870s and 1880s.

24. Keller, *Adirondack Wilderness,* 127–28.

25. Charles Brumley, *Guides of the Adirondacks: A History* (Utica, NY: North Country Books, 1994), 28.

26. Ibid.

27. Though Murray was not the first to take the Adirondacks as a subject, his prefatory material is considered an early guidebook and is cited in subsequent guidebooks. See, for example, Edwin R. Wallace, *Descriptive Guide to the Adirondacks, and Hand-book of Travel. . . .* (New York: Forest and Stream Publishing, 1872), and Seneca Ray Stoddard, *The Adirondacks: Illustrated* (Albany, 1874).

28. Field discussed her experiences in the Adirondack region in a two-part article titled "Among the Adirondacks": "To come into the Wilderness and not camp out would be to me as unnatural as to bathe in a diver's water-proof suit" (*New York Daily Tribune,* 12 August 1869). The second part, "Saratoga Seen with Another Eye (It Being a Man's)," appeared on August 21.

29. Donaldson observes in *History of the Adirondacks* that the book's "exaggerations are so obviously such that a literal construction of them reflects on the reader rather than the author" (1:198).

30. "Headley in the Woods: Letters from the Adirondacks," *New York Observer,* 2 September 1869.

31. Murray, *Adventures in the Wilderness,* 8.

32. "The Murray Mirage," *New York Circular,* 9 August 1869.

33. Charles Hallock, "The Raquette Club," *Harper's New Monthly Magazine* 243 (August 1870): 323.

34. Ibid., 338.

35. Murray, *Adventures in the Wilderness,* 32–33.

36. Ronald J. Zboray, "Antebellum Reading and the Ironies of Technological Innovation," *American Quarterly* 40, no. 1 (March 1988): 80.

37. Murray, "Reminiscences," 279.

38. "Rev. W. H. H. Murray," *Every Saturday: A Journal of Choice Reading,* 25 November 1871.

39. "An Hour at the Lecture Bureau," *Every Saturday: A Journal of Choice Reading,* 28 January 1871.

40. Ibid.

41. "Milford Lyceum: Murray," *Amherst (MA) Farmer's Cabinet,* 20 October 1870.

42. In the preface to *Mamelons and Ungava: A Legend of the Saguenay* (Boston: DeWolfe, Fiske, 1890), Murray states: "Through [Norton], as my mouthpiece, I tell whatever of knowledge I have of woodcraft, whatever appreciation I have of Nature, and whatever wisdom I may have been taught by my communings with her silence" (xviii).

43. William Henry Harrison Murray, *Adirondack Tales* (Boston: Golden Rule, 1877), 14, 63.

44. Ibid.

45. Ibid.

46. Ibid., 221–22.

47. Ibid., 320.

48. William Henry Harrison Murray, *Lake Champlain and Its Shores* (Boston: DeWolfe, Fiske, 1900), 12–13.

49. Murray printed multiple copies of his Canadian lectures, which he then cut and pasted into small notebooks for use as reading copies. These printed lectures do not appear to have been intended for anyone but himself, and the material in the lectures was never published.

50. From 1885 onward, Murray directed interested parties to contact his wife, "Miss. F. M. Murray," to secure engagements.

51. "To Mr. White," William Henry Harrison Murray Papers, Adirondack Museum Library, Blue Mountain Lake, NY (hereafter, Murray Papers).

52. "Murray's Illustrated Canadian Lectures," Program, Murray Papers.

53. "Lecture No. 2," Murray Papers.

54. Ibid.

55. William Henry Harrison Murray, *Daylight Land: The Experiences, Incidents, and Adventures, Humorous and Otherwise . . .* (Boston: Cupples and Hurd, 1888), 144–45.

56. Ibid., 145. James Doyle aptly reads such passages as "essentially an exposition of the doctrines of Manifest Destiny, prophesying the inevitable Americanization of the Prairie Provinces and British Columbia"; Doyle, "The Post-Ultimate Frontier: American Authors in the Canadian West, 1885–1900," *Essays on Canadian Writing* 22, no. 6 (June 1981): 16.

57. William Henry Harrison Murray, preface to *Doom of the Mamelons, with a Description of Lake St. John and Saguenay Region,* Tourist's Edition (Quebec: Morning Chronicle Office, 1888). In *The Canadian Guide-Book: The Tourist's and Sportsman's Guide to Eastern Canada and Newfoundland* (New York: D. Appleton, 1891), Charles G. D. Roberts recommends Murray's book to "the tourist who contemplates doing the Lake St. John region and the Saguenay" (101).

58. "Personal," *New York Herald-Tribune,* 21 September 1885; "Illustrated Canadian Lectures," loose in scrapbook, Murray Papers.

59. "Canadian History. Interesting Lecture by 'Adirondack' Murray Last Evening," *Montreal Gazette,* 15 September 1885.

60. "Personal," *Boston Evening Journal,* 18 September 1885.

61. "Boston and Vicinity," *Boston Daily Journal,* 3 November 1870.

6

William James's "True American Theory"

The Varieties of Religious Experience and Transatlantic Intellectual Culture

Paul Stob

William James should have been the first American to deliver Scotland's prestigious Gifford Lectures on Natural Theology. He was, after all, the first American invited to deliver them. But a variety of factors—health problems, time constraints, anxiety about finding the right message for this intellectually imposing venue—prevented James from delivering the lectures before Josiah Royce, a California native and James's Harvard colleague, could occupy the podium.[1] Perhaps it was best that Royce became the first American to deliver the Gifford lectures. Not only did the delay give James time to get healthier and to find his message, it also increased expectations among the people of Scotland for James's presentation. Josiah Royce was no William James, especially on the public platform. Whereas James was known for "incomparable moral eloquence and passion" and the ability to connect with diverse groups, Royce was known for much the opposite.[2] With language that was "archaic even for his time," he had trouble connecting with listeners.[3] So when Royce delivered the Gifford lectures, the people of Scotland responded predictably. The audience for Royce's opening lecture was around sixty people, but by the time the series concluded, only about fifteen attendees remained.[4]

Royce knew that part of the problem involved audience expectations. "You are unquestionably by far the best known of all American philos'rs here," he reported to James, "and your lectures will be eagerly awaited, and glowingly received." When the people of Scotland imagined American thought, they imagined James, not Royce. "Everywhere they ask about you," Royce elaborated, "and regard me only as the advance agent of the true American Theory. *That* they await from you. I received endless kindness; but they have still far more, I am sure, in store for you."[5]

To say the least, the pressure was on for James to deliver something distinctive, something novel, something American. And by all accounts, he succeeded. "The Varieties of Religious Experience," as James's Gifford lectures were titled, were far more popular than any previous Gifford series. The audience for the opening lecture filled the auditorium—about three hundred strong, which was "more numerous than had been expected." By the end of the series, four hundred people managed to cram into the space, lining the walls, perching on window sills, and doing whatever they could to catch a glimpse of America's best-known intellectual. After James uttered the final line of the series, the audience burst into applause and delivered a rousing rendition of "For He's a Jolly Good Fellow."[6]

James's Gifford lectures were published the same day the series concluded, and the book became an immediate success.[7] Since then, generations of readers have explored the rich and various examples of religious experience contained in the text. Those who study *Varieties of Religious Experience* for its scholarly contributions have regularly discovered new details and insights in James's philosophical project.[8] What's more, in 1999 a committee assembled by the Modern Library ranked it the second-best nonfiction book of the twentieth century, behind only *The Education of Henry Adams*.[9]

The number of well-documented interpretations of *Varieties* illustrates the richness of James's prose and the depth of his insights. Yet for all the interpretations, we lack a full picture of the book as a series of public lectures, as what Donald Scott calls "a form of intellectual theatricality."[10] Scholars have, of course, long recognized that *Varieties* came from James's 1901–2 Gifford lectures, but no one has yet accounted for the lectures as a performance in their historical moment; no one has yet accounted for the lectures qua lectures.[11] What James said and did in Scotland was intimately linked to the audience before him and to the complex, transatlantic intellectual culture around him.

Accordingly, my project in this essay is to return *Varieties* to the nexus of thought and performance at the turn of the twentieth century, exploring the rhetorical dynamics of James's inquiries with the people of Scotland. In so doing, I aim to expand the dynamics of lecture culture discussed in the present book. James was an American speaking to a foreign audience.

He was not an American speaking to Americans about faraway lands and cultures, nor was he a world traveler helping fellow citizens imagine life abroad, nor was he a foreign lecturer speaking to local American communities. He was an American philosopher—indeed, a supposed spokesperson for American thought writ large—whose job was to explore natural theology in an up-and-coming, European, academic venue. In this situation he seemed out of place. James was not, to be sure, the first American intellectual to address a European audience; the previous generation's "men of letters" had participated in a significant transatlantic intellectual exchange.[12] But the highly specialized and relatively elitist character of the Gifford lectures, centered as they were on rigorous philosophical and theological inquiry, put James in a distinctive situation. His challenge was to make true American Theory compelling in one of Europe's prestigious academic venues.

What I hope to show is how James responded rhetorically to this challenge. The analysis that follows advances two primary claims. First, James used the Gifford lectures to demonstrate the legitimacy of an American style of thought. In particular, he presented religious experience as an epistemology—as, in fact, the fullest, most complete source of knowledge available to humankind. This experiential epistemology gave the audience—Scotland's great philosophers and theologians as well as those demanding true American Theory—a mode of inquiry that seemed rugged, individualistic, practical, egalitarian, and democratic. Second, James's demonstration of American thought functioned ultimately as an argument for a more cosmopolitan intellectual culture. His presentation of true American Theory effectively demanded that American voices be included in the world's conversations about religion, science, and philosophy. As an American speaking to a European audience, as someone who purportedly personified American thought, James was able to articulate the cosmopolitan desire "to transcend the limitations of any and all particularism in order to achieve a more complete human experience and a more complete understanding of that experience."[13]

To be sure, transcending the limitations of particularism does not mean the complete loss of particularism. Cosmopolitanism, as Kwame Anthony Appiah has explained, need not be rootless.[14] In James's Gifford lectures, in fact, we catch a glimpse of the link between "solidarity and cosmopolitanism" that David Hollinger has explored at length. To borrow Hollinger's language, James demonstrated a "willed affiliation" with an American perspective that did not deny other perspectives. Instead, his willed affiliation encouraged "the voluntary formation of new communities of wider scope."[15] *Varieties* thus worked to widen Europe's philosophical community, which proved to be a commentary on cosmopolitanism itself. James's lectures suggested that the need for intellectual cosmopolitanism was not limited to the United States. Extending an American style of thought to the philosophical temples of Europe was a matter of extending the boundaries of international exchange, giving American thinkers, even ordinary Americans, a voice in intellectual culture abroad.

In the next section, I explore the transatlantic intellectual culture that shaped James's journey to the Gifford lectures. I then explore the Americanness of *Varieties* before showing how true American Theory helped build a more cosmopolitan perspective on religious experience. In each section I approach James's work for its rhetorical characteristics; that is to say, by situating *Varieties* in its historical moment, I focus on the relationships James tried to cultivate with his listeners. Ultimately, I am less concerned with the technical, philosophical details of the lectures than I am with how the audience, most of whom were not experts in philosophy, may have experienced America's most prominent intellectual. What James *said* in the Gifford lectures was undoubtedly important, but what he *did* to connect with his listeners is the primary focus of this essay.

The Opportunity for True American Theory

Lord Adam Gifford, a wealthy Scottish judge, hoped to enrich the intellectual lives of the Scottish people. The best way to do so, he believed, was to endow a series of lectures on natural theology. Gifford demanded that the lectures bearing his name be "public and popular, that is, open not only to students of the Universities, but to the whole community without matriculation, as I think that the subject should be studied and known by all, whether receiving University instruction or not."[16] In many ways, his dream was the same dream of nineteenth-century lecture culture writ large; namely, leveling the barriers between intellectual classes by bringing ordinary people into conversations about important issues.[17]

Because enriching the lives of the Scottish people was no simple task, Gifford endowed four lecture series, not just one. At each of Scotland's most prestigious universities—Edinburgh, Glasgow, Aberdeen, and St. Andrews—lecturers would try to unlock the secrets of "the Infinite, the All, the First and Only Cause, the One and the Sole Substance."[18] Because natural theology required at least twenty lectures to explicate properly—or so Gifford believed—most speakers would spread their talks over two years, giving ten lectures one year and ten more the next.[19] Fortunately, they would be paid handsomely for their commitment, upwards of $350 per lecture (or $9,000 per lecture in today's currency).[20]

The first scholar to reap the rewards was Friedrich Müller, who launched the lectures in 1888, a year after Lord Gifford's death. Müller was a German philologist and a pioneer of comparative religion, and he used his lectures to instruct the people of Glasgow on "Anthropological Religion." In the decade after Müller spoke, other prominent European thinkers—including James Stirling, Andrew Lang, Edward Caird, John Caird, Andrew Fairbairn, James Ward, and Alexander Bruce—joined the Gifford fraternity. They addressed such topics as "Philosophy and Theology," "The Making of Religion," "The Evolution of Religion," "The Fundamental Ideas of Christianity," "Naturalism and Agnosticism," and "The Providential Order of the World."[21]

The early lecturers effectively fulfilled Gifford's hope for knowledge of the Infinite and All. However, they largely failed in making their talks popular. Drawing an audience of fifty was cause for celebration, but most presentations averaged around a dozen attendees.[22] One of the primary reasons these early lectures failed to captivate popular audiences was that the speakers seemed interested above all in debating one another. Most lecturers were philosophical idealists, concerned with capturing the unity of experience and showing "how this undifferentiated unity becomes differentiated into all its various modes."[23] They were not all idealists of the same kind—some were personal idealists whereas others were Absolute Idealists—but idealism strongly defined the tone, tenor, and contours of Gifford discourse.[24] Speakers aimed at nothing less than "overcoming false dichotomies between subject and object, mind and matter, the individual and the community, and the self and God."[25]

It was not surprising that early Gifford lecturers conducted dense idealistic conversations, for Western philosophy at the time was defined by a kind of "idealistic consensus."[26] The consensus was particularly strong in England and Scotland, for many prominent English-speaking philosophers attempted to show how "the Absolute Spirit made the world and revealed itself in human consciousness."[27] Yet Americans also did their part in advancing the idealistic consensus, so that from "the Civil War until almost World War I idealism dominated the emerging profession of philosophy" in America.[28]

William James was not part of this idealistic consensus. In fact, he seemed to recognize that "the Hegelianization of natural theology by means of Gifford lectures" created the opportunity for someone to change the conversation in Scotland.[29] And when his invitation to become a Gifford lecturer arrived in early 1897, he began thinking of how he could alter the philosophical dynamics then pervading the Western world. But there was a slight problem: James's invitation came from Aberdeen, not Edinburgh.[30] Aberdeen was not a poor destination, but if James was going to make his oratorical mark on Europe, he wanted it to be in what many considered the "Athens of the North."[31] Edinburgh was the best place to change the philosophical conversation. So in February 1897, James withdrew his name from consideration at Aberdeen.[32] At the same time, he took it upon himself to recommend a replacement. Considering the idealistic bent of the Gifford lectures, he could think of no better candidate than his friend, neighbor, and colleague Josiah Royce. Royce was America's idealist extraordinaire, famous among philosophers for a full-throated defense of the Absolute.[33]

When James declined the Aberdeen offer, he ensured that Royce would become the first American Gifford lecturer. This news did not sit well with Alice James, William's wife, who exclaimed: "Royce!! He will go [to Scotland] with his Infinite under his arm, and he will not even do honour to William's recommendation."[34] Alice also knew that Royce's invitation greatly complicated William's chances of receiving another invitation. "It is hardly probable," she concluded, "that so rare a prize will be given to an American two years running."[35] She well understood the international dynamics at play, but she was wrong about William's offer. After hanging in Gifford limbo for over a year, James received word that he would deliver the lectures at Edinburgh.[36]

That Royce became the first American Gifford lecturer gave James time to plot his course. Royce was really a European thinker who happened to be born in California, and when he spoke in Aberdeen, he gave the audience more of what they had come to expect. Over the course of two years, he argued for "the unity of finite and of infinite, of temporal dependence and of eternal significance, of the World and all its Individuals, of the One and the Many, of God and Man."[37] James knew that Royce was extending the idealist conversation, and he recognized his opportunity. With "one eye on the page, and one on you," he told Royce, he would strike a new tone in Scotland. Accordingly, James worked to infuse his talks with as much "variety and vitality" as possible. The lectures, he insisted, were "pretty certain to be more popularly entertaining than most previous Gifford courses have been."[38]

After years of preparation, James arrived in Scotland in May 1901 to deliver the first half of his Gifford lectures. His anxiety was palpable. Knowing full well the extent of expectations for his performance, he worried about anything and everything. He even fretted about what clothes he should wear, joking to a friend that he might "have to lecture in my pajamas," which would certainly provide "a cachet of american originality."[39]

Pajamas as American originality—there was more truth to this joke than James cared to acknowledge. On the one hand, the people of Scotland expected him to brim with American ideas and deliver true American Theory. On the other hand, an American thinker seemed somewhat out of place in the prestigious academic halls of Europe.[40] To be sure, intellectual exchange across the Atlantic was nothing new by the time James traveled to Edinburgh. As Leslie Butler has demonstrated, America's great Victorian intellectuals—including Ralph Waldo Emerson, Charles Eliot Norton, Thomas Wentworth Higginson, James Russell Lowell, and George William Curtis, among others—participated in an expansive transatlantic network of ideas.[41] The social, cultural, and political reforms they championed "lent a distinctly cosmopolitan spirit to their contributions to learning, which they pursued as self-conscious members of a larger republic of letters."[42] In many ways, Victorian intellectuals brought the spirit of American sociopolitical reform to international contexts.

But the value of an American perspective in academic philosophy and theology at the end of the nineteenth century was ambiguous at best. In philosophical circles, "civilized Europe" was still "counterposed to philistine America."[43] With the rise of an academic culture defined by professionalism and specialization, American philosophy seemed to lack rigor and precision, especially when compared with the all-encompassing idealist tradition. It was a problem of appearances that surrounded James's Gifford performance, and his pajamas were a perfect symbol for the tensions that marked the academic relationship between America and Europe. James himself was acutely aware that many European intellectuals viewed American philosophy as unrefined, somewhat backward, and noticeably unsophisticated.[44]

He could have responded to this problem of appearances by delivering lectures that were technical, specialized, and rigorous. But James knew that nonacademics in Scotland were clamoring for true American Theory, and he had no intention of letting them down. He took the art of lecturing seriously, and he identified with Lord Gifford's dream of reaching "all classes of the community."[45] As a result, James had to connect with the nonacademic portion of the audience while simultaneously demonstrating the value of his philosophy to European academics. To navigate this situation, he positioned himself and his work as distinctly and proudly American, but he did so in a way that argued for intellectual inclusivity. Performing true American Theory on the Gifford stage underscored the importance of a more cosmopolitan philosophical community.

True American Theory in *The Varieties of Religious Experience*

At over four hundred pages in length, the published version of *The Varieties of Religious Experience,* which is close in content to the lectures James presented in Edinburgh, contains too many ideas, dimensions, and nuances to cover in a single analysis.[46] Moreover, given the work already done on what James said, it seems unnecessary to account for every facet of the text. But to better understand what James did in Edinburgh, it is necessary to explore the Americanness of the text. Attuned to the expectations and perceptions of Scotland's academic and nonacademic communities, James knew that a successful lecture series required him to demonstrate the value and distinctiveness of an American style of inquiry.

The Americanness of *Varieties* began simply enough. Because the lectures were delivered to a live audience, those who first encountered the text received it through the sound vibrations in the air. What were those vibrations like? Those who knew James described his voice as "peculiarly attractive" and "singularly sweet," with "resonant tones" that made for a "brilliant, high-strung, dynamic, vivacious, resilient, unexpected, unconventional, picturesque" presentation.[47] Then, of course, was his American accent. Sitting in the auditorium week after week, Gifford attendees heard someone who sounded different from them and from most Gifford lecturers.[48] Here was a speaker whose vocal qualities, mannerisms, pacing, and delivery reinforced the appearance of distinctive thought.

Beyond the quality of his voice, James chose to confront the international dynamics of the situation at the very beginning of the series. Before such a "learned audience," he noted, he felt significant "trepidation" at "talking whilst the Europeans listen."[49] James noted further that he felt humbled to lecture in Edinburgh, which called forth so many "illustrious names" and produced in him "a sense of dreamland quite as much as of reality." He then laid out his vision for intellectual exchange in the future: "As the years go by, I hope that many of my countrymen may be asked to lecture in the Scottish universities, changing places with Scotsmen lecturing in the United States; I hope that our people may become in all these higher matters even as one people" (12).

James's opening statements foreshadowed the kind of cosmopolitan appeal that would emerge more clearly later in the series. Yet the mere mention of nationality reinforced his distinctive position as an American philosopher speaking to Europeans. This distinctiveness was extended further when James noted that his scholarly focus was somewhat novel: he was "neither a theologian, nor a scholar learned in the history of religions, nor an anthropologist." Given that previous Gifford lecturers fell more or less into these categories, James felt compelled to explain that "psychology is the only branch of learning in which I am particularly versed," and "as a psychologist, the natural thing for me would be to invite you to a descriptive survey of" the religious propensities of human beings (12).

By marking himself as an American psychologist, James authorized a new approach to natural theology. In particular, he authorized a turn to "individuals for whom religion exists not as a dull habit, but as an acute fever" (15). This individual focus separated James's work from that of philosophical idealists trying to overcome the problems of individualism. Their philosophy was an attempt to move past personal peculiarities into consideration of unified impersonal experience.[50] For James, such a goal was misdirected and unattainable, and he told his Edinburgh listeners as much. After critiquing the work of John Caird, one of Scotland's leading idealists and a previous Gifford lecturer, James declared that idealists could never make "religion universal by coercive reasoning"; they could never transform it "from a private faith to a public certainty" (358). For James, the truth of religion was to be found in "the facts of personal experience," that is, in the lives of individuals and their bewildering peculiarities (360).

To the extent that the Edinburgh audience recognized the longstanding individualist focus of American thought, James had the chance to give his listeners what they hoped to hear.[51] And he seized this chance, infusing the lectures with an individualistic tone and emphasis. When addressing "The Religion of Healthy-Mindedness," for example, James positioned divine connection as an act of individual will: "The great point in the conduct of life is to get the heavenly forces on one's side by opening one's own mind to their influx" (93). When speaking on "The Sick Soul," he equated "the practically real world" with "the effective world of the individual" (127). When explaining the process of conversion, he affirmed "a small man's salvation" as "a great salvation and the greatest of all facts *for him*" (195). And when discussing the topic of "Saintliness," he went so far as to put himself in the perspective of the individual subject he was defending: "The person is infallibly aware when he has struck it in the right proportion *for him*. This, he feels, is my proper vocation, this is the *optimum*, the law, the life for me to live. Here I find the degree of equilibrium, safety, calm, and leisure which I need, or here I find the challenge, passion, fight, and hardship without which my soul's energy expires" (241).

To speak of James's work as defending an individualist perspective runs the risk of positioning *Varieties* as outmoded, naive, or crass. But it is necessary to view James's defense in its historical context. Nowadays, individualism carries negative connotations that it did not carry for James. As he saw it, individualism was a necessary response to industrial society and to impersonal philosophical systems. This was not individualism at the expense of communal well-being; nor was it a promotion of the self over and above others.[52] But it was a proud affirmation of the sanctity of subjects in the midst of sociopolitical "bigness."[53]

In Edinburgh, the turn to individuals was not only a way of signaling American thought but also a way of affirming the concept of experience. And it was in this affirmation of experience that James fully separated his work from the idealistic consensus sweeping the philosophical world. In *Varieties,* experience was not just a key term but the heart of a distinctive epistemology, as James made personal experience the epicenter of religious understanding. It was the beginning and the end of religious knowledge. Furthermore, by crafting this experiential epistemology, James made religious insight an aspect of everyday life. "Commonplace persons," as he called them, were able to claim knowledge of God as much as any theologian, philosopher, or scientist could (165). The great idealists of Europe did not control the circle of religious knowledge. True insight was open to everyone, which meant that *Varieties* was not just about individualism; it was also about egalitarianism. The ideals of democratic life were now prominent on the Gifford stage.

In explaining his experiential epistemology, James defined religion as "*the feelings, acts, and experiences of individual men in their solitude, so far as they apprehend themselves to stand in relation to whatever they may consider the divine*" (34). Whatever "the individual feels impelled to respond to solemnly and gravely, and neither by a curse nor a jest," constituted a religious experience (39). For James, it did not matter whether this thing eliciting a response was "real" in the traditional sense. What mattered was

> that curious sense of the whole residual cosmos as an everlasting presence, intimate or alien, terrible or amusing, lovable or odious, which in some degree everyone possesses. This sense of the world's presence, appealing as it does to our peculiar individual temperament, makes us either strenuous or careless, devout or blasphemous, gloomy or exultant, about life at large; and

> our reaction, involuntary and inarticulate and often half unconscious as it is, is the completest of all our answers to the question, "What is the character of this universe in which we dwell?" (36–37)

In this passage, James began with sensation and perception and ended with knowledge—with the "completest" answer to the character of the universe. Moreover, the movement from perception to knowledge took place at the level of the individual. Every individual could answer the question "What is the character of this universe in which we dwell." This did not mean that everyone had to arrive at the same answer, or that all answers were equally beneficial; subsequent experience helped sort out levels of benefit.[54] But it did mean that everyone had a right to answer in his or her own way, and those answers constituted knowledge.

James, of course, was not the first to put experience at the heart of a philosophical project. Nor is experience somehow a thoroughly American concept. In the nineteenth century, Ralph Waldo Emerson had made experience the epicenter of knowledge, and Emerson himself had borrowed heavily from European romanticists. Moreover, as Martin Jay explains, experience has "played a role in virtually every systematic body of thought" since the Greeks.[55] What James was doing in *Varieties,* however, was relatively novel among philosophers at the turn of the twentieth century in Europe. Given that most philosophers at the time had little respect for personal experience as a source of knowledge, James was able to color his experiential epistemology as American.[56]

But how cognizant were the people of Edinburgh of this Americanness? Although a definitive answer is difficult to come by, James's listeners would likely have perceived the American character of the lectures through the evidence James employed. *Varieties* was brimming with quotations and testimony about the power of religious experience and the knowledge obtained through that experience. In fact, the printed text of the lectures presented no fewer than two hundred accounts of people's intercourse with the unseen world, and most of the accounts came from Americans. The length of James's testimonial evidence ranged from a single sentence to several paragraphs. At times, he simply strung together pages of testimony, with a couple sentences of his own to transition from one example to the next. In the lecture on the religion of healthy-mindedness, for example, he quoted a couple hundred words from Theodore Parker, then several hundred from Walt Whitman, then a page from Henry Wood, then almost a page from Ralph Waldo Trine (74–92). Elsewhere in the series, James quoted Mrs. Jonathan Edwards about Christ's presence in her life. He offered Emerson's thoughts on the impotency of abstract theology. He drew on Theodore

Parker and Walt Whitman to demonstrate the value of religious optimism. He also turned to Charles Finney, Alexander Gardiner, Henry David Thoreau, John Woolman, William Ellery Channing, Edward Everett Hale, Cotton Mather, Charles Sanders Peirce, Joseph Smith, and many others. In the end, a cacophony of American voices filled the Edinburgh stage.

But the American voices of *Varieties* were not only those of great American thinkers; the "common person" in James's lectures was often an American, too. Many of his quotations came from the manuscript collection of Edwin Starbuck, one of his former students and a Stanford scholar who collected hundreds of religious histories from average Americans.[57] An unnamed clergyman, a Christian man "aged forty-nine," a man "twenty-seven years old," a woman of unspecified age, a man of unspecified age, one of "Starbuck's correspondents," people who witnessed heavenly light during conversion experiences—all were given the chance to contribute to the world's intellectual conversation. To be sure, James quoted many others besides Americans. But there was no doubt that American voices had plenty to contribute to Europe's philosophical and theological conversations.

If the audience had not yet understood the value and distinctiveness of James's American perspective, the culmination of the lecture series likely did the trick. In lecture eighteen, James announced that he wanted to introduce the work of "an American philosopher of eminent originality"—Charles Sanders Peirce, the father of "the principle of *pragmatism*" (350–51). Pragmatism, James explained, was a philosophy for common people, for democratic life. And it had much to offer the formal academic strictures that defined European inquiry. Pragmatism defined beliefs as "rules for action," arguing that the life of the mind ought to be directed at discovering "what conduct" an idea "is fitted to produce; that conduct is for us its sole significance" (351).

To illustrate exactly what pragmatism offered the audience, James turned to theological discussions of the attributes of God, attributes such as "aseity," "necessariness," "immateriality," "simplicity," "indivisibility," and "actualized infinity." These were just the kinds of attributes previous Gifford lectures had spent time exploring. But James approached them pragmatically, which allowed him to reach a striking conclusion: "I must frankly confess that even though these attributes were faultlessly deduced, I cannot conceive of its being of the smallest consequence to us religiously that any one of them should be true. Pray, what specific act can I perform in order to adapt myself the better to God's simplicity?" (351–52).

Here was a long-standing American demand for intellectual practicality.[58] But to extend the Americanness of pragmatism further, James told a story from his childhood. As a young boy, he explained, he used to read books by the novelist Mayne Reid, whose work typically explored life in the American West. Reid championed "out-of-door adventure" and was "forever extolling the hunters and field-observers of living animals' habits." Reid also kept up "a fire of invective against the 'closet-naturalists,' as he called them, the collectors and classifiers, and handlers of skeletons and skins." To Reid, closet naturalists purported to know about nature but never got their hands dirty, forever avoiding the mud of the frontiersman's trail. James then revealed the point of the story:

> Surely the systematic theologians are the closet-naturalists of the deity, even in Captain Mayne Reid's sense. What is their deduction of these metaphysical attributes but a shuffling and matching of pedantic dictionary-adjectives, aloof from morals, aloof from human needs. . . . One feels that in the theologians' hands, [God's attributes] are only a set of titles obtained by a mechanical manipulation of synonyms. . . . What keeps religion going is something else than abstract definitions and systems of concatenated adjectives, and something different from faculties of theology and their professors. All these things are after-effects, secondary accretions upon those phenomena of vital conversation with the unseen divine, of which I have shown you so many instances, renewing themselves . . . in the lives of humble private men. (352)

James's approach to religious knowledge was the same approach Mayne Reid had taken to the American West. Reid was a frontiersman of the trail; James was a frontiersman of the mind. Blazing trails in the wilderness of thought, cutting new paths through the overgrowth of idealist philosophy, James offered his listeners an intellectual adventure. Perhaps he should have lectured in his pajamas; then he could have provided a visual adventure to mirror the verbal one.

True American Theory and Cosmopolitan Intellectual Culture

However extensively James promoted American thought in *Varieties,* it would be a mistake to conclude that his Gifford lectures were merely the assertion of an American perspective. In fact, considering the performative nature of the lectures, the presentation of true American Theory was above all a way of broadening the intellectual horizons of Gifford attendees. When James asked the people of Scotland to consider American voices, he asked for inclusion, for recognition, for the consideration of something new. Even when critiquing idealist philosophy, his goal was not to deny European thought but to make room for American thought. The rhetorical underpinning of *Varieties,* then, was an argument for intellectual cosmopolitanism. To get a handle on religious experience and the rich varieties thereof, natural theology needed, James suggested, to get bigger and broader. It needed to listen to voices from across the Atlantic and elsewhere. European academic culture could greatly benefit from new insights and perspectives, particularly those that ran against the idealist grain.

If cosmopolitanism refers to a "means whereby national and global cultures can be mediated, where dialogues can be initiated and transboundary issues resolved by those who can see above their national parapets," James's Gifford lectures take the form of a cosmopolitan project.[59] More specifically, *Varieties* advanced a kind of "rooted cosmopolitanism," which Kwame Anthony Appiah describes as attachment "to a home of one's own, with its own cultural particularities, but taking pleasure from the presence of other, different places that are home to other, different people."[60] David Hollinger further develops this kind of cosmopolitanism by noting that it "urges each individual and collective unit to absorb as much varied experience as it can while retaining its capacity to achieve self-definition and to advance its own aims effectively."[61] James's Gifford lectures were an assertion of American identity and culture as well as an attempt to expand the boundaries of collective experience. The presence of a distinctly American style of thought enabled the people of Edinburgh to encounter other and different places and people.

But James did not want this cosmopolitan encounter to be limited to Scotland. As he made clear at the beginning of *Varieties,* he hoped to see a more global, dynamic lecture culture. After declaring his hope that Americans and Scotsmen would lecture in each other's countries, he shared his desire that "the peculiar philosophical temperament, as well as the peculiar political temperament, that goes with our English speech may more and more pervade and influence the world" (12). In this vision, American and Scottish interactions would lead to a higher, more robust perspective, which would in turn influence the direction of the world. But the influence depended on the rise of American thought, of Americans lecturing abroad; only then would Europeans be prepared to respond.

Like other instances of cosmopolitanism, the cosmopolitanism of *Varieties* did not entail the loss of national identity, nor did it stop with national identity. Under James's direction, American voices became part of a transnational network testifying to the power of experiential knowledge. In the second lecture on conversion, for example, James began with a long quotation from Henry Alline, an American, then moved to a long quotation from Colonel James Gardiner, a Scotsman, then to M. Alphonse Ratisbonne, a "freethinking French Jew" who converted to Catholicism, then to John Wesley and Jonathan Edwards (178–88). He completed the lecture with the words of "the eminent French Protestant Adolphe Monod," Martin Luther, Jonathan Edwards again, the "illiterate English evangelist" Billy Bray, five unnamed Americans from the Starbuck collection, and Charles Finney, America's famed revivalist (198–209). This potent mixture allowed Americans to stand side by side with their European counterparts, giving the people of Edinburgh a cross-cultural view of religious conversion.

Other lectures in the series provided the same cosmopolitan vision of religious experience. In the first lecture on saintliness, James pointed to "a Fox, a Garibaldi, a General Booth, a John Brown, a Louise Michel, a Bradlaugh" as the type of saintly character for whom "the obstacles" of life were "as if non-existent" (214–15). In the lecture on "other characteristics" of religious experience, he noted that George Müller of Bristol had an "intensely private and practical conception of his relations with the Deity," but when "we compare a mind like his with such a mind as, for example, Emerson's or Phillips Brooks's, we see the range which the religious consciousness covers" (371). In the concluding lecture of the series, James made the cosmopolitan ideal even clearer: "If an Emerson were forced to be a Wesley, or a Moody forced to be a Whitman, the total human consciousness of the divine would suffer" (384). The key to a robust view of religious life was perspectival diversity. Americans had a place in this diverse chorus, and, *Varieties* suggested, the people of Edinburgh would benefit greatly from listening to them in relation to others.

To be sure, James's cosmopolitanism was not as cosmopolitan as it could have been. His testimonial evidence came primarily from Americans and Europeans, resulting in a predominantly Western perspective. The perspective was not exclusively Western, however, nor was it exclusively Judeo-Christian. In fact, for a white, privileged, turn-of-the-twentieth-century American professor, James was surprisingly interested in alternative traditions. To that end, he put "Emersonian optimism" alongside "Buddhistic pessimism" to create a novel juxtaposition (36). He told the story of an Englishman's encounter with a "royal Bengal tiger" in India (212–13). He noted that "Hindu fakirs, Buddhist monks, and Mohammedan dervishes unite with Jesuits and Franciscans in idealizing poverty as the loftiest individual state" (255). In a single paragraph, he paraphrased the *Bhagavad-Gita,* Saint Augustine, Ramakrishna, and the Buddha (288). But his greatest cross-cultural display came in the lecture on mysticism when he discussed yoga training in India, the empirical focus of the Vedantists, the four stages of contemplation for Buddhists, the Sufi tradition of Islam, and the work of the Persian philosopher and theologian Al-Ghazzālī (317–21).

That James spent considerably less time on non-Western religious traditions makes a good deal of sense when considering the situation in which he spoke. His goal was to make room for American voices and perspectives in a European academic context, which he did by demonstrating that Americans had significant ideas and experiences to contribute to the world's conversation. This was a limited cosmopolitanism, but it was at least more cosmopolitan than much of what had previously occupied the Gifford stage.

The success of *Varieties* reveals more than just James's brilliance as a thinker and speaker. It reveals the direction in which nineteenth-century lecture culture had moved by the turn of the twentieth century. That James delivered his true American Theory to a Scottish audience was most fitting, given that the popular lecture movement had begun in Scotland in the early nineteenth century before arriving in America and captivating audiences there.[62] When James spoke in Edinburgh on the legitimacy of American thought, his lectures served as a kind of report on intellectual progress across the Atlantic. His assertion of an American perspective communicated to the Scottish people that their interest in public lectures and the performance of thought had resulted in a worthwhile tradition. Americans had something important to say, and the world's intellectual culture would be stronger as a result.

Moreover, the phenomenon of an American in Europe arguing for a more global perspective indicated just how cosmopolitan nineteenth-century lecture culture had become. For much of that century, Americans had gone abroad, soaked up foreign experience, and returned to the United States with lectures about the value of life on the other side of the Atlantic. A cosmopolitan lecture meant giving Americans an oratorical view beyond their own shores.[63] James reversed this relationship. His Gifford lectures gave Europeans an oratorical view of American thought and experience, showing that the dynamics of life in America were valuable and worthy of consideration. Such a perspective was particularly important in academic contexts that tended to view "American philosophy" as oxymoronic. European philosophers and theologians, James suggested, had a ways to go in expanding their own conceptions of religion and religious experience. They could stand to be more cosmopolitan in their approaches to knowledge. And a good place to start would be the proudly democratic appeals of American thought.

NOTES

1. For an overview of James's journey to the Gifford stage, see William James, *The Varieties of Religious Experience* (Cambridge: Harvard University Press, 1985), 520–55; and Robert D. Richardson, *William James in the Maelstrom of American Modernism* (Boston: Houghton Mifflin, 2006), 368–416.

2. Ross Posnock, "The Influence of William James on American Culture," in *The Cambridge Companion to William James,* ed. Ruth Anna Putnam (Cambridge: Cambridge University Press, 1997), 326.

3. Bruce Kuklick, *Josiah Royce: An Intellectual Biography* (Indianapolis: Bobbs-Merrill, 1972), 99. For other reactions to Royce's lectures, see Robert V. Hine, *Josiah Royce: From Grass Valley to Harvard* (Norman: University of Oklahoma Press, 1992), 123.

4. See John Clendenning, *The Life and Thought of Josiah Royce,* rev. ed. (Nashville: Vanderbilt University Press, 1999), 240.

5. Royce to James, 12 January 1899 and 7 February 1900, *The Letters of Josiah Royce,* ed. John Clendenning (Chicago: University of Chicago Press, 1970), 381, 401.

6. On the Gifford lectures, see Stanley L. Jaki, *Lord Gifford and His Lectures* (Edinburgh: Scottish Academic Press, 1986), 8–12. Quote is from William James (hereafter, WJ) to Henry James Jr., 16 May 1901, in *The Correspondence of William James,* 12 vols., ed. Ignas K. Skrupskelis and Elizabeth M. Berkeley (Charlottesville: University Press of Virginia, 2004), 170; on the size of the audience, see WJ to Theodore Flournoy, 9 June 1902, in *Correspondence,* 10: 55. For the report from the *Boston Evening Transcript,* see James, *Varieties of Religious Experience,* 549–50.

7. For James's comments on the popularity of the book, see WJ to Giulio Cesare Ferrari, 13 October 1902, and WJ to William James Jr., 26 January 1903, *Correspondence,* 10: 144, 185. For an overview of the success of *Varieties of Religious Experience,* see Richardson, *William James,* 419–23.

8. See, for example, Henry Samuel Levinson, *The Religious Investigations of William James* (Chapel Hill: University of North Carolina Press, 1981); Ann Taves, *Fits, Traces, and Visions: Experiencing Religion and Explaining Experience from Wesley to James* (Princeton: Princeton University Press, 1999); Wayne Proudfoot, ed., *William James and a Science of Religions: Reexperiencing "The Varieties of Religious Experience"* (New York: Columbia University Press, 2004); and Jeremy Carrette, ed., *William James and "The Varieties of Religious Experience": A Centenary Celebration* (London: Routledge, 2005).

9. Dinitia Smith, "Another Top 100 List: Now It's Nonfiction," *New York Times,* 30 April 1999, E45.

10. Donald M. Scott, "The Popular Lecture and the Creation of a Public in Mid-Nineteenth-Century America," *Journal of American History* 66, no. 4 (March 1980): 806.

11. It should be noted that Larry Witham provides an adept reading of the lectures in *The Measure of God: Our Century-Long Struggle to Reconcile Science and Religion* (San Francisco: HarperSanFrancisco, 2005), 81–116. However, Witham is more interested in the content of James's philosophy than in the performative aspects of the lectures, including the presentation of Americanness that animated James's work in Scotland.

12. Leslie Butler, *Critical Americans: Victorian Intellectuals and Transatlantic Liberal Reform* (Chapel Hill: University of North Carolina, 2007).

13. David A. Hollinger, "Ethnic Diversity, Cosmopolitanism and the Emergence of the American Liberal Intelligentsia," *American Quarterly* 27, no. 2 (May 1975): 135.

14. See Kwame Anthony Appiah, *Cosmopolitanism: Ethics in a World of Strangers* (New York: W. W. Norton, 2006), xvi–xvii.

15. David A. Hollinger, *Cosmopolitanism and Solidarity: Studies in Ethnoracial, Religious, and Professional Affiliation in the United States* (Madison: University of Wisconsin Press, 2006), xi, xx.

16. "Lord Gifford's Will," in Jaki, *Lord Gifford and His Lectures,* 74.

17. See Witham, *Measure of God,* 24–27.

18. "Lord Gifford's Will," 72.

19. Ibid., 74.

20. For James's discussion of his own pay, see WJ to Henry James Jr., 21 February 1898, *Correspondence,* 3:23.

21. For the complete list of Gifford lectures, see Jaki, *Lord Gifford and His Lectures,* 43–65.

22. Ibid., 9–10.

23. David Boucher, ed., *The British Idealists* (Cambridge: Cambridge University Press, 1997), xi. See also David Boucher, ed., *The Scottish Idealists: Selected Philosophical Writings* (Exeter, UK: Imprint Academic, 2004).

24. For a discussion of different kinds of idealism, see Jeremy Dunham, Iain Hamilton Grant, and Sean Watson, *Idealism: The History of a Philosophy* (Durham, UK: Acumen, 2011), esp. 144–89. For an overview of idealism in the Gifford lectures, see Witham, *Measure of God,* 28–54.

25. David Fergusson, ed., *Introduction to Scottish Philosophical Theology, 1700–2000* (Exeter, UK: Imprint Academic, 2007), 16.

26. Bruce Kuklick, *The Rise of American Philosophy: Cambridge, Massachusetts, 1860–1930* (New Haven: Yale University Press, 1977), 138.

27. Witham, *Measure of God,* 39.

28. Bruce Kuklick, *A History of Philosophy in America, 1720–2000* (Oxford: Clarendon Press, 2001), 111.

29. Jaki, *Lord Gifford and His Lectures,* 17.

30. WJ to Andrew Seth Pringle-Pattison, 25 January 1897, in *Correspondence,* 8:223–24.

31. Witham, *Measure of God,* 300.

32. WJ to Andrew Seth Pringle-Pattison, 7 February 1897, *Correspondence,* 8:231.

33. For an overview of Royce's *Absolute Idealism,* see Kuklick, *History of Philosophy,* 111–28, 150–78.

34. Quoted in Gay Wilson Allen, *William James: A Biography* (New York: Viking Press, 1967), 387.

35. Alice James to Henry James Jr., 4 February 1899, quoted in *Varieties,* 522.

36. Andrew Seth Pringle-Pattison to WJ, 12 January 1898, *Correspondence,* 8:608.

37. Josiah Royce, *The World and the Individual* (New York: Macmillan, 1901), 2:378.

38. WJ to Josiah Royce, 26 September 1900; WJ to Henry James Jr., 21 June 1899; WJ to Andrew Seth Pringle-Pattison, 27 September 1900, *Correspondence,* 9:320; 3:64; 9:323.

39. WJ to Frances Rollins Morse, 15 May 1901, *Correspondence,* 9:483.

40. For an overview of American intellectuals in the nineteenth century attempting to find their place relative to the intellectual traditions of Europe, see Andrew Taylor, *Thinking America: New England Intellectuals and the Varieties of American Identity* (Durham: University of New Hampshire Press, 2010).

41. Butler, *Critical Americans,* 1–16.

42. Ibid., 43. Butler's remark is directed specifically at Andrews Norton and George Ticknor, but it applies equally well to all the figures she surveys.

43. Richard Hofstadter, *Anti-Intellectualism in American Life* (New York: Vintage, 1963), 412.

44. As Bruce Kuklick has pointed out, James felt particularly insecure around his European colleagues, and he became determined to "secure scholarly esteem"; Kuklick, *Rise of American Philosophy,* 181.

45. "Lord Gifford's Will," 75.

46. For the relationship between the lectures and the printed text, see James, *Varieties,* 555–82.

47. See Linda Simon, ed., *William James Remembered* (Lincoln: University of Nebraska Press, 1996), 13, 138, 236.

48. Even into the 1980s, the chance to hear an American deliver the Gifford lectures proved exciting to many in Scotland. See, for example, Alvin Plantinga's anecdote quoted in Witham, *Measure of God,* 4.

49. James, *Varieties,* 11. Subsequent page references will be cited parenthetically in text.

50. This is not to say that idealists agreed on the issue of individuals and the larger unity. For differences in positions, see W. J. Mander, *British Idealism: A History* (Oxford: Oxford University Press, 2011), 356–97, 463–88.

51. For a discussion of individualism and religious experience long before James spoke in Edinburgh, see the discussion of religious revivalism in colonial America in Hofstadter, *Anti-Intellectualism in American Life,* 55–80.

52. See Francesca Bordogna, "Selves and Communities in the Work of William James," *Streams of William James* 6 (2004): 30–37. Also see Francesca Bordogna, "Inner Division and Uncertain Contours: William James and the Politics of the Modern Self," *British Journal for the History of Science* 40 (2007): 505–36.

53. For more on James's opposition to "bigness," see WJ to Sarah Wyman Whitman, 7 June 1899, *Correspondence,* 8:546. See also George Cotkin, *William James, Public Philosopher* (Urbana: University of Illinois Press, 1989), 123–51.

54. The "science of religions" that James describes in the final lectures of *Varieties* is essentially a way of sorting, cataloguing, and interpreting religious experiences and their levels of benefit; see James, *Varieties,* 342–60, 385–403.

55. Martin Jay, *Songs of Experience: Modern American and European Variations on a Universal Theme* (Berkeley: University of California Press, 2005), 4.

56. For elaboration, see Jay, *Songs of Experience,* esp. 102–10; and Martin Kusch, *Psychologism: A Case Study in the Sociology of Knowledge* (London: Routledge, 1995).

57. See James, *Varieties,* 522–24. Also see Starbuck's discussion in Simon, *William James Remembered,* 168–71.

58. Hofstadter, *Anti-Intellectualism in American Life,* 45–46.

59. Steven Vertovec and Robin Cohen, eds., "Introduction: Conceiving Cosmopolitanism," in *Conceiving Cosmopolitanism: Theory, Context, and Practice* (Oxford: Oxford University Press, 2002), 17.

60. Kwame Anthony Appiah, "Cosmopolitan Patriots," *Critical Inquiry* 23 (1997): 618. See also Bruce Ackerman, "Rooted Cosmopolitanism," *Ethics* 104 (1994): 516–35.

61. Hollinger, *Cosmopolitanism and Solidarity,* xviii.

62. See Carl Bode, *The American Lyceum: Town Meeting of the Mind* (Carbondale: Southern Illinois University Press, 1968), 4; and Bernard Aspinwall, *Portable Utopia: Glasgow and the United States, 1820–1920* (Aberdeen, Scotland: Aberdeen University Press, 1984), 80.

63. The travel lecture was the representative cosmopolitan lecture of nineteenth-century America. Delivered most often by "Americans returning from international excursions," it provided "an oral rendition of first-hand experience, imparting esoteric knowledge about distant places or peoples"; Tom F. Wright, "The Results of Locomotion: Bayard Taylor and the Travel Lecture in the Mid-Nineteenth-Century United States," *Studies in Travel Writing* 14, no. 2 (June 2010): 113–14.

PART III

INTERNATIONALISM OR IMPERIALISM?

7

"Barnum is undone in his own province"

Science, Race, and Entertainment in the Lectures of George Robins Gliddon

Susan Branson

In the spring of 1850, the *Hartford Daily Courant* informed its readers that George Gliddon, former American vice consul to Egypt, renowned scholar, and collector of Egyptian antiquities, planned to unwrap an Egyptian mummy at Boston's Tremont Temple. The notice ended with the following comment: "Barnum is undone in his own province, and unless he can get up another Joyce Heth, may as well succumb."[1] Gliddon, a respected authority on ancient Egyptian culture, had recently concluded a six-year lecture tour in the United States. Why were Americans so interested in a time and place so distant from their own? And why was Gliddon linked with P. T. Barnum, that purveyor of spectacle and low entertainment, the individual to whom the term *humbug* was most often applied? Placing Gliddon's lectures and public activities within the context of the lyceum movement in the mid-nineteenth century illuminates this otherwise puzzling association of culture with spectacle.

The popularity of Gliddon's Egyptian lectures suggests how the lyceum phenomenon was an American cultural practice indebted to, and embedded in, transnational events and issues. The lyceum ideal of promoting American intellectual development and education rested on the assumption that Americans were part of a global community; knowledge of other cultures was a crucial way to understand, and interpret, ideas and practices fundamental to American society. In this regard, the lyceums, societies and associations that sponsored lecturers in the second quarter of the nineteenth century created an important venue for exposing Americans to the intellectual building blocks required to develop and define American society.[2] As Tom Wright suggests in the introduction to this book, "transcending the national was to be the culmination of nationhood."

Lyceums may not have created this interest in the world beyond America's borders, but they consolidated it, packaged it, and created opportunities for audiences to interact with people and ideas. Incorporating images, objects, and artifacts, George Gliddon's lectures embodied the central tenets of the lyceum ideal: placing American society within a global framework. He made the exotic familiar by tracing the historical origins of the cultural, religious, and political practices of the United States, thereby linking it with great civilizations of the past. Gliddon's lectures on ancient Egypt and Egyptians were part of the cosmopolitanism that characterized the outlook of American audiences. He challenged Americans to think about their place in the world from a historical perspective, that is, how Americans were linked by culture and lineage to civilizations and peoples beyond their own borders.

New Yorker Philip Hone wrote in his diary on November 15, 1841, that "lectures are all the vogue, and the theaters are flat on their backs."[3] The nineteenth-century drive for knowledge, what David Jaffee terms the *village enlightenment* in early nineteenth-century America, fostered the creation of many organizations that sponsored lectures.[4] In Boston, for example, Daniel Webster, John Lowell Jr., and others formed the Society for the Diffusion of Useful Knowledge in 1828. Lowell's interest in popular education led him to bequeath a substantial sum to fund a lecture series on the "philosophy, natural history, the arts and sciences, or any of them, as the trustees shall, from time to time, deem expedient for the promotion of the moral, and intellectual, and physical instruction or education of the citizens of Boston."[5] This was the venue for George Gliddon's first lectures during his tour in the early 1840s.

Lowell's generous funding guaranteed that the lecture series attracted luminaries, American and foreign, in a variety of disciplines. The fee paid to Yale professor Benjamin Silliman for his twelve lectures on geology in 1836, for instance, exceeded his yearly salary.[6] Each of Silliman's lectures attracted between fifteen hundred and two thousand people, a testimony to the interest in knowledge of all kinds. As Gliddon's editor noted, "Profundity is not, nationally speaking, an American characteristic, but there is no people more readily receptive of general information."[7] Though perhaps not everyone had the same motivation for attending lectures on geology or even Egyptology. As Angela Ray suggests, public lectures enabled community members to "'pay twenty-five cents' to hear 'remarkable' people lecture, 'with the privilege of looking at them for an hour and criticizing them for a week.' The pleasure of watching one's neighbors watch the lecturers and, perhaps, planning for later discussion or teasing added value to the experience."[8]

George Gliddon was invited to lecture on Egyptian history and culture at the Lowell Memorial Lectures because Americans already possessed some knowledge of, and had a great deal of interest in, that ancient empire. John Lowell, for example, spent more than a year in Egypt just prior to his death in 1836.[9] The increasing exchange of goods, information, and ideas between the United States and the rest of the world in the early nineteenth century fostered a desire in individuals like Lowell to see such places for themselves. Still, the connection between nineteenth-century America and ancient Egypt is not an obvious one. Americans looked primarily to classical Greece and Rome as models for political ideals, civic culture, and architectural inspiration. The grand tour taken by wealthy Americans in the eighteenth century was primarily to Europe, not the Middle East. Even Thomas Jefferson traveled no farther than southern France, relying on Roman remains in Nîmes and Avignon for his firsthand study of ancient monuments. Nonetheless, the construction of American national identity in the late eighteenth century encouraged the appropriation of symbols that reflected Americans' sense that the United States had inherited a legacy of greatness from past civilizations. The obverse side of the Great Seal approved by Congress in 1782, for example, depicts the Eye of Providence atop a pyramid composed of thirteen courses (for the original states). Such iconographic borrowing is testimony to this national ambition.

Americans who purchased imported books, or who had access to libraries, learned of Egyptian history and architecture through travel accounts and works on historical design.[10] But widespread acquaintance with ancient Egypt largely depended on geopolitical events in the Atlantic world at the end of the eighteenth century: the advent of American interest in Egypt is directly linked to Napoleon's invasion of the region in 1798. Although the military consequences of the French army's occupation were disastrous for the French, the scientists and artists who accompanied the expedition subsequently published a comprehensive work, *The Description of Egypt* (1809). Several libraries in the United States purchased the twenty-three heavily illustrated volumes.[11] Popular interest in ancient Egypt, generated by newspaper reports of the Napoleonic Wars, stimulated the production of neo-Egyptian objects Americans could see, touch, and display.

American acquaintance with neo-Egyptian design came primarily via Britain. Nelson's victory over the French at the battle of Abukir had heightened British enthusiasm for ancient Egyptian style. Josiah Wedgwood produced hieroglyph-covered canopic jars (stylized versions of the real thing, which had yet to be translated), vases adorned with obelisks, and a tea service with a crocodile teapot handle.[12] British designer Thomas Hope's book *Household Furniture and Interior Decoration* (1807) included an Egyptian room complete with furniture and ornaments. Hope's book, along with Thomas Sheraton's *Cabinet Dictionary* (1803), provided American craftsmen with illustrations of Egyptian-inspired furniture. In Philadelphia, cabinetmaker Ephraim Haines displayed Egyptian-style furniture in his shop and crafted chairs for merchant Stephen Girard. Benjamin Henry Latrobe designed a room, and the furniture to go in it, for another Philadelphian, William Waln. There was enough consumer interest in Egyptian style for the 1817 edition of *The New-York Book of Prices for Manufacturing Cabinet and Chair Work* to describe furniture with "tapered therms with mummy heads and feet."[13]

American interiors were not the only spaces that received an exotic makeover. By the time George Gliddon delivered his Lowell lectures in Boston in the winter of 1842–43, visitors to Mount Auburn cemetery passed through a gateway modeled after an Egyptian temple. Railway passengers in Massachusetts disembarked at New Bedford and Pittsfield into Egyptian-styled depots. Prisoners incarcerated in the New Jersey State Penitentiary (1832) or the New York City House of Detention and Halls of Justice (1835) served out their sentences in neo-Egyptian fortresses.[14]

Given the abundance of sources from which Americans learned about ancient Egypt, it is not hard to understand how the Land of the Pharaohs caught the imagination of those who saw the United States as a similarly great empire. Americans referred to the Mississippi River as the "American Nile."[15] Developers along the river christened new towns Karnak, Thebes, and Memphis. Planners hired architect William Strickland to design the entire town of Cairo, Illinois, with an obelisk as its most prominent feature.[16] The architects for these projects sought a design that people would correctly "read." In other words, neo-Egyptian buildings testify to the familiarity of Egyptian style by the 1840s. Americans could interpret these buildings correctly because they understood, after reading books, viewing paintings of Egyptian ruins, and, for a handful of individuals, traveling to Egypt itself, the monumentality and authority that pharaonic design conveyed.

For most Americans, their visual acquaintance with Egypt came in the form of entertainment: transparencies, panoramas, and museum collections. Great cities, dramatic battles, and exotic locales were illustrated in spectacular fashion. In 1809 viewers in Charleston, South Carolina, saw images of the Nile at the Cosmorama on Meeting Street.[17] At the celebration of peace between America and Britain in February 1815, the Temple of Peace erected on a stage at New York's City Hall included an Egyptian pyramid.[18] That same month Scudder's Museum offered New Yorkers "a grand view of the banks of the Nile," featuring Cairo and the pyramids, at the Optical Cosmorama.[19]

But views of the Nile, however evocative, could not compare with the experience of seeing an ancient Egyptian in the flesh. Mummies were the highlight of museum displays, lectures, and traveling entertainments in the early nineteenth century (and still are today). Objects and body parts found their way into early museum and library collections. American painter Benjamin West sent a mummy's hand (delivered by Francis Hopkinson) to the Library Company of Philadelphia in 1767.[20] Ship captains donated a variety of artifacts to the East India Marine Society in Salem, Massachusetts, including a mummified ibis presented in 1803.[21]

The Massachusetts General Hospital, capitalizing on this popularity, exhibited their mummy, Padihershef, as a fund-raiser in 1823.[22] This ancient Egyptian then traveled to other eastern cities. In the summer of 1824 Ruben Peale's Baltimore museum exhibited the mummy and made a substantial profit (including proceeds from the sale of mineral water and fruit to visitors).[23] The Charleston, South Carolina, museum advertised another mummy on display in 1826.[24] Mummies and mummy imagery appeared in newspaper articles, commentaries, and even political news. Under the headline "Spring Opened at Washington," from 1824, was the observation that Virginia congressman John Randolph "has *shed* the enormous *Drab* coat in which he has, like the mummy, been encased during the whole brumal season."[25]

Public unwrappings and dissections were also crowd pleasers. Rubens Peale staged a partial unwrapping of two mummies in his New York museum in 1826.[26] Six years later, P. T. Barnum, Peale's competitor down the street at the American Museum, did the same.[27] Mormon founder Joseph Smith claimed to have translated demotic texts found within the wrappings of mummies he purchased in Ohio in 1835. Smith displayed the mummies to the curious—Mormons and non-Mormons alike, including Charles

Frances Adams and Josiah Quincy—for twenty-five cents.[28] Theaters staged mummy-themed plays: Thomas Dartmouth Rice's *Virginny Mummy,* written in the 1830s, was performed for the next thirty years in theaters from Boston to New Orleans.[29] A satire on mummy purveyors, mad scientists bent on reanimation, Rice's play also catered to racial prejudices and stereotypes, confirming in a lowbrow form the same ideas and prejudices with which Gliddon infused his lectures. Thus saturated with Egyptomania, Americans were primed and ready for George Gliddon.

Because Gliddon's lecture series spanned more than a week, he was able to construct an elaborate setting for his talks. The audience sat in a hall adorned with a floor-to-ceiling curtain painted with colorful tableaux: sarcophagi, tomb paintings, and hieroglyphs.[30] On tables at the front of the room lay an abundance of creatures and objects from the tombs: mummified hawks, owls, ibises, cats, jackals, serpents, fish, and a ram as well as linen fabric, pottery, glass beads, copper mirrors, and leather shoes. Glidden also displayed bits and pieces of ancient Egyptians—heads, hands, and feet—along with one complete human mummy in its still brightly painted sarcophagus.[31]

Gliddon's lectures were comprehensive in scope, ranging from the history of Egypt's empires, religious beliefs, and written language to the daily life of men and women in the villages along the Nile and the desert tribes of Egypt and Libya.[32] Gliddon combined the exotic with the familiar: side by side with Old Testament accounts of individuals and events, he added corroborating (or sometimes conflicting) details derived from his translations of the hieroglyphs found on monuments and temples. His second lecture, for example, "Connections between Biblical and Pharonic History" addressed Bishop Usher's claim to the timing of the Flood and the subsequent repopulation of the earth. Gliddon's lectures would have appealed to social progressives among his listeners. Perhaps in acknowledgment that many of his audience members were women, Gliddon asserted, "We have the most positive and incontrovertible evidence, in a series of monuments coeval with Egyptian events for 2500 years, to prove that the female sex in Egypt was honored, civilized, educated, and as free as among ourselves; and this is the most unanswerable proof of the high civilization of that ancient people. . . . Let us render to the ancient Egyptians the proud honor of being the first nation who appreciated the moral capabilities, social virtues, intellectual attributes, and civil rights of woman."[33] Gliddon's listeners, all of them familiar with Bible stories and historical claims, thus had a hook onto which they could hang, and comprehend, this exotic world peopled with pharaohs and pyramids.

Gliddon's popularity rested not only on the novelty and exoticism of his displays but also on the style of his presentation. He conveyed a sense of connection between his listeners and the ancient past: from the table before him, Gliddon held up a human foot and hand: "The gentle owner of this exquisite foot danced in girlish gladness to the sounds of harps which were struck long ere David sang. . . . Or ask this scorched though gilded hand, to trace in hieroglyphics upon papyrus paper the memoirs of a lady, whose will its delicate fingers obeyed at a date when the Hebrews possessed no *alphabet,* when the Pentateuch was yet unwritten."[34] The "gilded hand" and "exquisite foot" that Gliddon used so evocatively were assumed to be those of white women. Race was threaded through all of Gliddon's talks; whether addressing biblical history, architecture and engineering, or women's status, Gliddon touched on current theories of race and human origins.

Gliddon had a long association with Samuel George Morton, one of the first practitioners of American ethnography, a study of humankind based on the theory of polygenesis, which stated that physically distinct humans originated in different parts of the world. Morton claimed that ethnic and racial distinctions were exhibited in cranial size and shape; race went hand in hand with superior, or inferior, intelligence. Gliddon aided Morton's investigations with a steady supply of ancient Egyptian heads shipped from Alexandria to Philadelphia in the 1830s.[35] By 1841 Gliddon had collected one hundred skulls and shipped them to Morton. This cranial bounty gave Morton the study subjects he needed to confirm his ideas linking skull capacity with race and to publish *Crania Aegyptiaca* in 1844.[36]

Gliddon infused his Egyptian lectures with Morton's ideas, arguing that ancient Egyptians, contrary to other theories, were Caucasians, not Africans. In his opening lecture, Gliddon told his audience that "he would return frequently to the subject of Ethnography, and sustain the *diversity of the human* race with hieroglyphical documents reaching as far back as 2000 B.C., and with plates, skulls, and other data gathered from the researches of his friend and colleague, Dr. S. G. Morton, of Philadelphia."[37] In his fifth lecture, one newspaper reported, Gliddon made frequent mention "of Ham, the twin brother of Shem, who, being beyond a possibility of doubt, as Mr. Gliddon thought, the father of that celebrated race whose long mystic movements we have so recently begun to interpret, was of pure and indisputable Caucasian parentage."[38] While holding up an ancient skull, Gliddon assured his audience,

> In this man's skull, one which, after 3,000 years of time, so perfect is his embalmment, would be recognized by us as an old acquaintance had we known him in his life-time, we behold one our ourselves—a Caucasian, a pure whiteman;

> not withstanding the bitumen which has blackened the skin. The same with this female head, of a girl of fifteen, whose hair, reddened though it be by embalmment, is soft and silky still. How surprised would both of these individuals be, could we recall them to life, to learn that we moderns have actually speculated in learned works, whether their countrymen were *Africans* or even Negroes—whether the color of their skins was not (as the Egyptian makes and females are painted on the monuments,) crimson, or yellow; or black as they now are with bituminous saturation—whether their ears were not placed on their heads higher than our own, even if they were as long—whether their feet were really canoe-shaped with the hollow reversed—or their hair actually wool!
>
> Could a people gifted with such facial angles, elevation of forehead, smooth hair and aristocratic noses as these, fail to be great men and great women?
>
> Was it in nature, or are anatomical laws so false, that a people with such physiognomical and osteological characteristics—a people whose mighty deeds are still erect in stone, and who are renowned beyond all others in sacred and profane history for their *wisdom*—should not possess a development of head and volume of brain commensurate with the grandeur of their works?[39]

Gliddon's elaborate proofs and protestations against the notion that Egyptians could have been anything but white must be situated within the context of American anxieties about race and slavery. As positions on abolition or proslavery hardened in the antebellum era, the question of whether men and women from a long-dead culture were, or were not, Caucasian served as a focus for contemporary ideas about race. Hence Gliddon's assertions were part of a modern argument that used ancient Egyptians as proof of racial superiority. Egyptians must have been white because they were civilized, intelligent, and, not coincidently, physically attractive. In this context, Gliddon's lectures, Morton's publications, theatrical farces such as the *Virginny Mummy,* and blackface minstrel performances all served the same end: to reify white superiority.[40]

Gliddon made Egypt both exotic and familiar at the same time; he impressed his listeners with knowledge and language skills possessed by only a handful of Westerners, and he supported the racial-origin theories of Samuel Morton. Gliddon showed his audience the marvelous: displayed across the width of the stage on which he lectured were large color images of "Tombs and Temples . . . Portraits of Pharaohs in their chariots, or in their royal robes—[and] Queens of Egypt from the Monuments, in their varied and elegant costumes."[41] When Gliddon's Boston lecture series ended in January 1843, he went on to New York and other eastern and then southern cities, traveling up the Mississippi from New Orleans to conclude his American tour in St. Louis in the spring of 1848.[42]

Gliddon returned to England just long enough to obtain further material for his second American tour, this time adding to his presentations a 900-foot-long moving panorama and still more objects, both human and inanimate. He strayed further into P. T. Barnum's territory of spectacle with mummy unwrappings in Boston and Philadelphia in 1850. Perhaps Gliddon thought listeners had had their fill of ancient Egyptian history and language. He invested money in the purchase and transportation of an English panorama and several mummies. He probably knew how successful the Massachusetts General Hospital and exhibitors such as Rubens Peale and P. T. Barnum had been with public unwrappings. By January 1850 he was back in the United States and ready to out-Barnum Barnum.

The venues chosen for his lectures and exhibits tell us much about Gliddon's intentions and his audiences' expectations. He opened his second tour in New York in January 1850 in what advertisements referred to as the "Chinese Building" on Broadway, a structure that had formerly housed the Chinese Museum.[43] In Philadelphia, Gliddon hired a space also known as the Chinese Museum (so called because Nathan Dunn's collection of Chinese art and artifacts had been exhibited there until 1843).[44] It is fitting (though perhaps only coincidental) that Gliddon displayed his collection in venues already associated with non-Western exoticism. More important, these locations were places people already went to *see* things.

Gliddon's advertisement for his exhibit emphasized the ocular treats in store for visitors. In addition to the "Brilliantly colored" 900-foot-long moving panorama, the "Egyptian Antiquities" included "*Four unopened human Mummies*, besides *Crania* of Ancient Egyptians, and several highly finished *Mummy-cases*." There were animal mummies—bulls, rams, dogs, cats, ibises, crocodiles—and "a beautiful *wooden model* of the Great Pyramid, exhibiting its interior chambers and construction."[45] "Oriental Music" accompanied the panorama as it moved; the broadside reproduced images from the panorama, including a drawing of the Dancing Girls of Esne—implying, perhaps, that they, too, might be on display.[46]

This visual experience distinguished Gliddon's 1850s exhibitions from his 1840s lecture tour: people were not required to sit through two hours of lecture, let alone a series of them. Nor did they have to pay nearly as much. Twenty-five cents bought admission to the exhibit. Gliddon lectured nightly for no additional charge, but visitors could skip the lecture altogether. They viewed the objects, the mummies, and the panorama while listening to music intended to evoke an Eastern culture. Gliddon borrowed this hybrid format that emphasized visual education from both Peale and Barnum. In doing so, he strayed from lyceum practice, but not from the lyceum ideal. Gliddon stated in the handbook that accompanied the panorama (on sale at the exhibit) that his "collection of varied materials, [are] calculated to render my future discourses in method of illustration more generally popular, no less than in character interesting and instructive."[47]

Gliddon promised his lecture audiences and exhibit visitors an even greater sense of immediacy and intimacy with ancient men and women. In 1850–51 he staged three mummy unwrappings, in Boston, Philadelphia, and New Orleans. The advertisements and subscription pages distributed in advance guaranteed audiences the spectacle of a mummy that revealed its secrets right before their eyes: Gliddon promised that "jewelry, trinkets, and papyri" would appear from within the folds of linen.[48]

Gliddon circulated a subscription paper, stating that three hundred subscribers, at $5 each, were needed to fund the unwrapping in Boston. He assured his potential audience that the mummy was of the "highest class" (no mere Egyptian commoner) and worth $1,500 on the open market. The event was spread over three afternoons at Tremont Temple Hall: on the first day the coffin was removed, on the second day the unwrapping took place, and on the third Gliddon expounded on "archaeological deductions . . . together with the Anatomical, Chemical, Ethnological, and other scientific results." Gliddon relied on local experts to assist at this ethnological striptease. Harvard professor Louis Agassiz and Oliver Wendall Holmes lent their names to the proposal.[49]

Newspapers reported each day's activities. On the first day, Agassiz unwrapped an ibis mummy. In preparation for the following day's unwrapping, the human mummy was to be removed from its coffin. When this proved unworkable because of the bitumen that adhered the body to its wooden case, Gliddon had a carpenter come up on the stage to saw away the box, eliciting a "burst of applause and a murmur of surprise from the audience."[50] On the second day, several medical men unwrapped the mummy as Gliddon looked on. On the third and final day, Gliddon summarized the results of the unwrapping, including the examiners' determination that the individual was male, not a female priestess as the hieroglyphs on the sarcophagus stated. Glidden explained that the body had probably been mistakenly placed in the wrong sarcophagus at the time of embalming. As the Boston newspaper stated, "His explanation was so ingenious and satisfactory that the audience received it with a burst of applause."[51] Gliddon's audience got their money's worth—scholarly lectures, a mummy unwrapped before their eyes, and even a bonus bit of controversy at the end. Attendees may also have taken souvenir mummy wrapping home with them.[52]

Gliddon encouraged publicity for the unwrappings: his prospectus for the Boston event advertised that "*A Reporter's* Ticket, and a desk close to the stage, [would] be furnished to each of the Boston daily Papers." This strategy encouraged individual ticket purchases for the second and third lectures (which were only fifty cents each), as well as attendance at the exhibition; the prospectus notes that the mummies were on display at the exhibit before and after the unwrapping. Gliddon was not disappointed in the press: papers as far away as California carried reports of the event. This was due in part to the mistaken identity of the mummy. Gliddon's reputation as a translator did not suffer from this circumstance, but the confusion fueled press reports of the event (and generated some really bad poetry). A San Francisco newspaper published a verse titled "The Boston Mummy." It begins

Humbugs are very much in vogue;
And people run, for every rogue
Enthusiastically mad—
For signs and wonders, always glad
To snatch at almost any bait
Like fishes; soon they curse their fate[53]

Another journalist-turned-poet, James Ewing Cooley, dedicated his long, vituperative rant against all lecturers from abroad, titled "Extracts from Humbugiana," to "George Rigamarole Gliddon":

Bow'd down beneath a loathsome load
Of worthless humbugs from abroad,
(Who, puff'd like bladders filled with wind—
With fashion's froth besmeared and slim'd—
Float lightly in the public dock,
And, with applauding breezes, rock,)—. . .
No one, perhaps, among the lot,
Hath more adroitly turn'd that spot
To shapes most strange, with stranger hues,
Than Gliddon, in his lecturing spews.[54]

Cooley singled out Gliddon for his splenetic attack because the two men had recently engaged in a heated exchange. Cooley's memoir of Eastern travels, *The American in Egypt with Rambles through Arabia, Petraea, and the Holy Land during the Years 1839–1840,* characterized Gliddon's father as pompous, lazy, and generally a useless consul. When Gliddon indignantly told Cooley he was "anything but a gentleman," Cooley punched Gliddon in the face. A New York court found Cooley guilty of assault but fined him a trivial amount, signaling that in the judge's opinion Cooley's attack on Gliddon was justified.[55]

Gliddon's activities inspired levity as well as enmity. In 1845 the *American Review* published "Some Words with a Mummy." This short story, by Edgar Allan Poe, is a satirical account of a group of inquisitive gentlemen who plan to unwrap and dissect an Egyptian mummy but inadvertently bring him back to life instead (by fooling around with electricity à la Mary Shelley). The mummy chats with his rejuvenators and offers opinions on American politics, architecture, and the popular pseudosciences of the day. The rejuvenators are able to communicate with their electrified friend because George Gliddon is there to translate for them. Poe's story appeared halfway through Gliddon's lecture tour, by which time he had been to most major cities on the East Coast. His name would have been familiar to many readers of the *American Review.*[56]

The Philadelphia and New Orleans unwrappings were not marred by the unexpected revelation provided by the Boston mummy. Afterward, Gliddon retired his skulls, mummies, and panorama and took up his pen to collaborate with Josiah Clark Nott in Mobile, Alabama, on the voluminous and heavily illustrated *Types of Mankind* (1855). This work elaborated on Samuel Morton's theories of polygenesis and racial hierarchies.[57] *Types of Mankind* reinforced a conviction, held by many Americans in every state, that blacks were "an inferior race."[58] Gliddon's public lectures laid the groundwork for interest in this publication and other "scientific" studies of human origins. The racism in these texts did not go unremarked; in pamphlets, books, and speeches, abolitionists countered the claims of the American ethnologists with arguments (and attacks) of their own. Most notably, on the lyceum circuit Frederick Douglass's speech "The Races" lent a powerful voice to the cause of freedom: "The fact that slavery can only be defended upon the denial of the manhood of the negro, and the whole doctrine of human Brotherhood, reveals the motive and explains why the South, the generally indolent and unscientific South, takes so lively an interest in the subject of Ethnology, as expounded by Doctors Nott and Morton, and by Glidden [*sic*], and Hamilton Smith."[59]

Ann Fabian has noted that Gliddon's "good cheer helped to smuggle ideas about racial hierarchy into American culture."[60] But smuggling was unnecessary; Gliddon merely confirmed what many already believed. The national lecture circuit gave him a venue, and his method of presentation assured him the public's attention. The explicit racism of Gliddon's lectures and publications did not reflect enlightened thought on the subject of race, but they did affirm public opinion. At first glance, this might seem a violation of the spirit of cosmopolitanism inherent in the lyceum ideal. Certainly Gliddon's lectures and publications were not forward-thinking (as we might wish them to be). But they were a symptom of an antebellum preoccupation. As Scott Trafton suggests, "the scientific and social interest in ancient Egypt for Americans in the nineteenth century was directly related to the tensions, concerns, and anxieties over the institutionalized uses of Africans and their descendants as the foundation of an entire economic and social system in the United States."[61] Conversations about the nature of race in this period of heightened anxiety therefore demonstrate the best qualities of the lyceum's cosmopolitanism. Gliddon and his audiences were cosmopolitan in their desire to engage with ideas, theories, and new discoveries that were part of a Western conversation about race.

As a writer in *Putman's Monthly* remarked in 1857, "The Lyceum is the American theater."[62] Gliddon's lectures and activities certainly fit the bill, packaging learning with spectacle and exoticism. To some, Gliddon was a showman and trickster, rather than a scholar and scientist: across the top of a copy of the Philadelphia broadside for Gliddon's 1850 exhibit someone wrote, "a tolerable humbug man."[63] Gliddon's mummies and Barnum's Joyce Heth (an elderly black woman whom Barnum claimed was George Washington's nanny) were equally suspect, just so much humbug. Perhaps it was the seamlessness with which knowledge and education glided into performance that elicited suspicion. Yet Barnum's success helps us understand the popularity of the lyceum. The lyceum achieved widespread participation and popularity because it fit well with existing modes of learning, both aural and visual. It gratified patrons' curiosity about science, nature, and humanity. In this regard, the lyceum was fundamentally a cosmopolitan space devoted to the pursuit of engaging Americans and their society with the larger world.

NOTES

1. *Hartford Daily Courant*, 29 May 1850, quoted in S. J. Wolfe and Robert Singerman, *Mummies in Nineteenth-Century America: Ancient Egyptians as Artifacts* (Jefferson, NC: McFarland, 2009), 147.

2. Angela G. Ray defines the lyceum in the nineteenth-century United States as "a discontinuous, culture-making rhetorical practice"; Ray, *The Lyceum and Public Culture in the Nineteenth-Century United States* (East Lansing: Michigan State University Press, 2005), 2.

3. Philip Hone, quoted in Samantha Taylor Long, "Rubens Peale's New York Museum and Gallery of Fine Arts and Its Place in the First Twenty-five Years of Museum History in the United States" (MA thesis, University of Houston, 1998), 45.

4. David Jaffee, "The Village Enlightenment in New England, 1760–1820," *William and Mary Quarterly* 47, no. 3 (July 1990): 327.

5. Edward Everett, *A Memoir of Mr. John Lowell, junior. . . .* (Boston: C. C. Little and J. Brown, 1840), 65.

6. The Lowell Lectures typically paid $2,000 for a lecture series, approximately three times what London societies could pay; Margaret W. Rossiter, "Benjamin Silliman and the Lowell Institute: The Popularization of Science in Nineteenth-Century America," *New England Quarterly*, 44, no. 4 (December 1971): 608.

7. In his introduction to George R. Gliddon's *Otia Aegyptiaca: Discourses on Egyptian Archæology and Hieroglyphical Discoveries* (London: James Madden, 1849), editor Luke Burke praised Americans for their curiosity and intellectual character, which was due to "a fine development of the anterior lobe of the brain, with a moderate or small proportion of the concentrive organs, [that] renders them not merely readily accessible to novelties, but also peculiarly quick in understanding all subjects that can be presented to them in a clear and simple manner" (4).

8. Ray, *Lyceum and Public Culture*, 34. "In Boston, all the boys and girls went to the Lowell Lectures. As many as five hundred at a time learned that acids were not alkalis and that Homer did not write the Iliad. It was quite the rage. The boys invited the girls, and after the lecture they walked home together, ending the evening with an oyster supper"; Van Wyck Brooks, *The Flowering of New England* (New York: Dutton, 1936): 173–74.

9. Lowell collected antiquities, including at least one mummy; Everett, *Memoir of Mr. John Lowell*, 44.

10. "G. B. Piranesi, the engraver whose prints of Roman views so many tourists took home with them, almost as they take home post cards today"; J. Stewart Johnson, "The Egyptian revival in the Decorative Arts," *Antiques* 90, no. 4 (October 1966): 489.

11. The timing of Napoleon's grand scientific venture was right: American libraries and societies were eager to expand their collections on exploration. The Athenaeum in Providence, RI, acquired the set and purchased a specially built Egyptian-style bookcase to house it; Donald L. Fennimore, "Egyptian Influence in Early Nineteenth-Century American Furniture," *Magazine Antiques* 137, no. 5 (May 1990): 1196.

12. According to Wedgwood historians, the majority of this production was for export, though I have yet to identify any Egyptianware in America during this era. See Michael Snodin and John Styles, *Design and the Decorative Arts: Georgian Britain, 1714–1837* (London: V&A Publications, 2004), 88–89.

13. Fennimore, "Egyptian Influence," 1196. Waln's furniture is now on display at the Philadelphia Museum of Art.

14. Richard G. Carrott, "The Neo-Egyptian Style in American Architecture," *Antiques* 90, no. 4 (October 1966): 485. John Haviland was well acquainted with ancient Egyptian design: he owned a complete set of the *Déscription de l'Egypte*.

15. "This noble river may, with propriety, be denominated the American Nile. . . . The general advantages of Memphis, are owing to its being founded on the Mississippi, one of the largest and most important rivers on the globe"; John Overton, advertisement for Memphis, TN, in *Port Folio* (1820), reproduced in John E. Harkins et al., *Metropolis of the American Nile: An Illustrated History of Memphis and Shelby County* (Woodland Hills, CA: Windsor Publications, 1982), 34, quoted in Scott Trafton, *Egypt Land: Race and Nineteenth-Century American Egyptomania* (Durham, NC: Duke University Press, 2004), 16.

16. Carrott, "Neo-Egyptian Style," 485.

17. *Charleston City Gazette and Daily Advertiser*, 29 August 1809. Cosmoramas were scenes viewed through a small opening, or window; several were displayed in a single room. See Ralph Hyde *Panoramania! The Art and Entertainment of the "All-Embracing" View* (London: Trefoil, 1988): 125.

18. *New York Commercial Advertiser*, 23 February 1815. This was probably because of the Battle of the Pyramids in July 1798, when the French defeated Mamluk forces.

19. Ibid.

20. George M. Abbot, *A Short History of the Library Company of Philadelphia* (Philadelphia: Library Company of Philadelphia, 1913), 9.

21. Gerry D. Scott III, "Go Down into Egypt: The Dawn of American Egyptology," in *The American Discovery of Ancient Egypt*, ed. Nancy Thomas (Los Angeles: Los Angeles County Museum of Art, 1995), 42.

22. Caroline Ransom Williams, "The Place of the New-York Historical Society in the Growth of American Interest in Egyptology," *Quarterly Bulletin of the New-York Historical Society* 4 (April 1920): 4.

23. William T. Alderson, *Mermaids, Mummies, and Mastodons: The Emergence of the American Museum* (Washington, DC: American Association of Museums, 1991), 44.

24. *Charleston City Gazette and Daily Advertiser*, 6 January 1826.

25. *Salem (MA) Gazette*, 13 April 1824.

26. Williams, in "New-York Historical Society," cites the announcement in the *New York Evening Post*, 30 March 1826; the mummy may have been sold to Barnum in 1846. See the mummy in the woodcut in P. T. Barnum, *Barnum's American Museum Illustrated* (New York, 1850), 20.

27. William Dinsmoor, "Early American Studies of Mediterranean Archaeology," in *American Philosophical Society Proceedings* 87, no. 1 (July 1943): 96.

28. Michael H. Chandler acquired four mummies in 1833, and after displaying them in Philadelphia and Baltimore, he took them on the road as far as Ohio; after being displayed in Cleveland in 1835, they were purchased by Joseph Smith in Kirtland, OH. The mummies moved with Smith and his Mormon community to Navoo, IL, where Adams and Quincy viewed them in 1844. Smith titled his translation of the demotic texts *The Book of Abraham*. See John Larson, "Joseph Smith and Egyptology: An Early Episode in the History of American Speculation about Ancient Egypt, 1835–1844," in *For His Ka: Essays Offered in Memory of Klaus Baer*, ed. David Silverman (Chicago: University of Chicago Press, 1994), 172.

29. W. T. Lhamon Jr., *Jump Jim Crow: Lost Plays, Lyrics, and Street Prose of the First Atlantic Popular Culture* (Cambridge: Harvard University Press, 2003), 425. Another play, *Mummy: or, The liquor of life! A farce, in one act*, by William Bayle, was performed as early as 1834.

30. Gliddon, *Otia Aegyptiaca*, 52.

31. "I have had but one complete *Mummy* in its Case, and one *painted coffin*, wherewith to elucidate this theme in the United States: where, excepting the choice but small cabinet of Egyptian Antiquities belonging to my esteemed friend, the Oriental traveller, Col. M. J. COHEN, of Baltimore, and the immense gallery of *Crania*, appertaining to the founder of Ethnology in America, Dr. S. Geo. Morton of Philadelphia, there is nothing entitled to the name of an Egyptian *collection*. Here and there a few trifles, chiefly sent by myself in former times from Cairo, exist at Boston, New York, Brooklyn, and Washington. The human mummy above referred to, (obligingly lent me by its proprietor, Mr. JOHN L. HODGE, of the Academy of Natural Sciences at Philadelphia,) . . ."; Gliddon, *Otia Aegyptiaca*, 52.

32. The title of Gliddon's lecture series is "Early Egyptian History, Archaeology, and Other Subjects Connected with Hieroglyphical Literature." The lectures were first published as an extra series of *The New World: A Weekly Family Journal of Literature, Science, Art and News* (New York), nos. 68 and 69, April 1843. Gliddon published a second, more comprehensive edition of his lectures as *Otia Aegyptiaca* in 1849.

33. Gliddon, "Early Egyptian History," *Otia Aegyptiaca*, 48.

34. Gliddon, *Otia Aegyptiaca*, 76.

35. While serving as vice consul in Egypt, Gliddon hired diggers to raid the cemeteries in Saqqara and elsewhere; he paid the Egyptian police to turn a blind eye to the looting. He may have been able to ship the body parts out of the country under the protection of his diplomatic status. See Ann Fabian, *The Skull Collectors: Race, Science, and America's Unburied Dead* (Chicago: University of Chicago Press, 2010), 106.

36. Morton's first book was *Crania Americana* (Philadelphia: J. Dobson, 1839).

37. Gliddon, *Otia Aegyptiaca*, 9.

38. Gliddon intended his lectures on hieroglyphs to be readily comprehended by his audience. He remarked that this was the "first time that hieroglyphical subjects have been developed in a series of popular lectures—His desire to render them instructive, easy and entertaining"; *New World*, 242.

39. Gliddon, *Otia Aegyptiaca*, 77.

40. As Scott Trafton puts it in *Egypt Land:* "Egypt thus became a semiotically folded space: a primary place of legitimation for both secular and theological accounts of the history of 'man' and a primary place of legitimation for both secular and theological accounts of the history of races"(50). An example of this self-congratulatory attitude is the diary entry by Sidney George Fisher, a wealthy Philadelphian. After viewing an exhibit of African and South American men and women at Barnum's museum, Fisher wrote in his diary on 13 March 1861: "brutified humanity, painful to look at. These, then, are lower states of what I am. Man in a state of arrested development"; Nicholas B. Wainwright, ed., *A Philadelphia Perspective: The Diary of Sidney George Fisher Covering the Years, 1834–1871* (Philadelphia: Historical Society of Pennsylvania, 1967), 382.

41. *New World*, 242.

42. George R. Gliddon, *Hand-book to the American Panorama of the Nile: Being the Original Transparent Picture Exhibited in London, at Egyptian Hall, Piccadilly* (London: James Madden, 1849), 17.

43. Ronald J. Zboray and Mary Saracino Zboray, "Between 'Crockery-Dom' and Barnum: Boston's Chinese Museum, 1845–47," *American Quarterly* 56, no. 2 (June 2004): 271–307.

44. This was the building that Charles Willson Peale's American Museum occupied until the early 1840s.

45. Gliddon, *Hand-book*, 25.

46. "Lands sacred & classical . . . ," broadside advertisement (Philadelphia: United States Job Printing Office, Ledger Building, 1850), American Antiquarian Society, Worcester, MA (hereafter, AAS).

47. Gliddon, "To My Friends in America," introduction to *Hand-book*. As Angela Ray asserts in *Lyceum and Public Culture*, "although the general trajectory of lyceum activity can be described as moving from education to entertainment, both functional impulses existed together, often in tension, from the 1820s forward. The word *lyceum* embodied the paradoxes of playful learning and serious fun" (6). The lyceum ideal was flexible enough to accommodate even the type of spectacle Gliddon provided: he unwrapped his third mummy at the Lyceum Hall in Lafayette Square, New Orleans, on February 28, 1851. Gliddon shared the proceeds with the New Orleans Lyceum and library. See Wolfe and Singerman, *Mummies in Nineteenth-Century America*, 165–66.

48. Gliddon, *Proposal* (Boston: Tremont House, 6 May 1850), broadside, AAS.

49. Ibid., 3. Among the first subscribers were Henry W. Longfellow, Benjamin Pierce, and Harvard president Jared Sparks.

50. *Boston Daily Evening Transcript*, 3 June 1850, quoted in Wolfe and Singerman, *Mummies in Nineteenth-Century America*, 151.

51. Quoted in Wolfe and Singerman, *Mummies in Nineteenth-Century America*, 151.

52. The American Antiquarian Society owns a handbill for the Philadelphia exhibit that was accompanied by piece of mummy wrapping. Handwritten on the back of the handbill: "This is cloth from the swathing or wrapping of the Theban Priestess named *Got Mut as- Ank*—This mummy was unrolled at the Chinese Museum by Mr. Gliddon Jan. 17, 1850 about 2500 years after its embalmment—The cloth therefore is at least that old"; "Lands sacred & classical," AAS.

53. "The Boston Mummy," *Alta California*, 31 October 1850.

54. James Ewing Cooley, *Extracts from Humbugiana: or, the World's Convention: A Satire in Four Parts* (Gotham [New York]: Gas, Green & Ginger, Shingleton Square, 1847).

55. Fabian, *Skull Collectors*, 110.

56. Edgar Allan Poe, "Some Words with a Mummy," *American Review: A Whig Journal*, April

1845; reprinted in the newspaper *Boston Museum,* 22 June 1850. Louisa May Alcott also tried her hand at a mummy story, "Lost in a Pyramid, or The Mummy's Curse," first published in Frank Leslie's magazine *A New World* (New York), 16 January 1869.

57. Josiah Clark Nott, *Types of Mankind: or, Ethnological Researches, Based Upon the Ancient Monuments, Paintings, Sculptures, and Crania of Races, and Upon their Natural, Geographical, Philological and Biblical History: Illustrated by Selections from the Unedited Papers of Samuel George Morton . . . and by additional contributions from Prof. L. Agassiz, LL. D., W. Usher, M. D., and Prof. H. S. Patterson, M. D. By J. C. and Geo. R. Gliddon* (Philadelphia: J. B. Lippincott Grambo, 1854).

58. "For the present, we can only say that we of the South should consider him [Morton] as our benefactor, for aiding most materially in giving to the negro his true position as an inferior race. We believe the time is not far distant, when it will be universally admitted that neither can 'the leopard change his spots, nor the Ethiopian his skin' "; Robert W. Gibbes, "Death of Samuel George Morton, M.D.," *Charleston Medical Journal* 6 (1851): 594–98, quoted in William Stanton, *The Leopard's Spots: Scientific Attitudes toward Race in America, 1815–1859* (Chicago: University of Chicago Press, 1960), 144.

59. The speech continues: "The South is not remarkable for its proficiency in scientific pursuits. It has done very little for Chemistry, Botany, Geology or Astronomy. It has done nothing for Metaphysics, Ethics or Theology, but it has shown great zeal in this modern science. The mental power of the Sunny South expends itself on the subject of negroes. Negro physiognomy, negro phrenology, negro craniology, and negro Ethnology, are the Chosen Studies of the scientific mind of the South. . . . The latest and most elaborate effort against the unity of the races, is a work by Nott and Glidden called the Types of Mankind. To the dealers in slaves and in the souls of men, the facts and reasoning of this Book are as clear and conclusive, as the book of Mormon is, to the polegamists of Utah"; Frederick Douglass, "The Races," transcribed in Ray, *Lyceum and Public Culture,* 215.

60. Fabian, *Skull Collectors,* 103.

61. Trafton, *Egypt Land,* 50.

62. Quoted in Donald M. Scott, "The Popular Lecture and the Creation of a Public in Mid-Nineteenth-Century America," *Journal of American History* 66, no. 4 (March 1980): 791–809.

63. "Lands sacred & classical," AAS.

8

The Lyceum as Contact Zone

Bayard Taylor's Lectures on Foreign Travel

Peter Gibian

One of the fundamental questions that divided Americans from the early postcolonial period through the antebellum era was a debate about the foundation and formation of cultural life in the young nation. This ongoing debate played out and heightened a schematic division between two sharply opposed conceptions of the process of nation building—pitting cultural independence against global interdependence; exceptionalist isolationism against expansive or expansionist outreach; a cultural nationalism that came to be commonly associated with the Young America movement against a cosmopolitan vision that came to be associated with the life and work of Washington Irving. Should the new nation develop its own forms of self-expression by turning its back on the world and erecting firm defensive barriers to seal the garden of its cultural distinctiveness and purity, or should it grow and mature by throwing open its doors to foreign interchange and influence?

In this essay, I explore some ways in which these midcentury cultural debates were played out or negotiated in the programming and the performances of lyceum lectures. Challenging a sense of the lyceum as a discursive and educational space defined by and fully allied with cultural nationalist imperatives, I first sketch a general overview of Washington Irving and his important legacy in nineteenth-century America as it framed an alternative vision of the goals of lecture culture, especially within the realm of the popular travel lecture. Bayard Taylor, a widely celebrated world traveler and travel writer who became one of the leading stars on the midcentury lecture circuit, then provides a vivid case study of the impact of this Irvingesque aesthetic vision on lyceum culture, bringing to the fore both its severe limitations and its great expressive possibilities. Indeed, in key moments in his lecture performances, Taylor transforms Irving's foundational model in important ways as he adapts it in response to the rapidly shifting international dynamics of a later historical period.

Taylor's example raises a second level of questions about the nature of the cosmopolitan vision that might be expressed in midcentury lyceum lectures. Travel writing and travel lectures—expressive forms that rose to an astonishing popularity in the mid-nineteenth century—are, in the most basic ways, globalizing forms, speaking for a strong contemporary fascination with and curiosity about modernizing developments that were bringing about increased contact between the world's formerly isolated and insulated cultures, tribes, or nations. But Walter Mignolo distinguishes two opposed modes of cosmopolitan vision that could arise in response to such developments: a "managerial" stance that promotes projects oriented toward mastery of the newly expanding world, and an "emancipatory" stance that aspires to new forms of "planetary conviviality."[1] How, then, does the midcentury lyceum travel lecture relate to these opposed modes of cosmopolitanism? Does it promote a global vision that serves as a vehicle for cultural forms of colonialism or imperialist expansionism, simply confirming the supremacy—the global reach and dominance—of Anglo-Saxon or Eurocentric cultures? Or does it offer to its audiences, in some modes or aspects, a cosmopolitanism aiming at cultural mediation rather than conquest, engagement rather than othering, interconnectedness rather than separation—seeking to effect a broadening of horizons, an opening to world influences, that might substantially transform a listener's sense of Americanness and of America's place in the world, developing as a vehicle for important critique of the narrowness of vision in the home culture?

Irving's *Sketch Book:* Template for a Cosmopolitan Tradition in American Arts

Widely celebrated as America's first great writer, and as the first American to make writing his profession, Washington Irving became, as one capsule history aptly puts it, "the central American literary figure between 1809 . . . and his death in 1859."[2] His visions of story, of the writer's or artist's stance, and of America's cultural position in an early postcolonial period shaped the work and thought of several generations of American authors, visual artists, and cultural critics. With his peripatetic life as an international traveler, aesthetic tourist, and diplomat, he emerged as a founding example of and spokesman for early Romantic notions of an aesthetic or cultural cosmopolitanism, introducing a hugely influential model of the American writer as an expatriate global traveler, a cross-cultural ambassador, a cosmopolite. Inaugurating an important tradition within the new nation's arts and culture, Irving evoked through all of his writings the paradoxical vision of an American identity that finds itself most fully in transnational, or international, situations.

Irving's literary career coincided with the beginning of a great age of American travel and of travel writing, a transitional moment when an earlier age of exploration was evolving into an age of tourism. Going abroad to mark the beginning of his serious commitment to professional authorship, and then living abroad in a succession of European locations for much of his adult life, he made himself the model of the American writer who writes about home while always moving away from it, speaking not from within a bounded and self-contained "home culture" but more often from a life of constant physical and spiritual movement through a series of homes-away-from-home: wayside inns, firesides, coffeehouses. The title of one of his later story collections, *Tales of a Traveller* (1824), captures this characteristic sense of Irving's writings as dispatches from a life on the road. And indeed his foundational work in this line, *The Sketch Book* (1819–20), turns around a vexed or paradoxical relation to home, home soil, or home culture. The two invented works of American-based folklore here—"Rip Van Winkle" and "The Legend of Sleepy Hollow"—mine the mythic potential in the Catskills and Hudson River area, showing how legend or story can arise out the native materials and native soil of an isolated, provincial American region, and so served as founding works breaking the ground for later literary movements of American regionalism or local color writing (as well as for Hudson River school painting and other native school work in the visual arts). But one cannot overlook the fact that these regionalist tales are presented within the frame of a book of foreign travel, as the meditations of an author searching for his place and his voice through voyages in other worlds.

As a narrative of foreign travel, *The Sketch Book* departed in fundamental ways from a dominant line of early travel writing that tended toward nationalistic chauvinism and a moralizing xenophobia. But *The Sketch Book* came to have a powerful legacy of its own, establishing the cultural stance, the conventions, the literary strategies, and the narrative structure—the genteel, sentimental, and picturesque aesthetic vision, and the openness to other cultural forms and influences—that would shape an important alternative line of American travel writing for generations to come.[3] And if they set a key pattern for American travel writing, Irving's travel-based books also set key patterns for American travel, for his celebrated works came to be widely used as literary tour guides defining itineraries and destinations for the voyages of generations of later aesthetic tourists.

Centrally inspired by Irving's portrait of the artist formed through foreign travel, aspiring writers, painters, and sculptors paid special, reverent attention to the autobiographical introductory chapters of *The Sketch Book*—"The Author's Account of Himself" and "The Voyage"—which express Irving's characteristic sense that to write is to embark on an oceanic voyage, and that legend arises not when one is rooted in the soil of one place or of one bounded culture but when one is at sea, alone in that sometimes terrifying gulf between worlds. In the book's first paragraphs, he tells us that his career as an artist had its germ in his youthful "rambling propensity"—an imaginative tendency always leading him outside the bounds of his home turf, toward the different, the exotic.[4]

These introductory chapters set the template for the image of the American writer or visual artist as a dreamy, idle, rootless bachelor traveler at sea, forever on the move and finding his aesthetic sources through experiences as a cosmopolitan mediator in cross-cultural encounters—always located at, and speaking from, the threshold between cultures. Opening up exploration of the international theme that would be so important to Nathaniel Hawthorne and Henry James, as well as to Herman Melville, Irving highlights a condition of cultural estrangement seen to be basic to the writer's predicament. Indeed, the two most celebrated and resonant American legends in *The Sketch Book* both associate story and story-telling with homeless, traveling figures in exile—Ichabod Crane and Rip van Winkle—who play out divergent aspects of Irving's own situation as an imaginative writer in postcolonial America, allowing him to meditate anxiously on the unsettling implications of his aesthetic stance even as he is introducing and defining it.

But whatever the complexity and ambivalence inherent in Irving's position, his vision became foundational to the self-definition of several generations of the nation's most popular authors—including Henry Wadsworth Longfellow, Herman Melville, Henry T. Tuckerman, N. P. Willis, Donald G. Mitchell, Bayard Taylor, Richard Henry Dana Jr., Edward Everett Hale, Bret Harte, and, later, William Dean Howells and Henry James—each of whom took up the voice, tone, imagery, and stance of the Irvingesque voyager, founding his literary career on writing grounded in travel and centering his work on exploration of the dynamics of cross-cultural interchange.

"The Great American Traveler": Bayard Taylor's Travel Lectures

Bayard Taylor, one of the major followers in the line of Irving, combined impulses to write and to travel more fully than any other American in his era, merging these two vocations so thoroughly and successfully that Larzer Ziff describes him as the "inventor" of the "profession" of "travel writer"; by the early 1850s he had, certainly, as many observers have noted, made himself the "best-known professional travel writer" in America as well as "the archetypal 'travel lecturer' of the period."[5] Stimulated by the careers and writings of Irving, Longfellow, and Willis, the young penniless Taylor followed their model for the formation of the American artist through foreign travel, but in the process he transformed that tradition significantly. First, his work spoke for and led to a dramatic democratization of such travel experience. Beginning his career as an adventurous youth addressing other similarly young aspiring travelers, Taylor produced writings that served in part as how-to manuals, showing through practical example that exotic foreign travel could be accessible not only to members of a well-heeled leisure class coming to see aesthetic tourism as a required display of cultural capital but also to youthful or working-class adventurers willing or even eager to seek out more bohemian down-and-out experiences in foreign lands—to rough it abroad "on the cheap." Then, responding in later writings to the requirement that a professional travel writer must always remain a step ahead of the tourist crowds, Taylor felt the need to seek out ever more far-flung experiences, further challenges to his own ability to rough it in exotic cultures under extreme circumstances. In this way, he also dramatically expanded the global scale of Irvingesque voyaging.

Setting out in 1844 on what would develop into more than a decade of almost nonstop foreign travel, venturing far beyond Europe to test himself physically as well as spiritually through rugged experiences of life in truly distant lands, amid truly exotic cultures, Taylor, as Tom Wright observes, covered "more ground than perhaps any other American of his age."[6] Beginning close to the *Sketch Book* model with a two-year walking tour of Europe, he then traveled to the American West in 1850 (as Irving had done in the 1830s) to witness on horseback the frontier life of Mexico and the California gold rush. In 1851, largely inspired by Irving's stay in Spain and his writings about Moorish culture and the Alhambra—"Your cordial encouragement confirmed me in my design of visiting the East, and making myself familiar with Oriental life,"[7] Taylor writes in dedicating his book *The Lands of the Saracen* to Irving—Taylor set out to explore the Middle East and North Africa, crossing the Nubian desert by camel and sailing down the White Nile from Cairo far past Khartoum before journeying on to Palestine, Asia Minor, and Spain. Then, in 1852, he passed through China and India on the way to a historic opportunity arranged by his publisher, Horace Greeley: the chance to become one of the first Americans to see Japan as an embedded journalist accompanying the 1853 mission of Commodore Perry to force the commercial "opening" of that isolated, exotic land. As a cap to this debilitating schedule of constant globe-trotting mobility, Taylor would make further voyages in 1856–58 meant to provide balance to his earlier experiences of southern lands, exploring first Scandinavia and the Arctic zone and then Greece, Russia, and Crete.

The journalistic letters he published in American newspapers while on these voyages soon made Taylor a celebrity at home. And he was quick to take advantage of the public fascination by publishing a series of eleven hefty travel books (collected as *Bayard Taylor's Travels* in 1874) that he managed to produce during any brief moments between trips. The European tour resulted in *Views Afoot; or, Europe Seen with Knapsack and Staff* (1846), which went through six printings in its first year and twenty by 1855; the buoyant, charming letters home from the California gold mines were brought together in *El Dorado* (1850); the extended voyage through North Africa, the Levant, Spain, China, India, and Japan resulted in a series of popular tomes: *A Journey to Central Africa* (1854), *The Lands of the Saracen; or, Pictures of Palestine, Asia Minor, Sicily, and Spain* (1854), and *A Visit to India, China, and Japan in 1853* (1855). And the prolific, hardworking, ambitious author also converted his later travels of 1856–58 into writing in *Northern Travels* (1859) and, finally, *Travels in Greece and Russia, with an Excursion to Crete* (1859).

Through these writings, Taylor succeeded in making himself one of most popular authors in his day, a literary sensation at least briefly holding a place in the pantheon alongside Irving, Longfellow, Emerson, James Fenimore Cooper, and John Greenleaf Whittier. (Over the course of a long career Taylor published seventeen volumes of poetry, four novels, dramatic works, story collections, books and essays in literary criticism, and important German translations—of Goethe's *Faust,* for example—but his status as literary star rested almost entirely on his preeminence as a travel writer.) To nurture this popularity, as well as to respond to it, Taylor soon found himself answering the call to appear on the lyceum lecture circuit—the "people's town hall" evolving in just this transitional period into a venue merging education and entertainment, instruction and showbiz, and increasingly centered on the celebration and amplification of the figure of the media star, the author as celebrity, the cultural spokesperson as "personality."[8]

In this travel-crazed period, American audiences from coast to coast were clamoring for the chance to see and hear in person the man now becoming a household name, in fact apparently coming to be widely known as "The Great American Traveler."[9] He then emerged as one of the preeminent voices on the lecture circuit throughout the 1850s, an indispensable fixture on the program of any ambitious lyceum. Lyceum historian David Mead describes how, through his lecture tours, Taylor became one of "the most admired and talked-about men in antebellum America," and a *Harper's Weekly* obituary, looking back at Taylor's life, paints a vivid picture of this midcentury moment when his "lectures of travel . . . were more charming and attractive to the public than any other Lyceum oratory; special trains were run, and no hall was large enough for the crowds that wished to hear him."[10] So, for Taylor, a life and literary career grounded in foreign travel quickly translated, in North America, into a life defined by even more rapid, restless, nonstop wandering from lectern to lectern.

Deluged with invitations to speak, for many years through the 1850s he endured, and became deeply frustrated by, a highly lucrative lecture season of nearly two hundred performances, lasting from fall to early spring, in a wide range of far-flung venues.[11] During the 1854–55 season he lectured 130 times, to full houses on each occasion, which would have earned him between $7,000 and $10,000. He told one friend that he had performed 278 times in eighteen months in 1859–60.[12] By another measure, Taylor apparently delivered nearly eight hundred lectures between 1850 and 1865.[13] His biggest successes came, though, with his series of travel lectures given from 1853 to 1858, in which he played variations on a repertoire of five main scripts about different exotic experiences and cultures: "The Arabs," "Japan and Loo Choo," "India," "Life in the North," and "Moscow," sometimes paired with a more generalizing effort, "The Philosophy of Travel."

It is easy to imagine how the preeminent traveler who had, in Ziff's words, "brought the world to the American fireside" would come to have a special fascination for average Americans in the 1850s.[14] In some ways Taylor does clearly perform the fundamental function so well defined by Mary Louise Pratt in *Imperial Eyes,* her seminal study of European travel writing since 1750: the stories of his personal experiences of the "contact zone"—Pratt's apt term describing "the space in which peoples geographically and historically separated come into contact and establish ongoing relations"—speak to the huge hopes and deep fears of an audience coping with a form of culture shock brought on by the rapid pace of globalizing movements forcing new openings to and interchanges with the broader world.[15]

Early movements tending toward such an expanded global awareness had been celebrated by Irving in his 1819 *Sketch Book*, where he voiced the hope that Americans might be especially well situated to lead the world in defining an "enlightened and philosophic" approach to this emerging cosmopolitan reality: "What have we to do with national prejudices? They are the inveterate diseases of old countries, contracted in rude and ignorant ages, when nations knew but little of each other, and looked beyond their own boundaries with distrust and hostility. We, on the contrary, have sprung into national existence in an enlightened and philosophic age, when the different parts of the habitable world, and the various branches of the human family, have been indefatigably studied and made known to each other."[16] But the developments that Irving had blithely hailed in 1819 had expanded dramatically in scope by the midcentury, and could be felt to be progressing at a dizzying pace.

Taylor's travel lectures, then, helped to bring home the abstract dynamics of globalization and imperialist expansion, as he enacted, in his own person, the unsettling drama of the interdependence and interconnectedness of the world's peoples, giving a human face to his audience's confusions and questions about the relation of their own bounded, "fireside" lives to the increasingly planetary movements of capital, power, and knowledge. And, while addressing the anxieties of his readers and listeners, Taylor's accounts could also reassure them, helping them to feel part of these planetary developments, offering them what Pratt sees as basic to the cultural work of travel writing in the era: "a sense of ownership, entitlement and familiarity with respect to distant parts of the world that were being explored, invaded, invested in, and colonized."[17]

The great attraction of Taylor's lecture performances seems in fact not to have been the chance to hear further accounts of marvelous sights in faraway places, or to be amazed by reports on the exotic lifeways of foreign peoples. All of that was already abundantly available in books and articles. Rather, what brought out the crowds was the opportunity to encounter and assess the enigma of the traveler himself: the representative American everyman who had left small-town Pennsylvania to immerse himself in a wild range of global cultures and now returns to tell about it. How would this speaker—who had learned foreign languages, eaten foreign food, worn foreign clothes, traveled with foreign peoples—have responded to or been transformed by his almost incredible experiences of Otherness?

Taylor often appeared on the platform in the costumes of the people he was speaking about—donning an oversized fur hat for the lecture "Moscow," or an Oriental turban and robes to deliver "The Arabs"—and his image came to be associated in the popular mind with these trademark

FIGURE 8.1. Bayard Taylor, from *Putnam's Monthly* 4, no. 4 (August 1854). *Courtesy American Antiquarian Society.*

foreign garments. The Bedouin robes, in particular, became central to the appeal of his lecture performances, as Carl Bode observes: "Dressed in his colorful Arab costume with a scimitar at his side, Bayard Taylor . . . found as ecstatic a welcome as any lecturer could wish"[18] (fig. 8.1). Indeed, the podium appearances of this bearded, athletic-looking speaker with his turbaned head, loose-fitting Bedouin gown and trousers, and curved Oriental sword were "reported to have made women swoon."[19] When the painter Thomas Hicks wanted to capture an epitome of Taylor's stance as traveler (and travel lecturer) in an 1855 portrait, he presented his friend in "Bedouin" costume, reclining with his Middle Eastern hookah above a view of Damascus—a vision then reproduced in Whittier's poetic portrait of Taylor:

"One whose Arab face was tanned . . . / And, in the tent-shade, as beneath a palm, / Smoked, cross-legged like a Turk, in Oriental calm."[20]

To twenty-first-century readers, Taylor's emphasis on costuming might be dismissed as a marketing strategy, an attention-grabbing gimmick reflecting the lyceum's turn to showbiz and entertainment. More seriously, it might suggest the shallowness of a vision that sees only the surfaces of foreign folkways and trivializes the complexities involved in cross-cultural interaction, making the difficult process of reciprocal exchange seem as simple as a child's game of dress-up. Hilton Obenzinger, for example, mocks the "orientalist theatricality" and "cultural transvestitism" of romantic midcentury American tourists like Taylor, whose wearing of Arabian Nights costumes seems to speak for a facile and complacent appropriation of the Other.[21] Donning that foreign dress could seem to imply an assertion of the ease of cultural dominance, with the globe-trotting Western adventurer displaying his Arab robes on stage as a sort of trophy—a commodified sign that Taylor has been to the desert, confronted it, conquered it, and returned as its possessor. Indeed, Hicks's painting *A Morning in Damascus* can be read in just this way: the painter imagines the American voyager naturally taking his place of privilege in a new incarnation as a Arab sheikh, surrounded by the accessories of his leisure, lording it over his barefoot native servant, and mastering the background Middle Eastern city from his position on a panoramic overview.

But this was not how Taylor's midcentury lecture audiences were meant to respond to his foreign costumes. On the contrary, the Russian hats and Arabic robes served during Taylor's performances as key elements in his effort to present himself as a personal embodiment of his central message—a message fundamental to his cosmopolitan vision—about the potential life-altering effects of cross-cultural travel. The point is not that Taylor has emerged from his international voyages as an imperial self able to project his values onto other cultures, and free to appropriate the cultural forms of others; on the contrary, the costumes are Taylor's stagey way of registering that he has himself been transformed by his interactions with the foreign. Conceiving of his travel lectures as a mission, a crusade to promote his cosmopolitan ideal to American audiences, Taylor appeared at the lectern as a figure who has recognized the globalizing dynamics of the contemporary world and has taken them on—not in the sense of resisting those developments, but in the sense of opening himself to them and incorporating them into a reformed, refigured personal and cultural identity. An American wearing Bedouin robes, familiar yet strange, Taylor appears before home audiences as an uncanny, hybrid figure, performing the transnational human identity he wants to evoke and celebrate. This consciously unsettling, provocative self-image is meant to challenge settled complacency and chauvinism in the home audience, provoking listeners into thought about their own self-definition.

In "The Philosophy of Travel," his most abstract lecture articulating the goals of what he called his "lecturing crusade,"[22] Taylor puts a central stress, in example after example, on what he sees as the foundational gift necessary to make possible the highest form of cross-cultural travel—the gift of being flexible, adaptable, resilient, which can help the traveler go beyond his own cultural limits and be reformed through international exchange: "He whose nature has not been harnessed by the moulds of custom, or warped by the prejudices of sect, is to some extent a microcosm, embracing within himself something of the characteristics of all the races of men." Quoting the words of "an old Arab poet" to reinforce this main, Irvingesque theme—"Fly thy home, and journey, if thou strivest for great deeds"—Taylor sums up the desired result of such an "enlarged experience of the world": the traveler "learns to overlook the narrow boundaries of creed and sect and to perceive that . . . there is some truth everywhere—that all the virtues of humanity are not monopolized by his own peculiar circle." And this broadening of horizons, opening into an expanded, cosmopolitan vision of how a global humanity expresses itself in a diverse range of cultural embodiments, begins for Taylor when the voyager is able to "penetrate the national character of each country he visits, and without losing his own, to identify himself as much as possible with new habits of thought and new standards of judgment."[23]

But, for Taylor's traveler as for Edgar Allan Poe's detective Dupin, this process of intersubjective identification with the object of investigation is not only intellectual or imaginative; the "penetration" of a "national character" is seen to operate through a physical playing of roles, with the traveler taking on not just foreign "habits of thought" but a foreign *habitus*—the language, foodways, gestures, bodily carriage, and everyday practices that define a distinctive way of inhabiting the world. "The true cosmopolite," Taylor tells his lecture audience, must be able to shift his "habits according to his locality," thus "making himself equally at home in all parts of the world": "He wears the Andalusian jacket, plays the guitar and dances the bolero, in Spain; he eats macaroni, and swears by Bacchus and by Hercules, in Italy; he drinks beer and smokes meerschaums in Germany; in England he wears stiff cravats, short whiskers, and a pink in his button-hole; in Turkey he sits cross-legged, hires a pipe-bearer, and assumes a grave countenance."

For Taylor the lecturer, then, the adoption of a foreign costume is seen not simply as an effort to imitate the external surfaces of other people's lives but as a performative way in to the visceral, lived experience of other people, other lives, other cultures: "You can establish no magnetic communication with another race, without conforming in some degree to their manners and habits of life. Unless you do this, you carry your own country with you wherever you go, and you behold new forms of life merely from the outside, without feeling the vital pulse which throbs beneath. The only true way of judging of a man's actions is to place ourselves in his situation, and take our bearings from that point; and the only way to understand a people thoroughly, is to become one of them for a time." Here Taylor takes up the theatrical dynamics central to Irving's model of aesthetic tourism only to transform the model in surprising ways. While Irving's bachelor traveler is always a detached spectator, appreciating the picturesque surfaces of local scenes at a distance, Taylor holds up the example of the "sympathetic traveler" who is able to play a role himself, in the manner of the local actors. This idealistic vision of travel as physical and spiritual self-transformation—as an attempt to become other, or to be able to pass fully as another—begins when Taylor's shape-shifting voyager cuts himself off from all contact with his native land (traveling alone or with locals, leaving compatriots behind, and avoiding letters or newspapers from home) in order to immerse himself in a new *habitus* and so to take on the new forms of a foreign life: "There is no home influence to attach him to his old self, and he speedily puts on the new nature which he travels to find."[24]

Competing Cosmopolitanisms in Taylor's Travel Writings and Lectures

In many contemporary reports, this does seem to have been recognized as the central effect and message of Taylor's travel lectures. He came to be widely celebrated as the era's epitome of the "cosmopolite" or "cosmopolitan," emerging not only as the prime spokesperson for the cosmopolitan ideal but as, in Tom Wright's words, a celebrity embodiment of that ideal, fascinating and provoking American audiences through his enactments of a "performed cosmopolitanism."[25] In a report on one talk, "The Arabs," a Wisconsin newspaper explained the compelling power of Taylor's local lyceum performance by relaying the speaker's presentation of his own situation, giving a sentimental, melodramatic, midcentury spin to the classic story of the cosmopolite "citizen of the world": "As a traveler, Bayard Taylor has no equal and probably never had one. The ties of home being early sundered by affliction—the world is his country, and all mankind his brethren. Whether turbaned like a Turk bestride a dromedary, traversing the pathless desert, or in the luxurious Capital of the Prophet, he is equally at home. In Japan or Africa, he is among friends whose customs he adopts, and whose opinions he respects."[26] A San Francisco report paints a similar picture, explaining that crowds naturally throng to hear "so universal a traveler," curious to assess the character and presence of a man who has come through such demanding cross-cultural experiences: "He is a tall, good-looking and still youthful man. Nobody would suspect that he had been in every quarter of the globe, and had described almost every representative country in the arctic, temperate and torrid zones, and almost every race of people."[27]

But beyond playing to the midcentury audience's basic curiosity about personal experiences of the global contact zone, what *sort* of travelers' knowledge would Taylor the cosmopolitan offer to the listeners who filled every seat at his lyceum performances?

It is difficult to answer searching questions about the implications of Taylor's cosmopolitan stance and message, largely because, in his travel writings as in his lectures, Taylor can seem to be almost schizophrenic—speaking, writing, and thinking at different moments in two distinct, and opposed, modes. Giving expression to the larger culture's dividedness on these central issues, he can oscillate between what seem to be contradictory stances and discourses even within a single moment in a particular travel report. Although many characteristic passages promote a globalizing vision that is Eurocentric, chauvinistic, imperialist, and hierarchical in its "scientific" ranking of the world's races, the vital expressive moments that Taylor was most known for—eloquently conveying to his audience the firsthand drama of being immersed in a fully foreign world—are designed to take his listeners on an imaginative voyage through an intercultural contact zone, speaking for disorienting and enriching experiences of interaction, reciprocity, and self-transformation that invite and enact an opening to the world in the service of a utopian effort to bridge the apparent differences between the world's peoples. Taylor undoubtedly offered his lyceum audiences a broadly cosmopolitan vision, then, as a counter to contemporary advocates of a bounded cultural nationalism or isolationism. But this cosmopolitanism could work in two very different ways. In some modes it operates as a tool to reinforce imperialist expansionism and notions of Western or Anglo-Saxon cultural supremacy; in an alternative vein, it develops as an oppositional discourse that can serve as the basis for unsettling critique of a narrowly Eurocentric or chauvinistically American worldview.

A Cosmopolitanism of Mastery: Mapping Hierarchies of Global Culture

Several critics have recently put a strong emphasis on key passages in Taylor's works that seem to define his cosmopolitanism clearly along the lines of the first mode described above: as an ideological tool providing a rationale to support contemporary movements working to extend Western economic, political, and military domination around the globe. The subtitle of his California book, *El Dorado, or, Adventures in the Path of Empire,* could be taken as a fitting summary for much of his thinking in this mode. And Taylor's direct participation in Commodore Perry's mission to "open" Japan would then stand as the epitome of this position. Of course this voyage was an anomaly in Taylor's work, since he was best known not for travel on the giant vessels of a huge military machine but for his low-tech, on-the-cheap, quasi-bohemian solo explorations on foot, camel, horseback, or reindeer sleigh. And the idea that he might be allowed to serve as the only embedded reporter accompanying the Perry mission did not originate with Taylor. Although he did personally win over the reluctant commodore during a private interview, the basic arrangements, giving Taylor a major journalistic coup, were made for him by his sponsoring newspaper, the New York *Tribune,* and its insistent editor, Horace Greeley. Also, in writing up his experiences with Perry's team, Taylor did register his confusions and questioning as he was being rushed along to join up with this imperial mission, offering withering criticism of the effects of British colonial rule in India as a prelude to his service as witness to his own nation's encounter with the Japanese.[28]

But Taylor's participation in the opening of Japan, narrated in his lecture titled "Japan and Loo Choo," does underline the potential relation between the travel writer's cultural cosmopolitanism and the powerful dynamics of American expansionism, expressed in this case through a brutally aggressive assertion of military and diplomatic force in the service of a blatantly exploitative form of economic globalization. Here a fundamental cosmopolitan ideal—the sense of the need for all human societies to open into intercourse with the community of other nations around the world—is coopted as a rhetorical rationale justifying the opening of new global markets to Western profiteering and the threatened invasion by military force of an isolationist local culture. In the official *Narrative* compiled by the Perry mission, Japan is put forward as an admonitory example of the necessary destruction of localist barriers; cosmopolitanism emerges as an inexorable, universalizing cultural and intellectual movement that requires the breaking down of those barriers—a force that dominates, that can be imposed: "Japan had no right thus to cut herself off from the community of nations" and must "obey the universal law of hospitality."[29] Though he refrains from full boosterish support for such a vision of this imperialist encounter, Taylor's written and spoken reports of it do narrate what Ziff describes as the Perry mission's "display of triumphant diplomacy" in a way that could pander to the jingoism of an American audience eager to hear of these latest movements in an expansionist destiny, a continuation of the national push to the West.[30]

Another more general, and perhaps more telling, way in which Taylor's vision of cosmopolitanism is linked to an imperialist model comes in his lecture "The Philosophy of Travel," in a rising passage celebrating "mobility" as the foundational dynamic basic to his sense of the "progressive" values inherent in a cosmopolitan model of culture: "If we note the course of History, we shall find that a country is progressive, in proportion as its people travel. None of the great nations of the ancient world ever grew up to power on its original soil. The Egyptians, the Hindoos, the Greeks and the Romans, all migrated to their seats of Empire."[31] Of course, Taylor goes on to trace the historical evolution through which these dynamics of ancient imperial conquest came to be refined in more contemporary movements of commercial travel, scientific travel, and travel for personal education. And the point of this historical lesson is to reinforce Taylor's main theme—his enthusiastic advocacy of the intellectual benefits of travel for individuals: "Travelling is, in fact, the world's greatest college. . . . These are the results which we seek to attain by going forth into the world:—the pleasure and profit to be derived from a wide range of experience; the enlargement of our intellectual vision; the cultivation of our entire nature."[32] But Taylor's history of the traveling impulse does underline his basic sense that cosmopolitan, traveling peoples (whether societies or individual members of those societies) are resolutely separate from and superior to local or sedentary ones, not just because of their "progressive" breadth of knowledge but because this travelers' knowledge is related to power: the power to move in and occupy the soil of others; the power of "conquest."

Here we mark a crucial transformation in the travel dynamic that Taylor inherited from Irving and Longfellow. While Irving and many of his initial followers made their journeys in an early postcolonial moment as visitors opening up new ties to lands that had been dominant colonial powers in their home country, Taylor's later voyages take him farther afield—to explore relations with lands and peoples that could in some ways be considered potential colonies of a rapidly expanding American power. Certainly

Taylor's writings on Mexico include strong, direct advocacy of national expansion into that territory.[33] And many of his reports from more exotic, truly Other lands conclude with blunt summary assertions of a Western cultural superiority that grounds current economic and political developments extending Western mastery over increasing areas of the globe. During his extensive tour of Egypt and North Africa, Taylor tells readers that, in the end, all that he has seen simply reinforces his appreciation of the virtues of the race that has produced the "progressive" civilization that he shares with his audience: "the highest Civilization, in every age of the world, has been developed by the race to which we belong."[34]

The celebration of "mobility" in "The Philosophy of Travel" similarly culminates in a vision of the great hierarchical typology of races: "With scarcely an exception, the inferior races are stationary, and the roving propensity increases as we ascend the scale, until it culminates in the Anglo-Saxon, which is now the ruling branch of the highest, or Caucasian race, and which has so scattered itself over all the lands and seas, that before many years its telegraph lines will be able to put a girdle around the Earth in forty seconds."[35] Where Irving's *Sketch Book* began with his evocation of the idiosyncratic "rambling propensity" that defined the American artist's mobile imagination and sent him out into the wider world as a homeless bachelor traveler testing his relation to the powerful traditions of other longer-established cultures, Taylor's vision is founded on a "roving propensity" that defines not so much a personal quality as the essential character of a race—a race of Caucasian travelers who have now begun to penetrate all the lands on the planet and whose technology will soon "girdle" the globe.

At such moments the message of "The Philosophy of Travel" develops in complex, confusing, contradictory directions: advocacy of personal travel as a broadening of horizons merges in problematic ways with promotion of travel as an expansion of national or cultural dominance; emphasis on the urge to learn from other cultures can morph abruptly into expression of the urge to rise above other cultures; enthusiastic evocation of the ideal of "planetary conviviality" can conclude with powerful support for "managerial" mastery; and a cosmopolitan celebration of the human potential shared by all peoples sits uneasily beside sudden turns to rankings of the world's peoples in relation to the ideal of cosmopolitan mobility: "In our day, the nations which travel are the Anglo-American, the English, the French, the German and the Russian, and these are the great powers of the Earth."[36] While the most extended argument in "The Philosophy of Travel" urges the desirability of crossing cultural boundaries—stepping into other lives and experiences without judgment, toward a goal of expanded universal understanding—Taylor can then invoke this internationalist vision to make essentialized distinctions between the world's nations or races, judged according to their native interest in or gift for intercultural travel and exchange. The shape-shifting abilities of Anglo-American globe-trotters, allowing them to gain a full panoramic sense of a universal potential in all humans, make them clearly superior to less-developed "inferior" peoples who remain "stationary"—bound to the singular, settled cultural forms of their ethnic or racial enclave: "The negro race of Africa, . . . have always clung to their original seats, and have never emerged from their original barbarism"; "When the Chinese shut themselves out from communication with the rest of the world, their life began to stagnate."[37]

In summary conclusions such as these, Taylor is offering American readers and lecture audiences a flattering sense that the mobile representatives of their progressive culture can bring back to them privileged access to a form of comparative cross-cultural knowledge that makes them masters of the world. They can feel that they are gaining a knowledge that differentiates them from others, opening up a totalizing global perspective that orients them in relation to others. This is the aspect of Taylor's books and lectures that leads Ziff to conclude that the cosmopolitan world traveler finally only confirms his audience in their provincial complacency: even though "he educated Americans about their place on a racial map of the world," thus undeniably broadening his audience's narrow frame of reference, "the message the famous traveler conveyed to his stay-at-home countrymen was that their cultural/racial superiority was confirmed by the ways of the world."[38] Taylor's travel lectures, then, can be seen in some ways to operate precisely along the overarching lines defined by Mary Louise Pratt in *Imperial Eyes*, her study of European travel writings—they "created the imperial order for [those] at home and gave them their place in it. . . . They made imperial expansion meaningful and desirable to the citizenries of the imperial countries"—or summarized by Bruce Harvey in *American Geographics*, his analysis of the cultural work of midcentury American travel texts: they "provide Western mastery of the non-Western."[39]

As we have seen, one key way in which Taylor works to forge meaning out of the world's multiplicity and diversity is to embrace currently popular hierarchies of nationality and race. It is surprising, in fact, to see the broadly educated Great Traveler, at certain moments, summarizing the results of a voyage by resorting to the most reductive forms of racial essentialism, referring to new "sciences" of craniology or phrenology to fit different human specimens into the neatly differentiated typological pigeonholes of a sort of natural history cabinet, on the basis of their bodily forms. This is not a cosmopolitanism of cultural relativism. In such moments, a form of cosmopolitan, cross-cultural knowledge is deployed not to bring out a sense of the connections between the world's peoples but, rather, to make possible invidious comparative judgments that help to establish radical separations between cultures and peoples. In his more generalizing travel lectures, Taylor could assert this physiological vision with blunt clarity: "Moral and mental traits are almost uniformly revealed in the physical appearance of a race. The African Negro is tall, but absolutely without grace or beauty. Correspondingly, he has no significant art."[40]

One of Taylor's chief concerns in *A Journey to Central Africa* is to argue, along these lines, for firm distinctions between the Negro or African race and the Egyptians or "Orientals" who are seen to be the ancestors of the Caucasian peoples: the "graceless" movements of African warriors help explain why the Negro race, unlike the Egyptians, has never been capable of the progressive development that would allow them to attain "a higher degree of civilization than is at present exhibited in Congo and Ashantee."[41] In his "Japan and Loo Choo" lecture, differences in physical appearance between the Chinese and Japanese define the moral superiority of the latter, as the "stolid, impassive" faces of the graceless Chinese speak for their "mental inertia" and the "stagnation" of their culture, whereas the graceful and curious (even Yankee-like) Japanese faces express that progressive race's "lively and active mind."[42]

Underlying these physiological judgments and codifications is an unexamined aesthetic vision; the standard of grace or beauty or symmetry often invoked here as a universally applicable measure is that defined by the progressive Western civilization. And at the top of this classificatory hierarchical typology comes, always, the white European, as could be made most apparent in the direct distillations of the basic message in Taylor's travel lectures: "Every important triumph which man has achieved since his creation belongs to the Caucasian race. Our mental and moral superiority is self-evident."[43]

How do we explain such moments within Taylor's work? Perhaps, most simply, he is here—usually in the concluding passages of lectures, articles, or books—trying to wrap things up neatly, assuring audiences that they will receive some pay-off, some take-home message. And he often does this by giving his midcentury listeners what he thinks they want, pandering to expectations of a rise to a patriotic point, or to strong-felt demands in this period that global knowledge should be expressed through increasingly precise schemes of "scientific" international classification. At midcareer Taylor also faced a crisis of confidence that led him to give a new value to what he saw as the "sciences" of travel. When he undertook a massive project of research and reading to make selections and prepare the preface for the *Cyclopaedia of Modern Travel* (1856), a hugely ambitious historical compendium of nineteenth-century travel writing, Taylor came to see the travel mode for which he had become known—the narrative of personal experience—as limited, inadequate, near-sighted, uninformed, leading to no new knowledge.

Overwhelmed by what he found in the writings of Alexander von Humboldt, the genius to whom the *Cyclopaedia* was dedicated, Taylor resolved to transform his own work by attempting to develop the basis of a true traveler's stance through study of the modern sciences of anthropology and ethnology. This impulse is also what led to his decisions to undertake his two later voyages, to the Arctic zone and Russia, in order to balance his earlier southern explorations and thus attempt to give his oeuvre the overall shape of a "human cosmos"—a compendium registering and mapping all the grand divisions of the world's humanity.[44] Park Benjamin's famous, damning witticism about Taylor, which has now perhaps come to have more currency than any of Taylor's own writings—"[Bayard Taylor] has traveled more and seen less than any man living"—seems to imply just the self-critical point that Taylor himself would begin to make about his own work: immersing himself in firsthand sensations and perceptual details, he often failed to provide a final overview, to arrive at a grand, outside perspective from which he (and his readers) could "see" the big picture. In fact, Taylor wrote that he would have agreed with Benjamin's remark (which he initially believed had been made by Humboldt) if he had said, "No man who has published so many volumes of travel has contributed so little to positive science."[45]

A Cosmopolitanism of Cultural Mediation: The Lecture Hall as Contact Zone

But Taylor's efforts to achieve what he came to valorize as positive, scientific knowledge in fact seem to have led him to turn away from his real strengths as a traveler and writer. In his books and articles, there is often a characteristic turning point when Taylor makes a sudden, signature transition from graphic, detailed re-creation of his own particular foreign experiences to attempts at generalizing, comparative cross-cultural analysis—to the "philosophy" or "science" of travel. This transition can be even more marked, and forced, in his lectures as Taylor leaps from accounts of close-up immersion in the life of a foreign land to the detached, outsider's overview of that life. And it is remarkable how often the concluding overview seems not only to be detached from the traveler's experiences just recounted but to contradict those experiences.

"The Vision of Hasheesh," a *Putnam's* article building upon a set-piece passage from *The Lands of the Saracen,* recounts the hallucinatory bafflement provoked by an excessive ingestion of hashish as a sort of microcosmic enactment of the plot of a standard travel narrative: we follow the narrator on a disorienting trip to a world in which no familiar standards apply. But, in the end, this essay offers a clear example of Taylor's tendency to turn away from his own insights and experiences out of a characteristic urge to conclude things in a state of mastery, of solidity, of safe return. After many pages of vivid, graphic, and hilarious description, in the dark romantic vein of Poe or Thomas De Quincey, conveying the overwhelming effects of this experiment in letting go, of yielding to the influence of mind-altering Middle Eastern drugs—where the ground is very clearly shifting under the feet of this naive pilgrim—Taylor steps outside the experience in the last paragraph to speak for a moralizing lesson that minimizes the mental travel into irrationality that has kept readers mesmerized: "It has taught me the majesty of human reason and of human will . . . and the awful peril of tampering with that which assails their integrity."[46] In a more directly travel-oriented case, Taylor's lecture "The Arabs" went on at length, in some performances, about his discovery of the richness of the Muslim religion and the value of its vision of the historical commingling of Muslim, Jewish, and Christian traditions—Arab culture suggests that "portions of the Divine Laws have been revealed not to us alone"—before concluding in its last few sentences with a paean to the superiority and distinctiveness of Christianity: "the religion of Mahomet has done its duty."[47]

The "Philosophy of Travel" is crucially marked by similar swerves. Though not based on any one travel experience, this lecture centers on an extended series of colorful, concrete, visceral evocations of the efforts of Taylor, and of other famed voyagers, to make contact with foreign lives by inhabiting foreign lifeways: "I have lived on red-peppers and black beans in Mexico; rice and curry in India; roasted sheep and raw onions in Central Africa; goat's flesh and garlic in Spain; and shark's fins and bird's-nest soup in China."[48] These catalogues of graphic travel scenes—meant to incite audience members to consider setting off for their own experiments in cross-cultural exchange—imply a performative notion of culture, as model Western travelers show by example that one can "cut loose" from the forms and practices that define one's "native character" to take on a role in the social theater of a foreign people, moving like them, dressing like them, eating like them, speaking like them, and so becoming "one of them, for a time."[49] But then, when Taylor feels the need to arrive at a general "philosophy" of such travel, he falls back on a deeply ingrained habit of cultural categorization: "In the floating society of travel, no less than in fixed communities, we get the habit of arranging men into classes, and after a little experience it is as easy to decide to which class a person belongs as it is to pronounce upon his nationality."[50] Where the Africans or the Chinese ignore the benefits of cross-cultural interaction, the Frenchman makes a good traveler "because his nature is essentially theatrical"; such impulses are also "the natural inheritance of the Saxon and Scandinavian races"; but "after the Germans and the Russians, the Americans are the most sympathetic of all travellers."[51] In such passages, the argument turns, once again, from a stress on the porousness and malleability of cultural constructions to an opposed emphasis on the immutability of distinctions in essential "nature" among different cultures or races.

Here, again, Taylor's celebration of the ease and desirability of cutting across cultural boundaries—following the example of the traveler who learns to "identify himself as much as possible with new habits of thought and new standards of judgment"—confronts the scientist's model of the planet as a natural-history cabinet defining firm barriers between each categorized national identity.[52] And with this move we turn, characteristically, from a nonjudgmental, relativistic exploration of diverse "standards of judgment" to a hierarchical ranking of global cultures. Indeed, by the end of the lecture, Taylor feels the need to stress his reintegration within the home culture and values of his audience, as he concludes by defending himself from any possible suspicions that his long history of participation in the lives of exotic peoples may have led him to go native, losing his original identity as a representative of the dominant civilization of the West: "I am a most earnest advocate of Civilization. . . . The coarse life of a savage is abhorrent to all our sympathies. . . . The true nobility of human nature only exists in civilized lands."[53]

In his book *Going Abroad,* William Stowe introduces a clarifying analysis of American travel writing according to the classic, tripartite structure of tribal-initiation ritual defined by Arnold van Gennep and Victor Turner, in which the voyaging persona moves through three phases: from separation, through a liminal/mixed/threshold stage, to a final reintegration within the home community. Stowe takes Bayard Taylor as his prime example of a traveler who only goes through the motions of the mixed, confusing "liminoid" experience of cross-cultural travel because, for him, the entire process is, from the outset, so fully oriented to the moment of reintegration as "an inevitable, foregone conclusion": "[Travel] changed him, however, not a whit." In Stowe's view, Taylor stands as the polar opposite of Margaret Fuller, whose trip to Italy developed as a transformative, "revolutionary odyssey." Taylor, by contrast, never really leaves home; the central persona in his travel writing is never capable of being transformed; and thus his travel accounts might be *in*formative but can never be *trans*formative for readers.[54] But while Stowe's vision does capture something of what I have been describing as the strong drive for an ending—or for reintegration into the home culture of American audiences—evident as one characteristic tendency in Taylor's travel narratives, I would argue that Taylor is in fact more appropriately understood as a *specialist* in the liminal, and that the most vital and intriguing moments in his work come not in the pat conclusions of his writings and lectures but in his introductions and intermediary passages—with his graphic and scenic re-creations of his personal sensations, experiences, and responses during the unsettling, destabilizing liminoid stages of his initiations into foreign cultures and his voyages through foreign lands.

From the first, what distinguished Taylor's approach to travel was not his desire to master or to dominate or to judge through external observation but his adaptability, his eagerness to connect with and to get a feel for other lives from within. Even Ziff highlights his remarkable gift for "submerging himself in local ways."[55] As we have seen, the central, and distinctive, message in Taylor's "Philosophy of Travel" is a celebration of the "sympathetic" traveler's willingness to give himself over to an experimental, perhaps utopian, effort at participatory immersion in the practices of foreign lives—as the basis for what he calls a "true" cosmopolitanism: "[The sympathetic traveler] . . . is the true cosmopolite, shifting his habits according to his locality, and making himself equally at home in all parts of the world. . . . You can establish no magnetic communication with another race, without conforming in some degree to their manners and habits of life. Unless you do this, you carry your own country with you wherever you go, and you behold new forms of life merely from the outside, without feeling the vital pulse which throbs beneath."[56]

Lecture performances of "The Arabs" began with a similar keynote message, not imposing a singular Western system of values but advocating the benefit in recognizing a relativity of cultural standards: "Those who have always lived in the same climate, and associated only with men of their own race, can form but little idea of the diversity of human character." Urging a stance of "charity to all," Taylor then went on to argue against easy, "one-sided," anti-Arab judgments: "We must adopt *their* highest ideal of excellence as the standard by which they must be judged, as men."[57] Rather than treat the Arabs as enemies, he says, he "associated and fraternized" with these people—"In their steps I followed"—and presents himself as someone who "loved them and desired to be their advocate."[58]

In his Europe book *Views Afoot,* he insists on the fact that his tour was undertaken mainly on foot, and that this meant he spent most days not with tourists or ruling elites but in the company of migrant, indigent, working-class commoners and itinerant students. In the same way, the preface to *A Journey to Central Africa* stresses, as his main motive for undertaking this demanding journey, Taylor's "desire to participate in their free, vigorous, semi-barbaric life." He also makes clear that, counter to currently dominant modes of Orientalist vision, his focus is not on a frozen memory of past existence in Egypt but on contact and interaction with the living, evolving present; his interest is "more in the live Arab than the dead Pharaoh."[59] And this cross-cultural interaction is most fully achieved after a major turn in the book, when Taylor leaves behind the luxurious mode of aristocratic tourism he had adopted while floating down the Nile in the company of a German count and his many servants—just observing the aesthetic show as he drifted by it at a protected distance—and, in a new phase, decides to head out on a camel for an extremely demanding desert crossing in the company of native camel drivers speaking only their native Arabic. Riding the camel for eight to ten hours a day, Taylor shifts from the role of Irvingesque tourist to that of Ledyard-like explorer, from spectator to participant, as he tests himself by immersion in this new life, and the focus turns (as it does in the later narratives of Lawrence of Arabia's initiation in the desert) to his own physical, emotional, and spiritual responses to the camels, to these Arab companions, and, especially, to the blowing sands and intense sun.

This tendency in Taylor then tends to erase, or at least to blur, what at other moments can seem to be a sense of absolute difference between the mobile cosmopolitan and his isolated, grounded, local subjects of study. In these scenes the accent shifts to areas of connection or resemblance between the American traveler and natives from other races. In the company of camel drivers crossing North African deserts, or common sailors crossing the Atlantic, or itinerant workers walking between European cities, Taylor can feel a special sense of comradeship or even identification with "locals" who are also fellow travelers—"free and roving peoples," as he puts it in "The Arabs." The "Wandering Arab" is a fitting type of that race, Taylor observes, expressing special reverence for the Bedouin camel drivers he relied on as "mariners" in the oceanic expanses of the desert.[60] Especially in the case of these Bedouin guides, who are seen to live an existence based on continual mobility—always on the move between more sedentary tribes or settlements—and who can surprise him with a comparative, travelers' knowledge not only of diverse tribes but also of other regions and cultures, Taylor presents his interactions with exotic natives not on the classic hierarchical model of emerging ethnography—as encounters between broad-minded cosmopolitan voyagers and bounded, limited locals—but as, in James Clifford's words, meetings between "discrepant cosmopolitanisms."[61] Looking back in later years at his time among the camel drivers crossing the Nubian desert, Taylor can even hold up those "mariners" as models of the best approach to travel, thus placing them as non-Western cosmopolitans figuring an alternative to the classic European cosmopolitanism of a Humboldt.[62]

Compared with most tourists or travel writers, Taylor stayed much longer in each land that he visited. And during his stays he did, as he says, eat the local foods, wear the local clothing, live (for the most part) in local dwellings. Over and over, this point is noted as the chief interest in reports on his lecture appearances. A San Francisco report on a performance of "The Arabs" notes that Taylor began with his usual emphasis on the fact of his own extended participatory immersion in the exotic worlds he will describe: "Eight months he lived with Arabs, as one of themselves. He spoke their language, dressed, ate, and drank with them, slept in their tents and wandered with them over their deserts."[63] Angela Ray notes that here Taylor was fulfilling in spectacular fashion what had become a basic requirement of lyceum performance: the sense that a lecturer be seen to be speaking from firsthand, eyewitness, personal experience.[64] Another news report promoted Taylor's "Philosophy of Travel" lecture in just these terms: "Certainly the author of the 'Journey to Central Africa,' the man who has traveled over a good part of a hemisphere and taken its 'views *afoot*,' who has taken *Hasheesh* by the quantity and traveled among the Arabs as a Bedouin, and who has seen the Elephant he told us of on Tuesday, in India, must have a system of philosophy on such things worth hearing."[65]

But in some ways the close-up, detailed reports of his immersive cross-cultural experiences could prove to be more profound than Taylor's efforts to arrive at systematic philosophical conclusions or to frame the results of his personal experiments in international travel within a comparative study of global cultures. Perhaps the most significant of Taylor's attempts at engaged participation in foreign lives came with his efforts to inhabit the local language. Following in the tradition of Longfellow, Taylor would, on most of his extended stays, take the time to develop something like fluency in the native tongue as well as in the local literary or aesthetic forms. As a result, his travel reports are distinctive in that they do not always operate unselfconsciously in one linguistic register, simply representing the lives of foreign peoples by translating them into Western terms or by imposing Western grids of expectation on them.

In *The Lands of the Saracen* and *A Journey to Central Africa,* Taylor's everyday encounters with foreign natives (who speak only Arabic) frequently revolve around questions about their language or discussions about their literary conventions and distinctive modes of expression. And the "Arabs" lecture gives a central place to reporting the results of these conversations through extended evocations of the distinctive, non-Western expressive modes that so fascinated Taylor: the intricate elaborations characteristic of the nonrepresentational mode of the arabesque; the magic and romance of *Arabian Nights* fable; the exhilarations and dangers latent in flights of a Middle Eastern fictional imagination—studied as a form of wild "exaggeration," which is itself explained as "the imperfect form of metaphor." Taylor is effusive in praising the artful musicality and gorgeous images of Persian poetry, which he knew well, having published *Poems of the Orient* (1854), a collection of his own work in the mode of the fourteenth-century poet Hafiz, in which his persona frequently speaks as a globally aware Muslim, expressing his Eastern worldview while refuting Western misperceptions of it. And in his effort to speak for the moral character of an Arabic verbal culture, Taylor also incorporates into the "Arabs" lecture a retelling of a number of short Arab prose parables.[66]

In Taylor's written travel narratives, peak moments of reciprocity are often marked by the exchange of stories—thus not simply imposing a mode of representation on the local culture but, in some ways, conveying a record of the local culture's own self-image in its own modes and figures. A major turning point in *A Journey to Central Africa* comes when the romantic traveler finds what has always been the highest goal of his Middle Eastern visit—"a living experience of the Arabian Nights." Here, after another discussion of local expressive modes, his Bedouin guide Achmet agrees to recite, in Arabic, an oral tale for Taylor, who reclines with his turban, pipe, and coffee to relish every word, which he then transcribes at length for his Western readers. Christoph Irmscher describes this extraordinary moment, when Taylor gives his book's narrative voice over to his local servant for the length of a chapter, as "an egalitarian exchange hardly to be found elsewhere in the American travel literature of the time."[67] Sealing a personal bond between the Western traveler and his local guide, this exchange of fables then leads to an intimate exchange of passages from sacred texts (mainly the Koran and the Bible) that culminates in a cosmopolitan sharing of religious principles—a recognition of "the one great and good God" beyond the differences of Prophet and apostle—making Taylor and Achmet close, tale-sharing comrades for the rest of the voyage.[68]

The ability to enter into some forms of two-way communication, then, means that often Taylor is able to present foreign peoples not only from the outside, through surface descriptions of their bodies, clothing, and behaviors, but also through re-creations of their roles as participants in a rich, highly defined culture. Unlike the Western travelers catalogued by Pratt, Taylor always stresses that the people he visits do have a religion, a complex code of conduct, an aesthetic vision, and so on. And because Taylor has developed at least a rudimentary ability in the local language, his travel experience becomes much more interactive than that of more standard tourists; in key moments, we see him not only judging his companions but learning *from* them.

In his eyewitness mode, Taylor characteristically presents himself not as an older voice of wisdom, able to make firm pronouncements about what he sees and knows, but in his original persona as an adventurous youth, open to the experience of an initiation into unknown ways of being. In this attitude, Taylor is not dominating but, more often, yielding as he comes slowly to a fuller sense of the ways of life around him. The drama in these moments is not so much about a final urge to know, to convert everyday interactions into knowledge, as it is about the traveler's experience of not knowing. Knowledge in Taylor's firsthand descriptions of his experiences of the contact zone is not the possession of the well-traveled visitor but of the local hosts. And in extended scenes tracing Taylor's slow processes of learning, initiation, and adaptation, *he* is the one who is being transformed—changing his manner of expression, his bodily *habitus,* his clothes. When Taylor appeared at some travel lectures wearing his Arabic robes and turban, or his Russian fur hat, he was, first of all, bringing lecture audiences back to the key moments they would remember from his travel books, in which he managed to follow guides who could help him to give up his learned values and everyday practices to immerse himself in local ways. As we have seen, the foreign clothing was meant as a sign that Taylor has incorporated some elements from his travel experiences into his reformed being; that travel has involved some reciprocal interchange; that, contra Stowe, Taylor has not returned from his journeys the same as he was when he began.

When Taylor emerges from these liminoid experiences to try to put into words what he has learned through this process, we get a remarkable series of strong statements advocating values diametrically opposed to those of the "scientific" and imperial Western vision. *The Lands of the Saracen* works to counter an unhealthy, obsessive American work ethic through extended celebrations of the value of "rest" and "indolence," of new experiences of the senses and of bodily sensuality, and a revisionary defense of what Taylor terms "animal existence." Touring Spain, Taylor compares "Orientals" to "Christians" and asserts, "One's sympathies are wholly with the Moors." If he were to begin anew and decide his own religious affiliation based on what he saw of the practitioners of all the world's religions when visiting Jerusalem, he says, "I should at once turn Mussulman."[69] Surprising audiences by reversing their conventional vision of Western values, Taylor would assert in the "Arabs" lecture his certainty that "Christian knights first learned their sense of honour and chivalry among the Saracens at the time of the crusades."[70] (The oppositional thrust of that point might be heightened as it was spoken by a lecturer proudly wearing an Arab sword said to have been made in 798 A.D. and to have been used in bloody battles against Christian crusaders.) In a later lecture on Egypt, Taylor told his audience that in North Africa he discovered that all that is best and most progressive in America's "progressive" civilization—"the best elements of our sciences, laws, morals, and religion," as well as the movements for temperance and women's political equality—had its basis in ancient Egypt.[71] As he said, Taylor wanted to counter anti-Arab sentiment and speak as their advocate. So the liminal initiation into other worlds can, at certain moments, especially when the topic is the Arab world, turn Taylor's native worldview upside down—and leave him speaking *for* the "foreign" *to* his countrymen. In this mode the traveler uses what he has learned abroad not just to flatter Western or American chauvinism but to critique it, making use of the comparative platform of travel writing to challenge and resist the self-limiting aspects of midcentury nationalism, and to denaturalize American values. In the last lines of his "Arabs" lecture, he summarizes for his listeners the most profound result of his experience among the "remarkable people" of the East: it has left him deeply skeptical of the "insatiable national vanity" that has led Americans "to think we are about as near perfection as men can reach."[72]

But more often Taylor's liminoid, firsthand experiences of being immersed in another world *cannot* be so clearly distilled into such summary value judgments—pro *or* con Western, "civilized" values—or into solid bits of take-home comparative knowledge. Instead, in the most compelling moments in his writing and lecturing, he seems to seek to put himself into confusing, disorienting, extreme situations that cannot be rationally, abstractly summarized and articulated, but instead can only be presented through close-up, blow-by-blow accounts of strong, strange sensations, quasi-hallucinatory visions, and, especially, immersive threshold experiences. These graphic firsthand accounts, for which Taylor was best known, do not center on rock 'em sock 'em physical adventure so much as on extreme tests of the traveler's self-identity—challenges that situate the individual spirit not in a state of imperial mastery but, rather, in something like abjection, or ecstatic, ascetic dispossession. In scenes re-creating his encounters with the light and sand of the desert, his efforts to endure the light and cold of the Arctic, his experiments with hashish, or his literal immersion in the Arabian baths, Taylor is not only documenting an exotic exterior environment with detailed, scientific empirical solidity but also recording *changes in himself,* in his interior life, testing his own epistemological and spiritual bearings.

In *American Geographics,* Bruce Harvey has shown how, for a line of early American travelers, the Holy Land of the Middle East became the site for tests of a voyager's theological and psychosexual virility.[73] Taylor, exceptionally fit, succeeded in joining this lineage, making himself, in Ziff's words, "America's first great popular Orientalist."[74] But while Taylor's physical exploits in following the White Nile in North Africa showed him pushing farther than previous explorers into dangerous new territory, and his desert crossings involved feats of extreme endurance beyond anything in John Lloyd Stephens, his writings and lectures urged an opposed approach to the experience of the cross-cultural voyage. Describing his ideal of "sympathetic travel" in "The Philosophy of Travel," he argues that "the most favorable physical temperament is that which is pliant and yielding, rather than that which accompanies bodily vigor. Men of large frames and great muscular strength are apt to suffer from changes of climate: their systems are resistant and set up an active opposition, instead of accommodating themselves to the change of circumstances."[75]

In *A Journey to Central Africa,* Taylor models this stance of yielding rather than conquest, accommodation rather than resistance, in his ecstatic descriptions of his physical ordeal of immersion in the desert sands and sun. He notes that most tourists feel the need for lined umbrellas, broad hats, or green veils to protect them, but Taylor wants nothing to come between him and the "fierce red Desert"; he wants not so much to see it (through the distorting frame of protective veils) as to feel it. And although the intense sun was painful, physically damaging his eyes—thus forcing him to give up a reliance on the dominant sense of vision—he describes the full-body immersion in its rays as a "burning baptism" through which he begins to be initiated into the life of the East: "You must let the Sun lay his scepter on your head, if you want to know his power."[76] Here Taylor does not adopt a stance of virile mastery but yields, passively, sensually, to the dominant force of a visceral experience arising out of the foreign environment.

The value of yielding to the mastery of the foreign is also dramatized in sensational fashion in the scenes of Taylor's experiments with hashish, which are narrated in an article in *Putnam's* and a key chapter in *The Lands of the Saracen* and re-created in central passages in the "Arabs" lecture. Although this ordeal is psychological rather than physical, the hashish is first taken as a cure for the severe eye problems caused by Taylor's immersion in the harsh North African sun, and the drug-inspired visions show how the traveler has internalized the dynamics of the desert crossing: "I was moving over the Desert, not upon the rocking dromedary, but seated in a barque made of mother-of-pearl. . . . I suddenly found myself at the foot of the great Pyramid of Cheops . . . [and] saw that it was built not of limestone, but of huge square plugs of cavendish tobacco!" In this hallucinatory reprise of his Egyptian experiences, Taylor takes his audience through an Arabian Nights experience of cross-cultural travel, of "wandering for years in some distant world." Far from dominating, the traveler is now seen to be "possessed," under the influence of a powerful Oriental drug that "masters" him and gives him a new bodily form: "I was a mass of transparent jelly, and a confectioner poured me into a twisted mould." This mental travel does expand his horizons—"the walls of my frame were burst outward and tumbled into ruin"—but the loss of a familiar frame here is fearfully disorienting, bringing Taylor close to madness.[77]

A much more positive vision of this mode of travel experience comes in another of the set-piece chapters in *The Lands of the Saracen:* "A Dissertation on Bathing and Bodies." The "peculiar institution" of the Eastern bath is celebrated as a "sensuous elysium," and Taylor counsels a literal immersion in its ritual practices as the most direct means of transforming oneself and beginning to inhabit the lifeways of the East. Here again the proper stance is not one of "stiff-necked" resistance but, rather, once again, of yielding to the mastery of foreign arts and influences: "The Oriental yields himself body and soul" to the heat and steam, and to the sometimes painful physical manipulations, of the bath process. To understand the bath, a Westerner must accept the pipe from the young attendant with "submissive lips" and lie "passively," like an infant, to respond to the molding and reformation of his body: "He must be as clay in the hands of a potter." Though an uptight initiate might be fearful of this deep massage, Taylor advises, "It is only resistance that is dangerous. . . . Give yourself with a blind submission into the arms of the brown Fate, and he will lead you to new chambers of delight." One will find that all these bodily ministrations, provoking "thrills of the purest physical pleasure," transform the soul as well as the physical frame. This visceral experience, then, inspires Taylor to effusive praise of the beauty of the naked human body, grounding what emerges as a strongly Whitmanian challenge to fundamental Western values—urging the importance of rest as an alternative to a compulsive mobility, idleness as a healthy complement to an obsession with productive work, and reverence for the body as temple to counter censorious Victorian attitudes toward sensual bodily enjoyment.

In his account of his own initiation into the bath, Taylor uses the pronouns "you" and "we" to draw his individual readers into the process, placing himself as a guide who can lead a newcomer, moment by moment, through the stages of this disorienting, transformative experience: "Come with me, and I will show you the mysteries of the perfect bath. Here is the entrance, a heavy Saracenic arch, opening upon the crowded bazaar. We descend a few steps."[78] The account is meant to work, then, not only as a report on Taylor's own past travels but as a present experience of travel for the reader who participates imaginatively in the scene.

This is the effect Taylor is aiming for during some peak moments of his travel lectures, especially in the "Arabs" lecture, which was based on the books *A Journey to Central Africa* and *The Lands of the Saracen* and weaves together reprises of those texts' set-piece essays on pipes, coffee, baths, bodies, hashish, and Eastern expressive modes. Working in this register, Taylor not only recounts a moment of personal experience but also attempts to present that moment in a way that places the reader or listener as a participant at the experiential center of what is being described. Tom Wright has noted how the sensually detailed, vivid, scenic firsthand reporting in the lectures is rarely presented in the first person. Instead, Taylor characteristically slips into the second person in these passages—"you see" this and "you sense" that—thus drawing the engaged listener in, placing him or her within the developing scene.[79] So here the travel lecturer may not be simply reporting *on* the experience of complex cross-cultural interactions in the contact zone but attempting to give some audience members the feeling of voyaging through the contact zone themselves.

And this voyage is not always solidly grounded, settled. Taylor brings in listeners in this way not only for his great set-piece panoramas, providing what Mary Louise Pratt terms an imperial "monarch-of-all-I-survey" vision, but also to conjure the effect of his more subjective experiences of dispossession and loss of mastery.[80] The "Arabs" lecture, for example, begins with strong attempts to convey the overwhelming intensity of noonday sun in the desert, as Taylor shifts away from a first-person syntax to situate his listeners within the landscape that in his view is the ground of Arab culture: "at times the eye can scarcely support" the "deep and dazzling colors" experienced in this "inmost heart of fire." Audience members are also meant to relive Taylor's original affective response to the bracing purity of the desert air, imaginatively taking it in themselves: "You breathe the unadulterated elements of the atmosphere."[81] In the same way, the "Moscow" lecture takes listeners through the process of a first entrance to the city—just as the "Baths" chapter guided initiates into the bathhouse waters—introducing each added detail in the second person so that the elements of this dazzling, disorienting visual spectacle slowly come together before the eyes of each audience member: "Your eyes, accustomed to the cool green of the woods and swamps, are at first dazzled with the sight."

But Taylor's goal here is never to arrive at a moment of perspectival mastery, when all becomes clear in overview. Rather, his tendency is to evoke the sense of foreign travel as an experience of overwhelming wonder: "There comes a moment when you doubt whether what you see belongs to this actual world, or whether some work of the genii, forgotten since the age of fable, has not been left to punish your modern unbelief." Taylor characteristically associates this effect of enchantment with his own experience of Arabian expressive modes. Introducing his Moscow lecture with reference to an Arab legend about a "marvelous city," he suggests that listeners who participate in the visual spectacle of his approach to Moscow will feel with him that this city "was built while the lamp was yet in Aladdin's hands" and observes that, in the Russian winter, these colorful buildings "appear as strangely out of place as a turbaned Oriental smoking his pipe on a block of ice."[82] A Taylor travel lecture, then, seeks to initiate engaged listeners into a romantic vision of cross-cultural travel, in which the dazzled voyager enters a wonderland where standards and proportions are constantly shifting, and it is difficult to tell what is real and what is Arabian Nights enchantment—or hallucination.

Another especially intriguing lecture passage that seems to work in this way comes in the middle of "The Arabs." Here Taylor is explaining how he became familiar not only with the words and grammar of the Arab language but also with some more profound aspects of the East's distinctive expressive modes, especially the tendency to "exaggeration" or "lying," a "vivid imagination" and "Orientalism of style" that, he claims, traces its roots to the use of Indian hemp or hashish. Western travelers who fear intimate association with Arabs, thinking the locals will take advantage of them through their infamous lies or exaggerations, need only prepare themselves: knowledge of native modes of communication is the key to success in cross-cultural interaction. Taylor then admits that, after many months of his own everyday conversational interactions with Arabs, he found himself transformed by these local habits, beginning to think and speak in the mode of fable, legend, or exaggeration: "To confess the truth, after I was able to converse with some fluency in Arabic, . . . I was frequently guilty of the most shocking enlargements." Though he assures his audience that he has now learned to tame this habit, having returned to a mode of Western "veracity" and to the "plain" truths expressed in English—"I am now strictly speaking the truth"—he nonetheless leaves the half-joking but provocative suggestion here that this return to Western "veracity" may be a ruse, and that perhaps much of this lecture has been an exercise in Arabian "exaggeration."[83]

This suspicion might then be strengthened when Taylor's lecture immediately turns away from the mode of "plain" truth to dive into further enthusiastic discussions of the extraordinary imagery in Arabian tales and the elaborate verbal ornaments in Persian poetry, only to move from there into an extended recounting of the hallucinatory visions that possessed Taylor during his experiment with hashish—an experiment he undertook in an attempt to understand the sources of the fantastic Arabic imagination. Perhaps Taylor has not only been providing knowledge *about* Arabic language but has been addressing his American listeners from within an Arabic expressive discourse that he has now internalized. Perhaps he is not only wearing Oriental robes but has also taken on the deep structure of the Orient's language. If it does work in this way, this complex lecture passage would involve a lyceum experiment in something like what Pratt calls "transculturation."[84] In the place of a knowing Western discourse *about* the Orient, we may be encountering an Oriental voice talking back, foregrounding the limits of the Western ethnographic project. Taylor here plays with the potential *heteroglossia* of the contact zone—seen to operate not only in his original experience but now in the experience of his listeners. Is this lecture offered as literature or science? Fiction or fact? An Arabic or a Western expression? The effect is to provoke and test members of the lecture audience, to pose a challenge to them, and perhaps to give them at least a taste of the disorienting experience of true travel into the mixed world of the contact zone.

What I have been evoking in these final examples is not the *only* voice in Bayard Taylor's writing or lecture performances, but it is one of the most distinctive elements in his work, and it does serve as the ground for an alternative form of cosmopolitan traveler's knowledge that unsettles the solidities of the system of power and knowledge inherent in the dominant mode of globalizing imperial vision—the vision that is so powerful in shaping the generalizing conclusions in many of Taylor's travel reports. This other, distinctive voice and perspective in Taylor's lectures could represent his most important, still-relevant legacy for twentieth-first-century readers as we continue to try to negotiate questions of cosmopolitan identity in an increasingly interdependent world.

NOTES

Access to autograph lecture manuscripts (archived at the Chester County Historical Society, West Chester, Pennsylvania) and to some newspaper reports on Taylor performances was made possible through the generosity of Tom Wright.

1. Walter D. Mignolo, "The Many Faces of Cosmo-polis: Border Thinking and Critical Cosmopolitanism," in *Cosmopolitanism,* ed. Carol A. Breckenridge, Sheldon Pollock, Homi K. Bhabha, and Dipesh Chakrabarty (Durham, NC: Duke University Press, 2002), 157–58.

2. Hershel Parker, introduction to *The Norton Anthology of American Literature,* ed. Nina Baym et al., vol. B, 6th ed. (New York: W. W. Norton, 2003), 960.

3. On the place of Irving's *Sketch Book* within the history of nineteenth-century American travel writing, see Alfred Bendixen, "American Travel Books about Europe before the Civil War," in *The Cambridge Companion to American Travel Writing,* ed. Alfred Bendixen and Judith Hamera (Cambridge: Cambridge University Press, 2009), 103–26.

4. Washington Irving, *The Sketch Book of Geoffrey Crayon, Gent.,* ed. Haskell Springer (Boston: Twayne, 1978), 8.

5. Larzer Ziff, *Return Passages: Great American Travel Writing, 1780–1910* (New Haven: Yale University Press, 2000), 119, 157; Bendixen, "American Travel Books," 118; Tom F. Wright, "The Results of Locomotion: Bayard Taylor and the Travel Lecture in the Mid-Nineteenth-Century United States," *Studies in Travel Writing* 14, no. 2 (June 2010): 112.

6. Wright, "Results of Locomotion," 120.

7. Bayard Taylor, *The Lands of the Saracen; or, Pictures of Palestine, Asia Minor, Sicily, and Spain* (New York: Putnam, 1855), iii.

8. On this point, see Angela Ray, *The Lyceum and Public Culture in the Nineteenth-Century United States* (East Lansing: Michigan State University Press, 2005), 36–41; and Carl Bode, *The American Lyceum: Town Meeting of the Mind* (Carbondale: Southern Illinois University Press, 1956), 201–23.

9. Bayard Taylor to James T. Fields, 17 February 1854, *Life and Letters of Bayard Taylor,* ed. Marie Hansen-Taylor, 2 vols. (Boston: Houghton, Mifflin, 1884), 1:269.

10. David Mead, *Yankee Eloquence in the Middle-West: The Ohio Lyceum 1850–1870* (East Lansing: Michigan State College Press, 1951), 113; "Bayard Taylor Remembered," *Harper's Weekly,* 11 January 1879. Both cited in Wright, "Results of Locomotion," 120. See also Bode, *American Lyceum,* 230–31.

11. Kent P. Lyungquist, "Lectures and the Lyceum Movement," in *The Oxford Handbook of Transcendentalism,* ed. Joel Myerson, Sandra Petrulionis, and Laura Dassow Walls (Oxford: Oxford University Press, 2010), 337.

12. Paul C. Wermuth, *Bayard Taylor* (New York: Twayne, 1973), 52, 61.

13. Wright, "Results of Locomotion," 120.

14. Ziff, *Return Passages,* 169.

15. For more on the concept of the "contact zone," see Mary Louise Pratt, "Criticism in the Contact Zone," in *Imperial Eyes: Travel Writing and Transculturation,* 2nd ed. (New York: Routledge, 2008), 8.

16. Irving, *Sketch Book,* 48–49.

17. Pratt, *Imperial Eyes,* 3.

18. Carl Bode, *American Lyceum,* 217.

19. Malini J. Schueller, *U.S. Orientalisms: Race, Nation, and Gender in Literature, 1790–1890* (Ann Arbor: University of Michigan Press, 1998), 32.

20. John G. Whittier, *The Tent on the Beach and Other Poems* (Boston: Ticknor and Fields, 1868), 16.

21. Hilton Obenzinger, *American Palestine: Melville, Twain, and the Holy Land Mania* (Princeton: Princeton University Press, 1999), 45. See also Hilton Obenzinger, "American Palestine: Mark Twain and the Touristic Commodification of the Holy Land," *Yale MacMillan Center Working Paper Database,* 1 September 2002, 121, http://opus.macmillan.yale.edu/workpaper/pdfs/MESV5-3.pdf.

22. Taylor to James T. Fields, 15 April 1854, *Life and Letters,* 1:274.

23. Bayard Taylor, "The Philosophy of Travel," 2, 7, 42–43, 28, lecture manuscript, Chester County Historical Society, West Chester, PA (hereafter, CCHS).

24. Ibid., 30, 31, 41.5.

25. Wright, "Results of Locomotion," 126.

26. "Bayard Taylor's Lecture," *Wisconsin Patriot,* 6 April 1855.

27. "Bayard Taylor's Lecture on The Arabs," *San Francisco Bulletin,* 2 September 1859.

28. Bayard Taylor, *A Visit to India, China, and Japan* (New York: Putnam, 1853).

29. Francis L. Hawks, ed., *Narrative of the Expedition of the American Squadron to the China Seas and Japan,* 3 vols. (Washington: A. O. P. Nicholson, 1856), 1:76, 273. Cited in Ziff, *Return Passages,* 142, 148.

30. Ziff, *Return Passages,* 146.

31. Taylor, "Philosophy of Travel," 5.

32. Ibid., 4, 7–8.

33. See Ray, *Lyceum and Public Culture,* 106.

34. Bayard Taylor, *A Journey to Central Africa, or, Life and Landscapes from Egypt to the Negro Kingdoms of the White Nile* (New York: Putnam, 1854), 237.

35. Taylor, "Philosophy of Travel," 6–7.

36. Ibid., 6. Walter Mignolo uses the terms "planetary conviviality" and "managerial" mastery to distinguish two competing visions of the cosmopolitan in "The Many Faces of Cosmo-polis," 157–58.

37. Ibid., 5–6.

38. Ziff, *Return Passages,* 140, 154.

39. Pratt, *Imperial Eyes,* 3; Bruce A. Harvey, *American Geographics: U.S. National Narratives and the Representation of the Non-European World, 1830–1865* (Stanford: Stanford University Press, 2001), 10.

40. Taylor lecture cited in Richard Croom Beatty, *Bayard Taylor: Laureate of the Gilded Age* (Norman: University of Oklahoma Press, 1936), 150.

41. Taylor, *Central Africa,* 336, 158.

42. Bayard Taylor, "Japan and Loo Choo," 4–5, lecture manuscript, CCHS.

43. Taylor lecture cited in Beatty, *Bayard Taylor,* 151.

44. On Taylor's vision of "scientific" travel inspired by Humboldt, see Ziff, *Return Passages,* 156–57; and Wermuth, *Bayard Taylor,* 51, 70.

45. Benjamin and Taylor cited in Ziff, *Return Passages,* 166–67.

46. Bayard Taylor, "The Vision of Hasheesh," *Putnam's Monthly* 3, no. 16 (April 1854): 408. Versions of this account are repeated in chap. 10 of Taylor's *Lands of the Saracen* and in his lecture "The Arabs."

47. Taylor, "The Arabs," 33–34, lecture manuscript, CCHS. See also "Bayard Taylor's Lecture on The Arabs," *San Francisco Bulletin,* 2 September 1859.

48. Taylor, "Philosophy of Travel," 36.

49. Ibid., 33–34, 31.

50. Ibid., 20.

51. Ibid., 31, 34.

52. Ibid., 28.

53. Ibid., 39–40.

54. William W. Stowe, *Going Abroad: European Travel in Nineteenth-Century American Culture* (Princeton: Princeton University Press, 1994), 22, 26. Stowe uses the word *liminoid* to distinguish Turner's vision of the potentially transformative middle stage as opposed to the more conservative function of van Gennep's "liminal" moment.

55. Ziff, *Return Passages*, 121.

56. Taylor, "The Philosophy of Travel," 30–31.

57. Taylor, "The Arabs," 1–3.

58. "The Arabs," *Texas State Gazette*, 4 April 1854.

59. Taylor, *Central Africa*, 2, 5. Malini Schueller points to passages like this when, in her survey of midcentury American writings about the Orient, she singles out Taylor for his definition of a self-conscious, historically aware traveler's stance that in many ways resists and critiques the era's conventional thinking about an exotic, dematerialized East; Schueller, *U.S. Orientalisms*, 32, 156.

60. Taylor, "The Arabs," 1–3.

61. James Clifford, "Traveling Cultures," in *Cultural Studies*, ed. Lawrence Grossberg et al. (New York: Routledge, 1992), 108.

62. "Bayard Taylor on the Arabs," *Macon Georgia Telegraph*, 14 February 1854. This vision of the Bedouin drivers also recurs at several points in Taylor's *Lands of the Saracen*.

63. "Bayard Taylor's Lecture on The Arabs," *San Francisco Bulletin*, 2 September 1859. Taylor's script for the lecture actually reads, "For seven months I was in almost daily intercourse with the Arabs"; Taylor, "The Arabs," 4.

64. Ray, *Lyceum and Public Culture*, 104.

65. *Milwaukee Sentinel*, 1 March 1855.

66. Taylor, "The Arabs," 19, 23–24, 29. On *Poems of the Orient*, see Christoph Irmscher, "Bayard Taylor and the Limits of Orientalism," in *The Limits of Literary Historicism*, ed. Allen Dunn and Thomas F. Haddox (Knoxville: University of Tennessee Press, 2011), 77–104.

67. Irmscher, "Bayard Taylor," 91.

68. Taylor, *Central Africa*, 240–41, 257.

69. Taylor, *Lands of the Saracen*, 425, 79.

70. Taylor, "The Arabs," 8; "Bayard Taylor on the Arabs," *Macon Georgia Telegraph*, 14 February 1854.

71. "Ancient Egypt," *Philadelphia Inquirer*, 9 March 1875.

72. Taylor, "The Arabs," 34. On this point, see Tom F. Wright, "Results of Locomotion," 125, 127.

73. Harvey, *American Geographics*, 107–8.

74. Ziff, *Return Passages*, 138.

75. Taylor, "The Philosophy of Travel," 41.

76. Taylor, *Central Africa*, 521–22, 495.

77. Taylor, "Vision of Hasheesh," 402–8. Also appears as a chapter in Taylor's *Lands of the Saracen*, 133–48.

78. All citations here and above are from chapter 10 of Taylor, *Lands of the Saracen*, 149–60.

79. Wright, "Results of Locomotion," 123.

80. Pratt, *Imperial Eyes*, 197–204.

81. Taylor, "The Arabs," 5–6.

82. Bayard Taylor, "Moscow," 1, 4–6, 20, lecture manuscript, CCHS.

83. Taylor, "The Arabs," 18–19; "Bayard Taylor on the Arabs," *Macon Georgia Telegraph*, 14 February 1854.

84. Pratt, *Imperial Eyes*, 7–8.

9

The Peripatetic Career of Wherahiko Rawei

Māori Culture on the Global Chautauqua Circuit, 1893–1927

Evan Roberts

Historians of cultural pathways in the nineteenth-century "English-speaking world" have mostly examined the separate connections between Britain and its colonies and Britain and the United States. Within the British Empire strong cultural ties—seen by many historians as being exported from the metropole to the colony—went hand in hand with formal political ties. Despite the severance of those ties, cultural interchange between Britain and the United States remained strong through the nineteenth century. Telling historiographical evidence of a transatlantic culture may be seen in the use of the term *Victorian era* to describe late-nineteenth-century culture in both Great Britain and the United States. Only in the past thirty years have scholars begun to document the web of cultural connections across the Pacific between New Zealand and Australia and the United States.[1] One consequence of this study has been a renewed emphasis on a broader English-speaking world that transcended the divisions of empire.[2] Much of the scholarship has focused on the export of American ideas and culture to Australasia.[3]

After the establishment in the 1870s of regular shipping service connecting Sydney and Auckland with Honolulu and San Francisco, Americans increasingly interacted with Australasia. Indeed, Australia and New Zealand became part of a southern grand tour.[4] Likewise, the United States became more accessible to Australasians, who found that returning to Britain via a boat to San Francisco, a train to New York, and another boat to London carved two weeks off an eight-week journey.[5] The increase in trade and cultural exchange across the English-speaking Pacific confirmed opinions in both New Zealand and the United States that despite differences of size and empire, the two countries had much in common.[6] The recognition of a shared colonial encounter with indigenous peoples prompted comparative discussion of the culture and capacity of Native Americans and New Zealand Māori.[7] Like Europeans and Australians, many Americans saw Māori as "the very first of uncivilized races" and the most "capable of improvement and Christian civilization."[8] Although around the turn of the twentieth century there was significant transpacific discussion about social problems and progressive politics, there was little interchange about the practice and politics of Euro-American interactions.[9] Nevertheless, in America there was substantial intellectual and wider public interest in the spectacle of other indigenous races, including New Zealand Māori. Māori art and performance were on display at both the Centennial Exhibition in Philadelphia, in 1876, and the Columbian Exposition in Chicago, in 1893.[10] In addition, historians of Chautauqua of the nineteenth and early twentieth centuries have noted the twenty-eight-year presence on the circuit of a Māori performer named Wherahiko Rawei.[11]

Rawei traveled on the United States' lecture and Chautauqua circuits from 1900 until shortly before his death, in 1928, and illustrates important themes in the history of the lecture, lyceum, and Chautauqua movement. After he first arrived in the United States in 1900, Rawei traveled mostly to large cities, such as Los Angeles, Chicago, Philadelphia, and New York, lecturing in churches and professing to educate more than entertain.[12] His wife, who went by the name Hine Rawei while on the circuit, lectured and performed with him; the educational address she gave in Chicago was published by the Art Institute in 1906 under the title *New Zealand Past and Present*.[13] Thus, the first eight years of the Raweis' appearances in the United States are consistent with the dual origins of Chautauqua in the educational ambitions of the nineteenth-century lyceum and the religious character of the Chautauqua that emerged after the Civil War. The last twenty years of Rawei's life and career were entwined with the rise and decline of the Redpath Chautauqua agency, with which he contracted after 1908. Rawei traveled with the Redpath circuit through small-town America for nearly twenty years, performing largely in the Midwest and the South. For fifteen years Rawei, often assisted by his wife and children, performed and displayed recent Māori history in a performance called "Cannibalism to

Culture." Then in 1922, at the request of the Redpath agency, he switched his stage biography significantly to perform "Uncle Sam's Samoan Islanders," the show he presented for the last five years he spent on the circuit. The dramatic transformation of Rawei's act as circuit Chautauqua peaked and declined in the 1920s highlights how both the lyceum and the Chautauqua movement blended a principled search for educational and spiritual uplift with a form of mass entertainment. The success of the lyceum and Chautauqua depended on the interaction between entertainment and education, and the goal was always to help the performances appeal to multiple audiences. For performers, the mix of entertainment and education allowed for flexibility and adaptation not only between individual performances within a season but also within a performers' career over time.

The circuit Chautauqua movement of the early twentieth century grew from the merger of two nineteenth-century forms of adult education: the lyceum and permanent Chautauqua. Both institutions drew on American demands for self-improvement and education. The American lyceum, which originated in New England in the 1820s and flourished in the next two decades, particularly in northern states, combined a local organization and physical space for hosting lectures with a national and, later, international network of speakers.[14] It aimed to provide educational opportunities and became a form of popular entertainment, particularly in the winter. After a hiatus during the Civil War, in the late 1860s the lyceum and lecture circuit resumed with increasing professionalization. Among the agencies that brought a new professional outlook was James Redpath's Boston Lyceum Bureau, founded in 1868 and renamed the Redpath Lyceum Bureau in 1874.[15] Increasing demand in the Midwest led the agency to open a Chicago office in 1876.[16]

The New York Chautauqua Institute began as a religious gathering on the shores of Lake Chautauqua in 1874; it remained fixed in the place for which it was named through the last quarter of the nineteenth century. It remained more rural, educational, and religious at a time when the lecture and lyceum circuit was becoming more urban, entertaining, and secular. As well as religious discussion and education, the Chautauqua Institute incorporated "practical programs of adult instruction and constructive entertainment" into its summer season. Many of the acts were booked through New York or Boston lyceum bureaus, including the Redpath. Inspired by the success of the New York Chautauqua, hundreds of small Midwestern communities organized their own.[17] The late-nineteenth-century community Chautauqua mostly displayed local talent but also included a range of traveling speakers, arranged through the lyceum bureaus.[18] The professionalization of the circuit included international tours, with traffic going both ways across the Pacific.[19] From at least the mid-1880s, the Redpath Lyceum Bureau had contacts with New Zealand, representing the interests of Major Henry C. Dane, a Civil War veteran who gave lectures in the North Island.[20]

Wherahiko Rawei first made his name on the New Zealand lecture and entertainment circuit in the early 1890s. Despite its small size and great distance from other parts of the English-speaking world, New Zealand in the nineteenth century was not culturally isolated. High literacy and income rates contributed to a demand for public music, lectures, and entertainment similar to that in the United States.[21] As in America, local or amateur talent was complemented by professional national and international acts that toured the country.[22] Likewise, performances took place in a variety of venues, from tents that would seat large crowds in summer to opera houses, halls, and churches in towns and cities. The first records of Rawei's appearances document him speaking in churches with the Salvation Army in the North Otago region of New Zealand in the early 1890s.[23]

Rawei's life before his emergence on the New Zealand lecture and preaching circuit is obscure. He claimed to have been born in Pipiriki, in the Whanganui River valley in the North Island, to a Māori mother and English father. After he arrived in the Otago area in the 1890s, his activities attracted some suspicion because, in addition to lecturing and preaching, he also solicited money for a mission to Māori in the King Country area, near where he was born.[24] The Salvation Army vouched for his story, stating that before arriving in Otago he had been working with them in Sydney, and that his mission and fund-raising were legitimate.[25] The cloud of suspicion soon passed, and through the southern winter of 1893 Rawei gave many lectures in small towns in the South Island. With his lecture "My Mother's People or Life in the King Country," Rawei claimed to provide an authentic perspective on Māori history and culture to a European population largely unfamiliar with that indigenous culture. Rawei's performance blended both education ("a true picture of native life . . . with a vast amount of really useful Information") and entertainment ("Beautiful Songs . . . fun and hearty innocent Laughter") in a fashion similar to contemporary lyceum and Chautauqua performances in the United States.[26]

With few exceptions, Rawei's early performances in New Zealand were well received as entertainment. One critic found him "abounding with repetitions" and likely to have "seen very little of Māori life."[27] But most reviews were positive, describing him as "no common man," his performance "interesting and instructive" and "entertaining."[28] Even the negative reviews praised his voice and manner, while the more numerous positive reviews saw the same appeal in his "clear, flexible voice" that made him an "accomplished singer and musician."[29] Rawei was appealing to European audiences in New Zealand because he appeared authentically Māori, dressing in native clothing, talking and singing in the Māori language, but in other ways conforming to European models of behavior. One newspaper credited his understanding to having "been for some years away from the people among whom he was bred, receiving in the interval a good education and a knowledge of the habits and manners of European life."[30] Audiences more knowledgeable about Māori language were sometimes skeptical of his authenticity, with the *Otago Witness* commenting that "the most jarring note was the pronunciation of the Māori by Rawei," attributing the flaw of dropping his *h*'s to Whanganui Māori being "notorious as the cockneys of Māoridom."[31] Thus the hallmarks of Rawei's career on larger stages around the English-speaking world were evident in his first year of public visibility. Acting authentically Māori to audiences who were unfamiliar with Māori culture and language, he parlayed his good looks and pleasant voice into positive reception of a performance that blended education and entertainment.[32] His performances also advanced the claim that Māori were the "native" race with the most potential for civilization, and that his own life showed the potential for Māori who came under the good influence of Europeans.[33]

In late 1893 Rawei took his act to Australia, communicating much the same message for the audience across the Tasman: Māori were a superior native race.[34] Yet the object of the tour was to make money, with Rawei starting to downplay the amount that would go to his mission to the King Country.[35] Rawei's commercialization of his performance brought him trouble in Australia, where he was summoned by a local plainclothes policeman for violating blue laws by charging admission on Sunday evening.[36] In late 1893 and 1894 Rawei was positively received by Australian audiences and received some praise for the addition of Hine Taimoa, who joined his performances shortly before the couple married in New Zealand on New Year's Day 1894.[37] Taimoa was his wife's stage name, with all legal documents showing her to be Emily Jean Sizemore. Like Rawei, Sizemore was of mixed European and Māori descent, tracing her genealogy to a European whaler, Richard Sizemore, who had married a Māori woman in Otago in 1846.[38]

In Australia, Rawei was also first reported to have added stereopticon, or magic lantern, scenes to his show.[39] Magic lantern technology had been available since the eighteenth century, but it flourished in the last quarter of the nineteenth as a way of projecting photographs. On the lyceum and

Chautauqua circuits, lantern slides were especially used in performances that described travel or exotic locations.[40]

Rawei and Hine spent most of 1894 performing in Australia. After their final performance of the year, which took place in Hobart on December 19, 1894, they returned to New Zealand, where a week later their daughter Frances Eva Rawei was born.[41] By the end of that year, all the elements of Rawei's later American performances were in place: the argument for Māori potential being realized with European guidance, the magic lantern show of photographs of New Zealand, and the involvement of his wife in the performances.

In 1895 Rawei and his family departed for England, still holding loosely to the idea that they were raising money for a mission.[42] Their performances were again well received, with reviewers commenting favorably on the "beautiful," "charming," "handsome," "cultured," and "gifted" couple with a "musical voice" who demonstrated how Māori had "scaled the ladder of civilization to such excellent purpose."[43] Despite the positive critical reception and reports of well-attended shows, New Zealand papers frequently reported that the Raweis' "expenses have far exceeded income."[44] Competition with amateur lecturers was reportedly much greater in Britain than it had been in New Zealand or Australia.[45] Rawei and his family persisted on the British lecture circuit until 1897, however, reducing their admission charges and passing a plate for donations at the end of performances.[46]

After nearly three years abroad the family returned to New Zealand at the end of 1897, continuing to claim that Rawei would ultimately start a mission in the King Country.[47] Rawei and his family, which now included a son born in England, returned to New Zealand via Australia.[48] Stopping first in Tasmania, where they had been well received three years earlier, they then spent several months in isolated but booming Western Australia.[49] Rawei again ran into minor trouble with the law when a supporting musician successfully sued for £7 in unpaid wages and commission.[50] They would spend most of 1897–1900 traveling in New Zealand and Australia. Renaming their show "The Land of the Māori," they returned to Australia for most of 1898, touring the east coast and Tasmania.[51] They brought the new show back to New Zealand in December 1898, touring in the southern summer and autumn of 1899.

At the beginning of his career, Rawei had advertised his appearances as fund-raisers for a mission in the King Country, south of Auckland. On returning to New Zealand, however, the family purchased property at Taumarere in the Bay of Islands, north of Auckland, where Rawei claimed in newspaper interviews that they would devote "their time to missionary efforts."[52] But advertisements for their 1899 performances made no mention of any missionary cause that the shows' proceeds would benefit.[53] Nevertheless, Rawei continued to express his support of the need for European missions to Māori, criticizing New Zealand Christians for sending missions to India while claiming that no European missionaries were working among the 30,000 Māori in the King Country.[54] His argument for the condition and prospects of Māori needed to balance conflicting imperatives, simultaneously claiming that Māori needed the help of European missionaries but could also be saved rapidly.[55] He drew a contrast with the fate of Tasmanian Aboriginals, who were widely believed to have been entirely wiped out, but then drew back from the extreme comparison, saying there was "no reason to despair of success" because Māori were "naturally brave, generous and hospitable, and with such materials to work upon much may be accomplished."[56] His own life, he averred, demonstrated what could be achieved under European influence.[57]

Before Rawei's tours of Australia and England, the New Zealand press had been skeptical of his background and mission. But in what would turn out to be largely a farewell tour of New Zealand in 1899, his entertainment and argument about the possibilities of Māori uplift through European influence gained some respect. The *Colonist* newspaper in Nelson called him "gifted" and possessed of "the inspiration of a great theme . . . [and] much knowledge."[58] In Auckland, where he had performed earlier in the decade, the papers found him "eloquent" and "talented."[59] But in the Hawkes Bay province, controversy about his objectives dogged his performances. Having quietly dropped the claim that he was raising money for a mission of his own, Rawei overstepped in response to criticism, denying that he had ever intended the proceeds of his work to go to a mission.[60] After a week of debating the issue in the press, he departed for Auckland and then the United States, where he would attempt to parlay his talents into more money than he had made on the lecture and performance circuit in Australasia.[61]

Rawei's ambiguity about his objectives—mission or entertainment—continued in the United States. Stopping in Honolulu on the way to San Francisco, he lectured at the Hawaiian Mission Children's Society, where he claimed that his lecturing tour of the United States was to "raise funds" to "elevat[e] his own people . . . [at] a home school for young Maoris." Inspired by his lecture, the society donated $65 to the cause he claimed to be raising money for.[62] After two weeks in Hawaii, Rawei sailed for the continental United States, where he attempted to break into the lecture circuit. As he had done in New Zealand, Australia, and England before, Rawei began by talking to churches and emphasizing his evangelical purpose. Finessing the difference between past ambition and present reality, he claimed to have spent the last dozen years "devoted . . . to organizing and conducting schools for the native children."[63]

Rawei would spend much of 1900 and 1901 in the United States, gradually making his way to the East Coast via Los Angeles, Salt Lake City, and Chicago. Publicity for his talks that appeared in the *Los Angeles Times* describes him as "remarkably gifted," though the audiences were also impressed by the stereopticon displays of New Zealand scenery.[64] Rawei's appearances in the United States were infrequent in his first visit, from 1899 to 1901. Often lecturing in churches, he was obliged to waive admission charges and hint, or more, at the supposed missionary purpose behind his travels.[65] The *Brooklyn Eagle,* for example, reported that he would "stay for a month . . . collecting money in aid" of the school in the Bay of Islands that provided a "Christian training home for Māori children."

Rawei's claim to be collecting money for a school spoke to a contemporary concern in the United States and Australasia to educate and "civilize" indigenous children. In New Zealand, state-supported native schools were first opened in 1867, replacing a system of government support for schools operated by missions. The native school system offered elementary or primary education in local communities.[66] As in the United States and Australia, boarding schools were common for secondary education of indigenous children.[67] Although an object of the native schools was assimilation, local communities had to formally request that one be established in their area.[68] The growth of the native school system displaced church-supported schools; New Zealand audiences, knowing that churches played a small role in Māori education, were likely to have been more skeptical of Rawei's appeal. But in Australia and the United States, where the history of New Zealand indigenous schooling was not common knowledge, a religious school for children was a plausible reason for seeking charitable support.

Though his purpose, reported to be missionary, was a draw for audiences, Rawei's appeal also lay in the stereopticon views of New Zealand scenery and "his mellifluous voice and choice English."[69] Thus, his entrance into the United States lecture circuit from 1899 to 1901 mirrored the way he had begun his career in New Zealand, Australia, and the United Kingdom. Speaking and performing first in churches, claiming to be a "Reverend" or raising money for a mission to Māori, Rawei put on performances that attracted positive reviews for being both educational and entertaining. His appeal, beyond his noted good looks, was that as a "half-caste" child, he appeared authentically Māori to foreign audiences, but his European upbringing made him a "fluent talker" who did not threaten English-speaking audiences.[70]

Rawei embodied his own message: with European help, Māori could become as cultured as Europeans. It was an argument that Rawei found easier to sell outside New Zealand, where other Māori, or Europeans familiar with the culture, did not question his authenticity or knowledge of his homeland. Rawei's message was reassuring to Americans and Australians, flattering and absolving them at the same time. It flattered them as white descendants of European immigrants by suggesting that with their help, *some* indigenous people could be as civilized as Europeans and their descendants. Yet it also absolved their own histories of interactions with indigenous peoples by arguing that the capability for civilization was inherent in particular races—not a function of how Europeans and indigenous peoples had interacted. Moreover, by claiming that the indigenous people with the most potential lived elsewhere, Rawei distanced Americans and Australians from their own histories of European–indigenous encounters. It is not surprising then that his reviews were uniformly positive in the United States and nearly entirely positive in Australia. At the conclusion of his first American sojourn in 1901, Rawei returned to Tasmania, where he rejoined his family and performed for the rest of the year.[71] The family then spent 1902 and 1903 in Australia and New Zealand, embarking on a lengthy Australian tour in the winter of 1903.[72] Legal troubles arose yet again, this time with a contracted assistant accusing Rawei of stealing a set of lantern slides.[73]

At the end of 1903 Rawei left for North America. His timing was fortunate, for the Redpath Chautauqua company began to package and commercialize the small-town Chautauqua circuit.[74] Yet Rawei and his family did not immediately make the Redpath Chautauqua program; from 1904 to 1912 they continued to speak frequently in churches.[75] During his first solo trip to the United States (1899–1901), Rawei had spoken mostly in large cities. On the family's return in 1904 and thereafter, they performed more often in small towns. Basing themselves in Chicago or Indianapolis in various years, they performed throughout the Midwest; from 1905 to 1910 they toured mostly in Iowa, Indiana, Illinois, and Wisconsin.

However, both Rawei and his wife, Hine Taimoa, made appearances in large cities. Rawei reported that he was going to the St. Louis World's Fair in 1904, but it is unclear if he performed there during the fair. Some of his challenges of traveling as a nonwhite person in the United States were reported by a public servant visiting the World's Fair for the New Zealand Tourist

Department. During the fair, Rawei and Taimoa were refused seating at a St. Louis restaurant because they were "coloured people." The Tourist Department employee intervened successfully, explaining to the waitstaff that although the Raweis were "coloured," they were "not Afro-Americans" and should be treated as whites.[76] While in Chicago, Hine lectured several times to the Cook County Teachers Association.[77] Both she and her husband expanded their lectures to cover aspects of New Zealand life other than Māori culture. In Chicago, Hine talked about the passage of women's suffrage in New Zealand.[78] In church settings, Wherahiko spoke more broadly about the social and industrial progress of New Zealand, including labor laws and municipal ownership of utilities.[79]

Earnest lectures to religious groups and preaching in churches were not highly remunerative activities for the Rawei family. Rawei made efforts to make his show more appealing to a wider audience, and to reshape the performance to one that would sell. The contrast between the supposedly savage Māori past and its civilized present, as represented on stage, was heightened by a gradual adoption of the title "From Cannibalism to Culture."[80] The title alone highlights the mix of education and entertainment that Chautauqua offered. Cannibalism appears salacious and entertaining, but the idea embodied in the title was the widely accepted contemporary notion that cultures evolved and improved over time. It was a concept that could equally be heard in the lecture halls of eminent universities and in learned anthropological journals. The retitled show emerged gradually beginning in 1907, and it appears to have been the Raweis standard performance after 1910. In approximately that year, the family moved onto the Chautauqua circuit, performing as a group, sometimes referring to themselves as "The New Zealanders" and other times as "The Raweis." Their daughter Eva Frances (at times referred to as Piwa) wed a Syrian immigrant in Indiana in 1912, after which she rarely performed with her parents.[81] From 1913 the Raweis contracted exclusively with the Redpath Chautauqua company in Cedar Rapids, Iowa, the dominant lyceum and Chautauqua agency in the Midwest.[82]

Redpath and its competitors transformed the Chautauqua industry, and the Raweis were part of the circuit heyday that lasted from approximately 1912 to the mid-1920s. The longevity of the Raweis was somewhat unusual and has been noted by many historians of circuit Chautauqua.[83] Although their extended presence and sustained relationship with Redpath was unusual, many aspects of their contract were standard. To offer a standard package of performances to small communities that had previously been unable to mount Chautauqua, Redpath reduced costs by signing acts early—up to a year ahead of schedule—and for a long season of exclusive performances. In their initial years with Redpath, the Raweis were engaged for twenty weeks at $150 a week, which represented both greater net earnings and more security than they had hitherto enjoyed. While on tour, the Raweis, like other performers, met their own accommodation, food, and local transportation expenses, with the Redpath Bureau paying for railroad travel between venues. While under contract, the Raweis were obligated to go where Redpath sent them. They typically received their traveling schedule two to four weeks ahead of performances; as the upcoming schedule materialized, Redpath would write to let them know the next weeks' engagements and itinerary. A telling indication of the fluidity in their schedule is a telegram addressed to Wherahiko Rawei "c/o Some Hotel, Muncie."[84] The Redpath Chautauqua company also retained the right to transfer the Raweis between circuits within the same agency. Thus, although the Raweis traveled mostly in the Midwest—especially Illinois, Indiana, and Iowa—they often opened the year on a southern circuit, with engagements in Kentucky, Oklahoma, Louisiana, Mississippi, and Texas, before spending summers in the Midwest.[85]

The Raweis performed their New Zealand act on the Redpath Chautauqua circuit from 1913 to 1921. It was an act that relied heavily on the apparent authenticity of the Raweis as Māori. Although they had been professional entertainers since the 1890s, they had to profess a continuing contact and affinity with New Zealand. To obscure how long they had been performing as Māori on foreign stages, their biography was updated, and in interviews they continued to hint at one day returning to New Zealand.[86] The tension between performing indigenous culture authentically and being a part of a professional circuit of entertainment was visible in their advertising. In official Redpath Chautauqua brochures, the Raweis were always depicted in indigenous Māori costume. Yet on the postcards and letterhead they had printed independently, they dressed in European clothing, as an assertion of their own professional identity.[87]

The final act in the Raweis' career on the Chautauqua circuit reveals some of the tensions that existed in the lyceum and Chautauqua between education and entertainment. Wherahiko Rawei had performed for nearly thirty years as a supposedly authentic Māori evangelist, but in 1922 the Redpath Chautauqua company asked him to do a new act called "Uncle Sam's Samoan Islanders." His stage biography was changed significantly to give a sheen of authenticity to this new act. Consistent with his previous biography as Māori, Rawei continued to state that he had been adopted as "an infant by an English officer and his wife." Yet for the Samoan act, the Redpath publicity material claimed he had been educated at Eton and Cambridge, trained as a medical doctor, and practiced in Samoa for fifty years before arriving in the United States.[88] The Redpath bureau claimed endorsements for Rawei's history as a "gifted Polynesian raconteur" from none other than Robert Louis Stevenson, whose supposed signature they printed on advertisements for Rawei's new solo performance.[89] With this new act, Rawei returned to many of the same towns he had appeared in before, but now with a completely different "biography" and performance.[90] If Chautauqua was just entertainment, it would have sufficed for Rawei merely to act the new part. The emphasis on authenticity reveals the continuing importance of education to the Chautauqua circuit as a whole. The purported authenticity of Rawei's Samoan act was his license to tell Americans about their distant South Pacific colony.

Although Rawei's performance as a doctor to the Samoans lacked the authenticity it claimed, it represented the peak of his own career as a professional entertainer at the height of circuit Chautauqua in the mid-1920s. After that date, both Rawei and the Chautauqua circuit declined rapidly. Rawei was injured in a car accident in Georgia in April 1925, and his health quickly deteriorated.[91] Concerned for his well-being, he moved to Colorado Springs and traveled a reduced circuit, performing the Samoan act in 1926 and 1927. With his weekly salary now only $110, he tried to interest the Redpath in employing Hine for a version of their previous New Zealand performance, but the company was not interested.[92] With his health still in decline, Rawei set out with her wife to return to New Zealand. During a stop en route in the New Zealand dependency of the Cook Islands, Wherahiko Rawei died at Avarua on January 27, 1928. His biography was ambiguous to the last, recording his age as "over 80 years old."[93] Yet his marriage license and probate records from New Zealand confirm that he was just 65. Despite more than 30 years as a professional entertainer, Rawei's probate listed his occupation as farmer. He left Hine just under £1,500 in savings in New Zealand bank accounts, the equivalent of several years' earnings at the average wage. He had not been particularly wealthy, the value of his estate placing him almost exactly at the average for men of his age who died that year.[94] After his death, Hine returned to New Zealand, where she would live another eleven years, dying in Wellington in 1939, also at the age of 65.[95]

Wherahiko Rawei's career and abrupt transition in biography and performance reveal starkly how the American lyceum and Chautauqua blended education and entertainment. The lyceum began as a venue for education and self-improvement. In its ideal form, it represented a meeting of people whose experience or study allowed them to teach a public authentically searching for knowledge and betterment. When Rawei entered the Chautauqua circuit at the turn of the twentieth century, eighty years after the founding of the first American lyceum, he was part of that tradition of traveling lecturers imparting knowledge. Yet to command attention, Rawei had to be entertaining as well, grabbing audience attention with overstated references to cannibalism and changing his act entirely when the audience for his initial show ran out. Chautauqua could be educational, but it also brought to rural areas the entertainment that could be seen in diverse venues in larger cities.[96] Rawei's transformation under his own name, from Māori evangelist serving his own people to Māori doctor in American Samoa, where he had only ever stopped en route to the United States, symbolized the tension in blending educational lyceum with entertaining circuit Chautauqua.

In "Cannibalism to Culture," Rawei performed and represented the encounter between Europeans and Māori. The argument of his performance that Māori were the most civilized, and civilizable, indigenous race accepted prevailing beliefs that Europeans and their colonial and American descendants sat atop the hierarchy of human civilization. Yet it was also an argument that flattered Māori, offering them a privileged, if still subordinate, place in European and American understandings of the world.[97] Rawei exploited these common Euro-American beliefs to carve out a lengthy and successful career on the Chautauqua circuit. His career was distinctive for both its length and its representation of Māori on the American stage. Yet Rawei was part of a popular global circuit that presented indigenous cultures to European and European-descended audiences in Europe, North America, and Australasia.[98] His performance of "Cannibalism to Culture" presented, in an entertaining format, accepted theories of sociocultural evolution and cultural hierarchies. The late career switch to the Samoan-themed performance demonstrated not only the mingling of educational and entertainment ideals on the Chautauqua circuit but also Rawei's own capacity to succeed in the competitive marketplace of early-twentieth-century American popular culture.

NOTES

1. The work of Ian Tyrrell has been particularly important. Ian Tyrrell, "American Exceptionalism in an Age of International History," *American Historical Review* 96, no. 4 (October 1991): 1031–55; Ian Tyrrell, "Reflections on the Transnational Turn in United States History: Theory and Practice," *Journal of Global History* 4, no. 03 (November 2009): 453–74.

2. James Belich, *Replenishing the Earth: The Settler Revolution and the Rise of the Anglo-World, 1783–1939* (Oxford: Oxford University Press, 2009) see for example the very favorable review in *Times Higher Education,* 27 August 2009, by Don McRaild, "Book of the Week: Replenishing the Earth," available at www.timeshighereducation.co.uk/story.asp?storycode=407876. Bernard Porter, "The Anglo-world of settlers, not dominators," *Times Literary Supplement,* 23 September 2009. A more concise but earlier statement of the argument is in James Belich, "The Rise of the Angloworld," in *Rediscovering the British World,* ed. Philip Buckner and R. Douglas Francis (Calgary: Calgary University Press, 2005), 39–52. See also Kate Darian-Smith, Patricia Grimshaw, and Stuart Macintyre, eds., *Britishness Abroad: Transnational Movements and Imperial Cultures* (Melbourne: Melbourne University Press, 2007).

3. Miles Fairburn, "Is There a Good Case for New Zealand Exceptionalism," in *Disputed Histories: Imagining New Zealand's Pasts,* ed. Tony Ballantyne and Brian Moloughney (Dunedin, NZ: University of Otago Press, 2008), 143–67; Joy Damousi, "'The Filthy American Twang': Elocution, the Advent of American 'Talkies,' and Australian Cultural Identity," *American Historical Review* 112, no. 2 (April 2007): 394–416.

4. Lydia Wevers, *Country of Writing: Travel Writing and New Zealand, 1809–1900* (Auckland, NZ: Auckland University Press, 2002); Lydia Wevers, *Travelling to New Zealand: An Oxford Anthology* (Melbourne; Oxford: Oxford University Press, 2000); Maturin M. Ballou, *Travels under the Southern Cross: Being a Second Edition of "Under the Southern Cross, or Travels in Australia, Tasmania, New Zealand, Samoa and other Pacific islands"* (Boston: Houghton Mifflin, 1887); Mark Twain, *Following the Equator: A Journey around the World* (Hartford: American Publishing Company, 1897).

5. Charles Wentworth Dilke, "Greater Britain," *The Living Age* 185 (28 June 1890), 779; G. W. Griffin, *New Zealand: Her Commerce and Resources* (Wellington, NZ: G. Didsbury, 1884). 38.

6. Theodore Roosevelt, *The Winning of the West: The Spread of English-Speaking Peoples* (New York: G. P. Putnam's Sons, 1889), 31.

7. J. G. Wood, *The Natural History of Man: Australia, New Zealand, Polynesia, America, Asia, and Ancient Europe* (London: G. Routledge and Sons, 1870). 119; Charles Wentworth Dilke, *Greater Britain* (New York: Harper & Brothers, 1869). 123.

8. I. C. Russell, "A Sketch of New Zealand, with Pen and Pencil," *American Naturalist* 13, no. 2 (February 1879): 73.

9. Peter J. Coleman, "New Zealand Liberalism and the Origins of the American Welfare State," *Journal of American History* 69, no. 2 (September 1982): 373–91; Daniel T. Rodgers, *Atlantic Crossings: Social Politics in a Progressive Age* (Cambridge: Harvard University Press, 1998). 55–67.

10. Jennifer Wagelie, "Maori Art in America: The Display and Collection History of Maori Art in the United States, 1802–2006" (PhD diss., City University of New York, 2007), 79; Margaret Werry, "'The Greatest Show on Earth': Political Spectacle, Spectacular Politics, and the American Pacific," *Theatre Journal* 57, no. 3 (October 2005): 355–82; Robyn Handel, *New Zealand through the Eyes of American Women, 1830–1915* (Frankfurt: Peter Lang, 2009), 44.

11. Charlotte M. Canning, *The Most American Thing in America: Circuit Chautauqua as Performance* (Iowa City: University of Iowa Press, 2007), 86–87; John E. Tapia, *Circuit Chautauqua: From Rural Education to Popular Entertainment in Early Twentieth Century America* (Jefferson: McFarland, 1997). 104–5.

12. "City Briefs," *Los Angeles Times,* 6 February 1900, I16; "Department for Illinois. Chicago and Vicinity," *Chicago Standard,* 4 August 1900, 1497; "Wherahiko Rawei of New Zealand Describes His People at Emmanuel Baptist Church," *Brooklyn Eagle,* 6 February 1901, 16; "Philadelphia," *Church Standard,* 17 November 1900, 74.

13. Hine Rawei, *New Zealand Past and Present* (Chicago: Art Institute of Chicago, 1906).

14. Canning, *Most American Thing,* 8; Angela G. Ray, *The Lyceum and Public Culture in the Nineteenth-Century United States* (East Lansing: Michigan State University Press, 2005).

15. J. R. McKivigan, *Forgotten Firebrand: James Redpath and the Making of Nineteenth-Century America* (Ithaca, NY: Cornell University Press, 2008). 119–20.

16. "Personal," *Chicago Daily Tribune*, 13 August 1876, 4.

17. Andrew C. Rieser, *The Chautauqua Moment: Protestants, Progressives, and the Culture of Modern Liberalism* (New York: Columbia University Press, 2003).

18. Tapia, *Circuit Chautauqua*, 8.

19. Matthew Wittman, "Empire of Culture: U.S. Entertainers and the Making of the Pacific Circuit, 1850–1890" (PhD diss., University of Michigan, 2010).

20. "Theatrical and Musical Notes," *Otago Witness*, 4 February 1892, 36; "Major Dane," *Auckland Star*, 27 June 1887, 5; "Farewell Compliment to Major Dane," *Auckland Star*, 24 April 1888, 5; Redpath advertisement in *Overland Monthly*, April 1883, 4.

21. Caroline Daley, "Modernity, Consumption and Leisure," in *The New Oxford History of New Zealand*, ed. Giselle Byrnes (Auckland: Oxford University Press, 2009), 426–30.

22. Rob Weir, "Vagabond Abroad: Mark Twain's 1895 Visit to New Zealand," *Journal of the Gilded Age & Progressive Era* 8, no. 4 (October 2009): 487–514.

23. "Oamaru," *Otago Witness* (Dunedin, New Zealand), 10 December 1891, 21.

24. "Rawei, the Native Evangelist," *Otago Witness* (Dunedin, New Zealand), 29 June 1893, 18.

25. "Rawei, the Native Evangelist," *Otago Daily Times* (Dunedin, New Zealand), 22 June 1893, 3.

26. Advertisement, *Bruce Herald* (Milton, New Zealand), 4 July 1893, 2.

27. "Rawei," *Bruce Herald* (Milton, New Zealand), 11 July 1893, 2.

28. "Town & Country," *Timaru Herald*, 28 July 1893, 2; *Bruce Herald* (Milton, New Zealand), 4 July 1893, 2.

29. "Rawei, the Māori Evangelist," *Tuapeka Times*, 12 July 1893, 5; "Rawei," *Mataura Ensign*, 14 July 1893, 6; *Clutha Leader*, 14 July 1893, 4; *Southland Times* (Invercargill, New Zealand), 17 July 1893, 2.

30. "Rawei, the Māori Evangelist," *Tuapeka Times*, 12 July 1893, 5;

31. "Wellington Wing Whispers," *Otago Witness* (Dunedin, New Zealand), 11 April 1895, 37.

32. On "good looks," see "Song, Stage, and Story," *Auckland Star*, 18 November 1893, 3; and "Notes and News. British and Foreign," *Mercury* (Hobart, Australia), 2 December 1893, 2.

33. "Rawei's Mission," *Southland Times* (Invercargill, New Zealand), 18 July 1893, 2.

34. "Australian Stage Gossip," *Otago Witness* (Dunedin, New Zealand), 19 October 1893, 37.

35. "Pass about People," *Observer* (Auckland, New Zealand), 11 November 1893, 11.

36. "News Items," *Colonist* (Nelson, New Zealand), 2 June 1894, 4; *Horsham Times* (Horsham, Australia), 11 May 1894, 2.

37. "The Māori Evangelist," *Mercury* (Hobart, Australia), 11 September 1893, 4; "Rawei," *Mercury*, 13 September 1893, 3; "Rawei," *Launceston Examiner*, 25 September 1893, 3; "Greenroom Gossip," *Illustrated Sydney News*, 21 October 1893, 17. On the marriage, see *Otago Witness*, 11 January 1894, 26.

38. Angela Wanhalla, "'one white man i like very much': Intermarriage and the Cultural Encounter in Southern New Zealand, 1829–1850," *Journal of Women's History* 20, no. 2 (Summer 2008): 48.

39. "The Māori Evangelist," *Sydney Morning Herald*, 26 October 1893, 4.

40. Xenophon Theodore Barber, "The Roots of Travel Cinema: John L. Stoddard, E. Burton Holmes, and the Nineteenth-Century Illustrated Travel Lecture," *Film History* 5, no. 1 (March 1993): 68–84; Tapia, *Circuit Chautauqua*, 77.

41. "Temperance Hall," *Mercury* (Hobart, Australia), 18 December 1894, 2.

42. "Telegraphic Shipping," *Auckland Star*, 20 April 1895, 4; "London," *Tuapeka Times*, 14 August 1895, 4.

43. *Colonies and India* (London, UK), 29 June 1895, 12–13.

44. "London," *Tuapeka Times*, 14 August 1895, 4; *Auckland Star*, 25 November 1895, 2; "Our London Letter," *Star* (Christchurch, New Zealand), 15 January 1896, 2.

45. "Anglo-Colonial Notes," *Star* (Christchurch, New Zealand), 3 June 1896, 2; "Mimes and Music," *Evening Post* (Wellington, New Zealand), 27 June 1896, 2. See also *Hawera and Normanby Star*, 24 August 1896, 2.

46. "Rawei at Westminster," *Timaru Herald,* 12 March 1897, 4; "Maoriland and the Māoris," *Colonies and India* (London, UK), 23 January 1897, 14–15.

47. "Church Intelligence," *Advertiser* (Adelaide, Australia), 22 December 1897, 5.

48. "Rawei," *Mercury* (Hobart, Australia), 9 August 1897, 2.

49. "Māori Life," *West Australian* (Perth, Australia), 2 September 1897, 4.

50. "Action Against Rawei," *Inquirer & Commercial News* (Perth, Australia), 15 October 1897, 8.

51. "The Land of the Māori," *Dubbo Liberal and Macquarie Advocate,* 13 April 1898, 2; "Music and Drama," *Launceston Examiner,* 17 September 1898, 4; "The Land of the Māori," *Mercury* (Adelaide, Australia), 3 December 1898, 4.

52. "Auckland News Notes," *Otago Daily Times* (Dunedin, New Zealand), 17 January 1899, 5.

53. For example, *Marlborough Express* (Blenheim, New Zealand), 25 March 1899, 3; *Grey River Argus* (Greymouth, New Zealand), 6 April 1899, 3; *Colonist* (Nelson, New Zealand), 29 April 1899, 2; *Evening Post* (Wellington, New Zealand), 25 May 1899, 3.

54. "Shorthand in Law Courts," *Wanganui Herald,* 30 May 1899, 2; "Local and General," *Evening Post* (Wellington, New Zealand), 30 May 1899, 4.

55. "Rawei at the Theater," *Colonist* (Nelson, New Zealand), 1 May 1899, 2.

56. "Missionaries and Māoris," *Evening Post* (Wellington, New Zealand), 9 June 1899, 2.

57. "The Land of the Māori," *Colonist* (Nelson, New Zealand), 16 May 1899, 2.

58. "Rawei, the Native Orator," *Colonist* (Nelson, New Zealand), 28 April 1899, 2.

59. "Rawei at the Central Mission," *Auckland Star,* 10 July 1899, 2; "Table Talk," *Auckland Star,* 28 July 1899, 1.

60. "Rawei," *Hawke's Bay Herald,* 26 June 1899, 3; "Who Is Rawei?" *Daily Telegraph* (Hastings, New Zealand), 27 June 1899, 2; "Hard Hitting," *Daily Telegraph* (Hastings, New Zealand), 27 June 1899, 2;

61. "Pars about People," *Observer* (Auckland, New Zealand), 22 July 1899, 6.

62. *Forty-Eighth Annual Report,* 4 June 1900, Hawaiian Mission Children's Society Honolulu, 13; "A Dying People," *Austin's Hawaiian Weekly,* 30 September 1899, 6–7.

63. "The Māori Race: Evangelist Rawei of New Zealand Tells of His People," *Record-Union* (Sacramento, CA), 4 December 1899, 4.

64. "City Briefs," *Los Angeles Times,* 6 February 1900, I16; "Tribes of New Zealand," *Salt Lake Herald,* 12 May 1900, 2; "Religious Announcements," *Chicago Daily Tribune,* 15 July 1900, 31; "Department for Illinois. Chicago and Vicinity," *Chicago Standard,* 4 August 1900, 1497; "Monday Globe Glances," *Saint Paul Globe,* 19 November 1900, 4.

65. "Religious Notices," *New York Tribune,* 19 February 1901, 7.

66. John Barrington, *Separate but Equal? Māori Schools and the Crown, 1867–1969* (Wellington: Victoria University Press, 2008).

67. Margaret D. Jacobs, "Indian Boarding Schools in Comparative Perspective: The Removal of Indigenous Children in the United States and Australia, 1880–1940," in *Boarding School Blues: Revisiting American Indian Educational Experiences,* ed. Clifford E. Trafzer, Jean A. Keller, and Lorene Sisquoc (Lincoln: University of Nebraska Press, 2006), 202–31.

68. Ngareta Timutimu, Judith Simon, and Kay Morris Matthews. "Historical Research as a Bicultural Project: Seeking New Perspectives on the New Zealand Native Schools System," *History of Education* 27, no. 2 (July 1998): 112.

69. "Wherahiko Rawei of New Zealand Describes His People at Emmanuel Baptist Church," *Brooklyn Eagle,* 6 February 1901, 16.

70. "An Ideal Government: Rev. Rawei's Lecture on New Zealand and Its Government," *Freeport (IL) Daily Journal,* 5 April 1905, 8.

71. "Māori-land," *Mercury,* 17 September 1901, 2; "The Land of the Māori," *Mercury,* 3 December 1901, 2.

72. "The Decay of the Māori," *Sydney Morning Herald,* 10 February 1903, 6; "Dramatic and Musical," *New Zealand Free Lance,* 14 March 1903, 7; "Theatrical and Musical Notes," *Otago Witness,* 10 June 1903, 60; "The Sierra," *Auckland Star,* 2 October 1903, 4.

73. "The Māori Entertainer in Trouble," *Morning Bulletin,* 27 June 1903, 5.

74. Tapia, *Circuit Chautauqua,* 25–31.

75. "Maori to Speak," *Minneapolis Journal,* 25 August 1904, 6;"Mrs Hine Rawei Speaks and Sings of New Zealand," *Sterling (IL) Standard,* 14 November 1905;

76. "A Converted Māori," *Minneapolis Journal,* 23 June 1904, 6; "All Sorts of People," *New Zealand Free Lance,* 1 April 1905, 3.

77. "Native New Zealand Woman Says Americans Are Worse Than Cannibals," *Chicago Daily Tribune,* 23 September 1906, D13; "Hine Taimoa Rawei of the South Seas," *Belleville (KS) Telescope,* 11 July 1912, 1; "The Rawei Company," *McCook (NB) Tribune,* 6 May 1912, 1; Rawei, *New Zealand Past and Present.*

78. "Māori Suffragettes, Having Everything Else Their Own Way, Come to America to Learn the Fashions," *Chicago Daily Tribune,* 3 July 1910, G3.

79. "New Zealand Progressive," *Marshall (IA) News,* 3 March 1906, 5. More generally, on the interest of Americans in New Zealand social policy, see Coleman, "New Zealand Liberalism," 372–91.

80. "Foreign Missionaries Speak," *Syracuse Post-Standard,* 26 April 1907, 8; "Whitley County Items," *Fort Wayne Journal Gazette,* 6 March 1908, 1; "American Fork," *Salt Lake Herald-Republican,* 28 November 1909, 6; "New Zealanders Lecture Subject," *Morning Examiner,* 9 January 1910, 7.

81. Marriage of Eva Rawei and Michael Mattran, Lake County, Indiana, 28 September 1912, Index to Indiana Marriage Records 1850–1920, Book T, p. 269, available at ancestry.com.

82. "New Zealand," *Lyceum Magazine,* October 1913, 92.

83. Harry P. Harrison and Karl Detzer, *Culture under Canvas: The Story of Tent Chautauqua* (New York: Hastings House, 1958). 184–85; Tapia, *Circuit Chautauqua,* 104–5; Hugh A. Orchard, *Fifty Years of Chautauqua: Its Beginnings, Its Development, Its Message and Its Life* (Cedar Rapids, IA: Torch Press, 1923). 284; Canning, *Most American Thing,* 86–87.

84. Contract between Raweis and Redpath Lyceum Bureau, 29 October 1914; Redpath Chautauquas to Francis Rawei, 18 April 1916, L. B. Crotty to Francis Rawei, 9 December 1915, all in Box 272, Series 1, Records of the Redpath Chautauqua Collection, 1890–1944, MsC150, University of Iowa Library (hereafter, Chautauqua Collection).

85. "A Night in New Zealand," *Denton (TX) Record Chronicle,* 19 June 1912, 3; "Chautauqua Program," *Durant (TX) Weekly News,* 18 June 1915, 8; "Features of the Big Redpath Chautauqua Program," *Central (TX) Record,* 25 May 1916, 8; Redpath Lyceum Bureau to Francis Rawei, 2 January 1925,Chautauqua Collection.

86. "Mrs Hine Rawei Defends Woman," *Indianapolis Star,* 28 March 1914, 9; "Pretty Dresses to Banish Savagery," *Cedar Rapids Daily Republican,* 10 July 1914, 12.

87. Letterhead, postcards, and publicity material in Chautauqua Collection.

88. "Uncle Sam's Samoans," *Knoxville Sentinel,* 3 June 1925;

89. "Uncle Sam's Samoan Islanders," *Lyceum Magazine,* September 1922, 19.

90. "Francis Rawei," *Davenport Democrat and Leader,* 4 August 1922, 6; "Male Quartet Gives Redpath Recital Today," *Logansport, Indiana, Pharos-Tribune,* 3 August 1925, 2; "Notable Lectures at the Redpath Chautauqua," *Waukesha (WI) Daily Freeman,* 22 May 1926; "Chautauqua, Inspiring and Informing," *Marshall (IA) Evening Chronicle,* 28 June 1927;

91. Telegram from Rawei to Redpath Chautauqua, 25 April 1925, Chautauqua Collection.

92. Rawei to Harrison, 10 September 1925, Chautauqua Collection.

93. "Dr Rawei Passes Away in New Zealand," undated newspaper clipping in "Rawei (Francis) Wherahiko (Dr.)," Chautauqua collection

94. Marriage certificate of Wherahiko Rawei and Emily Jane Sizemore, 1 January 1894, NZ Marriage Registration No. 1894/829, Probate of Francis Rawei, 1928, BBAE/1570, Box 40, 266/1928, Archives New Zealand, Auckland. Figures on average values of estates from "Private Wealth," *New Zealand Yearbook* (Wellington: Census and Statistics Office, 1929), section 35.

95. "Deaths," *Evening Post* (Wellington, New Zealand), 16 October 1939, 1.

96. Canning, *Most American Thing,* 216–23.

97. For a comparative summary of these arguments at the turn of the century, see Donald Denoon, Philippa Mein Smith, and Marivic Wyndham, *A History of Australia, New Zealand, and the Pacific* (Malden, MA: Wiley-Blackwell, 2000), 37, 51–68.

98. See, among others, Coco Fusco, "The Other History of Intercultural Performance" *Drama Review* 38, no. 1 (Spring 1994): 143–67; Adria L. Imada, "Transnational *Hula* as Colonial Culture," *Journal of Pacific History* 46, no. 2 (September 2011): 149–76; Shari M. Huhndorf, *Going Native: Indians in the American Cultural Imagination* (Ithaca, NY: Cornell University Press, 2001); Lester G. Moses, *Wild West Shows and the Images of American Indians* (Albuquerque: University of New Mexico Press, 1996); Joy S. Kasson, *Buffalo Bill's Wild West: Celebrity, Memory, and Popular History* (New York: Macmillan, 2001).

CONCLUSION

COSMOPOLITAN MEDIUM

10

Humanist Enterprise in the Marketplace of Culture

THOMAS AUGST

IN THE early twenty-first century, we are witnessing the evolution of genres of discourse that, as with previous eras of "new" technologies of communication, reconfigure the relations between writing and speech in ways that seem to bend once finite boundaries of received forms of knowledge. Books with covers become e-books on screens; practices of writing that once assumed formality and deliberation have become tactile exercises of speed and efficiency that we call "texting"; more or less formalized exchange of messages across geographic distances performed by correspondence or telegrams now draw expressive power from wit and spontaneity once valued by educated classes in rituals of conversation, in genres of online practices we call "chats." Most radically of all, digital tools for the recording, streaming, relaying, and preserving of the contents of our culture have made the screen a ubiquitous site for not only "desktop" skills of reading and writing but also real-time capture of social co-presence, or what nineteenth-century Americans often called the "living word." In the density of human exchange afforded by social media, as well as the global flows of information fostered by the Internet, digital tools have captured polis and cosmos for the personal use of individuals around the world.

And on screens large and small, the lecture continues to thrive as a genre of learned communication, from high-end TED talks selling "ideas that matter" in an era of information overload to free college courses available through academic initiatives in online learning. Our contemporary media ecology continues to be organized by cultural boundaries that first emerged in the nineteenth century, designing the human interface with sources of information that, with the expansion of printing, would become newly abundant and diverse. Those boundaries were effects of media technology, for prior to the age of electronic broadcasting, live speech could travel only as far as human voice and acoustic spaces permitted. The more important and enduring boundaries, however, were institutional: sites and practices of cultural production that vested particular forms of advanced literacy with practical use and symbolic authority, across sectors of education, entertainment, and devotion. Technologies transform experiences of reading and writing, of speaking and listening. In doing so, they challenge institutional boundaries and conventions of learning, raising questions about where and how students, consumers, and citizens access and value knowledge. What might the institutional history of the lyceum teach us about building social infrastructures for advanced literacy in the contexts of mass communication, about forms and values of humanist enterprise in multimedia environments?

The lyceum was part of a larger institutional landscape, encompassing academies and common school, libraries and athenaeums, as well as the early American college, that mediated the meanings and uses of literacy amidst the development of printing as an industrial technology of mass communication. Nineteenth-century lecturers took many pathways through this landscape, in careers that paralleled generational changes in the public lecture as a genre of learned communication, a mode of performance, and a professional occupation. As a social institution, the lyceum stood at the crossroads of historical forces that would shape how we produce and value knowledge in liberal democracy, influencing the development of civil society, mass entertainment, and higher education. The lyceum was a contested field of cultural production, where a traditional genre of learned discourse with roots in the medieval university was democratized, where middle-class audiences cultivated tastes for self-improvement and entertainment, and where forms of intellectual and literary labor would, by the twentieth century, be reorganized by the emergence of the research university and the modern professions.

A Civic Institution: The Mission of Public Culture

We have become accustomed to thinking about the development of modern media in terms of the geographic reach of communications technologies. Print helped to foster imaginative communities among readers distant from one another in time and place; the Web is worldwide, as Internet addresses remind us. But networks of communication are also local, mediated by norms, practices, and spaces that constitute the social infrastructure for the circulation of knowledge among particular communities. Historically, these included the physical spaces in which cultural goods were produced and the shared habits and expectations that drew patrons to these spaces. In nineteenth-century America they included the diverse motives and styles of performers who crossed paths on the platform, in careers as educators and entertainers that kept their names and words in the public sphere for years, even decades. And most important, the development of the lyceum as a social institution depended in its early years on the values that animated the lyceum as a civic project: the idealism and cooperation of citizens who staffed lecture and lyceum committees in small towns across the United States, mounting seasons of learning and sustaining lives of the mind amidst the social and economic developments of capitalist modernity.

In a frequently reprinted manifesto that he published in *American Journal of Education* in October 1826, Josiah Holbrook outlined the goals for what he called a "society for mutual instruction." The local provision of lectures through voluntary associations would "do more for the general diffusion of knowledge, and for raising the moral and intellectual taste of our countrymen, than any other expedient which can possibly be devised. And it may be questioned whether there is any other way to check the progress of that monster, intemperance, which is making such havoc with talents, moral, and everything that raises man above the brute, but by presenting some object of sufficient interest to divert the attention of the young from places and practices which lead to dissipation and ruin."[1] Holbrook became a tireless impresario of the lyceum in the late 1820s and 1830s, motivated not only by enlightenment faith in the "diffusion of knowledge" but by an organizational pragmatism about the means of its transmission.

As Holbrook's words remind us, the building of educational and cultural institutions in nineteenth-century America was motivated by widespread concern about problems of social welfare and public health that accompanied the economic and political development of the new nation. In that sense, it was one of many experiments in institution building, which used the expansion of education to establish modes of governance suited to liberal democracy. What Holbrook defined as the moral utility of the public lecture—its capacity to improve the tastes of individuals and the qualities of public life—depended not simply on the knowledge one acquired there, but on its powers of attraction within a larger habitat of "places and practices." Appealing to antebellum energies of voluntary societies and the democratic ideals of self-improvement, Holbrook and other educational reformers made a cosmopolitan genre of learned discourse, identified with associational practices and scholarly protocols of transatlantic enlightenment, the vehicle for building local infrastructures for civic life. In attending lectures by professors and ministers, as well as managing the provision of lectures, citizens would learn to govern themselves and the communities in which they lived. In this regard, public lectures sponsored by literary or library societies and lyceums were not simply another source of knowledge; they were engines of civil society, ritual spaces that mobilized communities around the symbolic value of education as a democratic good.

In its earliest years, the development of the lyceum depended on the moral authority and social prestige of the traditional learned professions. Ministers in particular "found the lecture platform the easiest to stand on," as Carl Bode observed, giving as much as half the content of advertised seasons, with lectures that resembled the form of the sermon.[2] In Portland, Maine, in the 1830s, a Unitarian minister named Jason Whitman began giving evening lectures out of a desire to improve his parish in its "external prosperity and condition," as one memorial wrote after his death. "In preparation for the regular services of the pulpit he brought himself as frequently as possible before the public both by means of the press and through courses of evening lectures adapted to attract and interest miscellaneous audiences. On these occasions his place of worship was always thronged and we have reason to believe that his labors were extensively useful especially among the young men of the city in the formation of sober temperate intellectual and serious habits and characters."[3] Whitman, and many other ministers who populated the lyceum seasons in its early years, extended their pastoral work beyond ministerial duties in ways that supported liberal Protestant engagement with increasingly secular languages of "character" and social reform. In addressing such perennial lecture themes as "Advice to Young Men," Whitman and other ministers were adapting a professional genre of discourse for general audiences who would gather at town halls and churches to hear them.

In the 1830s, the lyceum mission was abetted by the work of "lecture agents" for increasingly bureaucratic temperance and abolition societies, who sought to extend the geographic reach of their movements by speaking at churches and town halls. In the organizational and professional networks they assembled through voluntary societies, periodical publication, and newspaper exchanges, reform lecturers helped to create systems for the promotion and circulation of oral discourse by which public lecturing flourished in the 1840s, and they helped popularize the public lecture itself as a medium of public discourse. Using the lecture as a vehicle of civic engagement and public outreach, they opened new pathways to the public sphere for a generation of men and women seeking to fashion literary and intellectual careers. By the middle of the nineteenth century, the occupation of lecturing had become a mode of professional enterprise: a vehicle by which members of the traditional learned professions of the ministry and the academy sought to format their learning for the interests of "miscellaneous audiences" and to acquire influence and authority as what we would now call public intellectuals.[4]

Freeing humanist discourse from the formalities and certainties of academic and literary tradition, the public lecture flourished as a hybrid genre of learned communication that was self-consciously directed to general audiences. As George William Curtis observed in *Harpers* in 1855, the public lecture "partakes of the pith of a sermon, the fluency of a speech, and the ease of an essay but it must hit a hundred audiences and please all," with the aim of holding every audience member in "breathless" absorption.[5] To do this required several kinds of translation—from the abstract to the practical, from formal or technical learning to everyday life, from the foreign to the familiar—that situated particular topics and themes within a "more comprehensive view that rendered thought and knowledge ultimately useful," as Donald Scott has observed.[6] In accomplishing these pedagogical strategies, the lecture platform proved to be particularly hospitable to nonfictional writing, to forms of learning authorized, implicitly or explicitly, by autobiography: the testimony of former slaves, of reformed drunkards, certainly, but also the reflections of Ralph Waldo Emerson or the observations of Bayard Taylor, which were similarly grounded in the authority of personal experience. By accommodating such diverse figures, the lyceum opened up an Enlightenment republic of letters, identified with aristocratic and scholarly modes of formal learning and advanced literacy, to a larger world—to wisdom grounded in the diversity of everyday life, both near and far. The knowledge parlayed by the public lecture was cosmopolitan in both its pragmatic regard for what books could not teach you, and liberal in its toleration, if not celebration, of the plurality of truths abroad beyond the classroom or the study, brought to life on the platform.

In its becoming a popular genre of learned performance, we might say that the public lecture encouraged and rewarded another kind of translation, in which we see the continuing influence of pastoral vocation and its secularization for the age of liberal democracy: the divination of moral authority in the live presence of individual speakers before audiences. If, as Scott notes, the lecture system "transcended intellectual fragmentation," bringing together "men of letters, science, and literature; reformers and conservatives; lawyers, physicians, professors, poets; editors; and statesmen,"[7] then the common ground they occupied had less to do with learning they may have shared than with the democratic theater of individualism in which they stood. A meritocracy judged by plebiscite, the lecture platform encouraged play with diverse forms of intellectual authority. On the lecture platform, the former Unitarian minister Emerson could experiment with conventions of written prose in ways responsive to exigencies of the lecture hall, to hone the expressive dimensions of aphoristic language whose drama unfolded at the sentence level, amid concentrated insights and intellectual surprises of "man thinking." Even with the travelogues of Bayard Taylor that traded so emphatically on cultural and social types, the meanings of cross-cultural differences were coded in performative effects: costumes, accents, anecdotes, and story-telling by which lecturers sought to reproduce the world rather than make general claims about it.

Importing wonders of individual performance to local communities, the civilizing mission of lyceum discourse, so often keyed to cultural nationalism and Anglo-Saxon racialism, was often belied by its mode of delivery. As Peter Gibian demonstrates, for example, the claims that Bayard Taylor offered about the meaning of social and racial difference during his virtual tours competed with his enactments of it. In the foreign manners that he inhabited for an hour or two, Taylor assimilated the cultural or racial Other within parochial ideologies of cultural essentialism, but he also performed identifications with global humanity, seeming to prove the capacity of individuals to become Other to local customs and beliefs to which we are born.[8] In their skillful performances of identity itself, Taylor and other lecturers made the platform hospitable to cosmopolitan realism. Descriptions of social and natural world, meditations on human nature, sentimental or sensational scenarios of the ordinary and exotic became authentic and natural by the personal sincerity and theatrical charisma of speakers addressing audiences.

What made the lyceum a civic institution was the function that local associations and professional networks had served as gatekeepers, keeping lower cultural forms, and the commercial motives that fed them, out of the town halls, churches, picnic grounds, and other public sites. Lecture committees had been guided in their selection of speakers by local and regional contexts of reputation, certified by institutional authority of the traditional learned professions as well as the trust that local elites had earned as stewards of public education and civic order. As they invited speakers and assembled seasons and courses, they were making qualitative judgments about lecture content meant to protect the platform from mere profit-seeking, and from the humbuggery and hoaxes that captured the imagination of penny-paper readers or patrons of P. T. Barnum's American Museum. As these committees faced exigencies of managing and promoting the lecture hall, however, they would be guided by quantitative measures of value: the imperatives of selling tickets to single lectures and subscriptions to seasons, of building and keeping audiences within regional and national markets for lecture talent. Those markets were increasingly tied to the cosmopolitan aura of celebrity—the experiences and reputations that lecturers accumulated with their travel as performers. As lecturers illustrated the diversity of science, history, culture, and personality for nineteenth-century audiences, an expanding universe of knowledge about the social and natural world was humanized by the presence of individuals in the lecture hall, in ways that routinized charisma for the age of mass media and secularized it for the age of liberal democracy.

A Media Platform: Popular Leisure and Mass Culture

The elaboration of lecturing as a social institution depended on many actors, who brought competing and sometimes contradictory motives to their roles as performers, entrepreneurs, reporters, critics, and audience members. Promoters and publishers sought to build reputations that authors had acquired off the platform. Newspapers and journals filled their pages with spoken words, broadcasting the content of lectures in summaries, reviews, and sometimes verbatim transcripts, and in their commentaries helped to define the platform's distinctive attributes as a performance medium. Audience members became intimate with the celebrity of speakers, citing their names, lives, and careers in their diaries and conversations over months, perhaps years. The historical record that all these participants in the lyceum left behind about their engagements with the public lecture, and the ways they expressed and acted on their interests in public speech, help us recover the vernacular languages in which individuals and communities engaged and invested their time and money in learned culture in nineteenth-century America. By helping us to understand these languages and the interests they expressed, literary and cultural histories of the lyceum help us understand the wider social and intellectual contexts in which lectures were valued as means of "raising the moral and intellectual taste of our countrymen," as Holbrook put it. The many actors who helped sustain the lyceum as a public enterprise may not have necessarily understood their participation in the same terms propagated by formal mission statements of organizational literature, but they nevertheless expressed what Hugh Heclo terms "institutional thinking," a general trust in cultural legitimacy and social authority that defines institutional identity in modern society.[9]

The lyceum was but one part of a civilizing mission that institutionalized forms of reading, writing, and speaking as related practices of self-culture, within a moralized geography of public leisure that was crucially shaped by the antebellum urban environments in which institutions of learning, print media, and philanthropic capital were centered. In 1842, for example, an editorial in the *New York Tribune* remarked on the "mighty revolution" in the "character and description of our Popular entertainment." Theaters had been closed during the winter, "while Popular Lectures have been multiplied and attended beyond all precedent, and the demand for our Current Literature has also largely increased." Linking the growth of lectures and literature to the temperance reformation then sweeping the land, the *Tribune* went on to observe that "now hundreds of firesides are nightly surrounded by happy family groups intent on the delightful acquisition of knowledge from the speaking page, who lately waited in terror the return of the husband and father intoxicated from the drunkard; and thousands of young persons now improve their evenings in hearing Lectures or in study, who but lately dissipated them amid the unhealthful excitement, the noxious influences of the Theater. Let Lyceums be formed in every village; let Reading and Debating Clubs spring up in every school District; let popular Libraries proffer their priceless treasures at every turn."[10] Within sites and practices of literary leisure, the public lecture offered "improved evenings" to "young persons," helping them avoid "unhealthful excitement" that was otherwise afforded by taverns in villages and small towns, and by theaters as well in urban centers of New York, Boston, and Philadelphia. In publishing and reviewing lectures and other forms of literary leisure, newspapers such as the *Tribune* were promoting the pursuit of education as a choice within an expanding marketplace for entertainment.

Whatever the contents of knowledge purveyed from the platform, the lyceum derived its moral authority as a civic institution within this broader context of social reform by successfully competing for audiences within a marketplace increasingly crowded with diverse forms of amusement. Where the transatlantic enlightenment cultivated cosmopolitan belonging in the circulation of texts and ideas across national borders, the liberal concept of the marketplace of ideas offered another model of cosmopolitan exchange, one that was grounded in laws of supply and demand. Public lectures would find many kinds of organizational sponsors throughout the nineteenth century: nonprofit chartered lyceum associations, working men's and young men's societies for mutual aid and self-improvement, literary and library associations and athenaeums, reform associations devoted to abolition or temperance or women's suffrage, for-profit outfits such as Barnum's Museum, tour-booking agencies such as the Redpath's lyceum bureau after the war, the Chautauqua and its later spin-offs, settlement houses, and university extension and adult education programs. These organizations had diverse motives in sponsoring public lectures—ideological, philanthropic, commercial—but they all shared a practical concern with developing the lecture's popularity as a form of public recreation.

Whether involving citizens in social reform and cultural uplift, or packing theaters with thousands of ticket-paying customers, the public lecture helped cultivate a popular taste for learning within a burgeoning marketplace of goods, leisure, and entertainment. Lectures were orally "published" from the stage, remediated in print journalism, periodicals, and especially printed editions of lectures. Beyond their many words that were published in speech and print, lectures acquired meaning from the aspirations for learning and hunger for diversion that participants brought to the institution. As Ronald and Mary Zboray demonstrate, for example, women who attended lectures about international travel were not simply passive auditors; they wrote about what they saw and heard in the lecture hall in diaries and letters, appropriating their experiences there to cultivate their own cosmopolitan sensibilities. As with books and periodicals people purchased or borrowed, lectures provided a staple of the cultural content women and men assembled and remade in their diaries. In attending to the aural and visual qualities of lecture performances, and differentiating their attributes of the lecture relative to modes of literary leisure with which they were engaged, ordinary people honed their critical tastes as students of mass media. In the interests women brought to travel lectures and the uses they made of them, we see more generally the ways in which the cosmopolitanism of the nineteenth-century lecture derived not only from the global expanse of lecture topics and the travels of the performers offering them, but also from the widened horizons of mental and emotional growth made possible by the expansion and diversification of advanced literacy.

As the lyceum opened up the lecture platform to a wider array of performers, who carried credentials from the academy as well as the "school of experience," it also opened up the enterprise of general education to values and practices of popular audiences who would drive the development of cultural recreation throughout the mid-nineteenth century. From learned societies, young men's associations, social and proprietary libraries, athenaeums and lyceums before the Civil War, to museums, public libraries, opera houses, and symphony halls after the war, once-elite forms of refinement flowed to ever-larger crowds of students, consumers, patrons, and citizens. These institutions fostered the consumption of culture as a public spectacle, accommodating forms of participation that might be as casual as they were self-improving or civic minded. At least a few young men thus considered lectures by temperance reformer John Gough to be good places to meet attractive women. The women they went to meet may have been drawn by the heart-rending personal biography and Christian conversion of a reformed drunkard. Like other forms of middle-class literary leisure, the lecture provided a respectable means for men and women to cultivate friendship within and across gendered boundaries of propriety. Indeed, as Edward Everett Hale observed in an 1871 editorial, the lyceum had become an institution of modern courtship.[11] So, too, the lyceum drew its institutional meaning for nineteenth-century Americans from the virtues of self-transformation, civic engagement, and social mobility exemplified by "self-made" success of speakers such as Gough and Frederick Douglass, who combined the missionary zeal of reformers, the dramatic eloquence of actors, and the creative discipline of entrepreneurs.

By attending lectures no less than reading books and periodicals, writing in their diaries, or having conversation, women and men were practicing cosmopolitanism—developing habits of self-cultivation and association that defined what it meant to be urbane or civilized for a growing middle class.[12] In that sense, the platform was a medium for the domestication of knowledge, which formatted experiences and insights of a global world for local consumption. In learning to engage and take pleasure in the diversity of knowledge increasingly available to them, nineteenth-century Americans acquired literary tastes and civic values that would animate "middlebrow" culture in the twentieth century.[13] In learning to educate and entertain diverse audiences, successful lecturers helped the lecture hall serve divergent needs of sociability, edification, and entertainment in the shared experience of live performance. The popularity of the platform as a public institution was built on this plurality of motives and dispositions that shaped the production and consumption of culture as a collaborative social enterprise. In this regard, the cosmopolitanism of the public lecture was found not only in the knowledge about the larger world it brought to local audiences, but also in the concessions to and investments in popular taste that it accommodated.

Attracting audiences of hundreds and thousands of people in every region of the United States, the lyceum was a crucible for the development of critical values and entrepreneurial practices that transformed the civilizing mission of culture into a mass enterprise. Lecture bureaus brought bureaucratic efficiency and corporate economies of scale to the marketplace for entertainment in ways that exploited celebrity to market speakers across national tour circuits and to brand cultural content across media platforms of speech and print. William Henry Harrison Murray bolstered the authenticity of his best-selling writings about the wilderness by appearing live before his readers, assuming the persona and appearance of a guide. As Virginia Garnett notes, "print gave him an audience, but oratory gave him authority," indexed to his corporeal presence on stage. For Murray, as perhaps for Mark Twain in the heyday of his platform career, published writings were advertisements for authorial personas and professional reputations peddled on the lecture platform. The bureaus also rationalized the provision of content on the lecture platform, supplying lecture committees with expanding menus of performers as well as commercial methods and values for circulating cultural goods to mass audiences. Embracing the organizational principle of variety, for example, James Redpath crafted "contract courses" that brought to the platform a new variety of performers, as well as a new variety of cultural content, responsive to popular tastes for recitation, humor, and music. As Sara Lampert makes clear, in using the lyceum bureaus to reach new audiences and develop local talent, musical impresario Camilla Urso designed programs with what she called "broad appeal": they emphasized familiar short pieces—what she termed "'*morceaux*' of the masters"—and the pleasures of solo virtuosity and melody over deeper appreciation for classical composition.

The mix of topics that had defined lecture "courses" evolved into eclectic seasons of entertainment that eroded the dominance of the literary and intellectual fare that, in its first decades, had established the lyceum as an educational institution. By the time elocutionist Helen Potter gained fame doing "personations" of other orators and actors in the later 1870s and 1880s, she was recording for posterity the theatricality of public speech, marked by individuality of style, more than the wisdom or art of their words. But then, the popular success of the public lecture had always depended on the sensations of performance. Whether impersonating famous orators or actors, unwrapping mummies, sporting orientalist garb, singing and reciting, or reenacting the delirium tremens, lecturers exploited the excitement of live performance on the platform, what *Littell's Living Age* described in 1848 as the "glare of the light, the presence of the ladies, the mere 'heat and stare, and pressure.'"[14] Complaints about the decline of the lyceum in the 1870s coincided with engagements of the platform with cultural tastes that seemed to eclipse the literary and learned attributes of rhetorical performance. As the lecture system became an increasingly centralized and commercial outlet for the distribution of cultural content, it became an undifferentiated medium of live performance: a platform for encounters with the human body and voice that would be supplemented, if not supplanted, by new technologies of cinema and electronic broadcasting.

A Pedagogical Tool: Professional Authority and Learned Communities

The lyceum's institutional success in the nineteenth century was measured by eulogies written to mourn its passing. In an 1898 article that appeared in the *Dial,* for example, Mark Lee Luther offered a capsule history of the movement, which sought to describe changes in the scale and content of the public lecturing over more than seventy years while interpreting its changing role in American life. An idea that was "now concrete only to the old and middle-aged," the lyceum had begun with Emerson and the other "men of letters" and "intellectual lions" who followed in his wake, whose appearances in cities and villages "the local thermometers of 'culture' registered high or low." As western lyceums sought to book lecturers from the east after the Civil War, "lecture brokerage" centralized the system, managing sought-after professional lecturers such as John Gough and Henry Ward Beecher. This phase brought a rise in prices and a "natural influx of mediocrity into the field" so that by 1874, signs of decline had become clear. The last phase, beginning around 1886, ushered in "the period of stars." In simpler times, the lyceum had been an outpost of civilization, connecting isolated communities to ideas, events, and people from elsewhere. "The fact that we are now intellectually almost one country and not several differing provinces," Luther observed, "has stripped lecturers of something of the glamour that attached to that which is foreign. His message has preceded him."[15]

Coming over the horizon of local worlds, lecturers had carried on their persons an aura of cosmopolitanism. As its traditional civic mission was overtaken by commercial motives, however, the lyceum had become another system of mass consumption. The lecturer himself had become standardized product, traveling the same centralized distribution networks as other goods of the industrial era. Meanwhile, the commercial expansion and centralization of the lecture had diminished the ability of educated scholars and writers to reach a general audience. "Our own men of letters still lecture but in the main before some convention or at some civic reform or liberal club dinner," noted Luther.[16] By the turn of the twentieth century, communities no longer seemed to graze on the same cultural commons, and the platform would become a site of nostalgia, for not only a lost sense of civic mission but for *shared* experience of communication that had been so intimately tied to the human body. One measure of the cosmopolitanism of the public lecture, after all, was long celebrated by the ancient arts of rhetoric: the ability to communicate with every member of an audience. The lyceum had sustained a liberal ideal of collective belonging, where any "miscellaneous crowd" might, in the moment of performance, discover their shared humanity, through the medium of one individual's voice and body before them. Strangers could become neighbors, forgetting their individual differences for an hour or two in the community of the lecture hall.

Luther's article used the history of the lyceum to tell a now-familiar parable about politics of culture in liberal democracy. Pitting learned elites against popular masses, centers of production against peripheries, private interests and public ends, that parable would become a comfortable response by scholars and writers to compromises of intellectual or artistic value or tradition that seemed to attend popular access to cultural goods. In social and cultural histories of the public lecture, however, we find other stories to tell about what the lyceum meant to those who participated in it, and new questions to ask about how these stories might help us value and engage diverse forms of knowledge in our contemporary moment. Did stars take the spotlight once occupied by "men of letters," or did men of letters abandon the public lecture for other forms of learned community? As both a self-conscious movement of educational reform that emerged in the late 1820s and 1830s, as well as a more general network of sites and rituals devoted to public lecturing that flourished in subsequent decades, the lyceum opened up access to general education, offering "courses" and "seasons" of lectures well before the twentieth-century boom in college enrollments made broad knowledge a familiar, if contested, credential for professional success and middle-class aspiration. Within an evolving landscape of literary and cultural practices, it offered what we might describe as liberal education: a kind of general learning that would become a staple of middlebrow culture and would flourish with expansion of college education, the specialization of scholarly disciplines of research, and the consolidation of modern professions in the twentieth-century university. Like Luther's history of the lyceum, the careers of nineteenth-century lecturers are historical artifacts of this evolving institutional landscape of higher education.

For decades after Luther wrote his eulogy to the lyceum, stars continued to carry the "glamour of the foreign" to both cities and small towns across Australia and New Zealand. Māori performer Whereahiko Rawei became a star on the twentieth-century Chautauqua circuit, as Evan Roberts documents. Rawei brought the exoticism of a Pacific culture to small-town audiences, introducing the redemptive power of Christian-themed entertainment to communities that were less familiar with the variety and sophistication of cultural tastes nurtured in the urban centers of cultural production. As Rawei traveled small towns in the early decades of the twentieth century, he was both an exhibit of the colonial enterprise and its salesman—a missionary of the civilizing project that accompanied and often justified the expansion of European and American colonial empires, of which the public lecture was both symbol and instrument. For communities more isolated and conservative in their social mores and Christian faith, Rawei perhaps offered a cosmopolitan literacy, bearing witness to Christian redemption while enacting each night his conversion to Anglo-American character—a star in the self-made universe. Like other lapsed ministers who pursued vocations as teachers outside the academy, Rawei leavened the rational duties of liberal Protestant self-culture with pleasures of theatrical performance in ways that anticipated the popular rhetorics of modern therapeutic culture.[17] Television talk shows and support groups, no less than the stadium sermons of "megachurches" or the motivational lectures of self-help gurus, have built communities around the spoken word dedicated to values of self-realization and authenticity.

Rawei's career may have echoed the intellectual drift of Emerson and Murray toward a natural theology animated by laws of social development and the fatalities of environment. So, too, the tools that Rawei used in this ministry were not so different from those used by George Gliddon, who like other amateur and academic scientists sought to regale popular audiences with a universe whose expanding historical horizons and physical laws scientific research had made newly visible. By the later nineteenth century, popular science would find a new home in brick-and-mortar institutions such as the American Museum of Natural History, as well as in periodicals such as *Popular Sciences* or *National Geographic,* that brought the glamour of the foreign to readers and auditors in images and stories of nature, and a cosmopolitan appreciation for the global scope of its history and the scale of its complexity.

In its primitive or pure variety, the wider world was domesticated by not only a burgeoning literary market for local color and regionalist writings but also the use of magic-lantern shows of travel and exploration, the dioramas documenting the laws of evolution that extended exhibition tactics of Peele and Barnum to modern forms of exhibition, as well as the stage minstrelsy of native informants in the colonial project. When seen in the evolving context of formats and venues dedicated to popular science, what might Rawei have taught his audiences? Did the spectacle of native difference that he both performed and erased on the Chautauqua circuit illustrate "laws" of social and racial progress, demonstrating the capacities for civilization that were unequally distributed to peoples and races across the world, or did it contradict them?

Although the tools public lecturers used throughout the nineteenth century remained tied to the medium of the human body, the meaning of these tools, and the senses of vocation that may have informed them for lecturers and audience members alike, would be transformed by the growing institutional power of the academy. Like the convention and the annual report, the lecture was a ritualized mode of learned communication that helped build philanthropic, professional, and academic associations dedicated to the diffusion of knowledge on both sides of the Atlantic through the early nineteenth century.[18] In that regard, it was not only a multidisciplinary genre shared by scholars in the contexts of learned societies and academies, but also a primary instrument of public outreach and institution-building in universities, where professorships such as the Gifford Lectures in Scotland were established with the obligation to give public lectures. William James's Edinburgh appearances in 1901 and 1902 certified his professional stature within an international republic of letters while also securing for the contents of his lecture formal recognition by an ancient academic institution, within meritocratic standards of scholarly achievement to which they claimed fealty.

The ceremony of oral delivery conferred a patina of institutional tradition on scholarly processes that, in their degrees of specialization and disciplinary methods, were recent inventions of the modern research university.[19] The oral publication of lectures also belied the virtual, symbolic nature of the "public" to whom scholars would address themselves in the modern academy. Emerson was writing for the audiences who gathered for his lectures, after all, in a way that William James was not. Affording occupational and intellectual possibilities unavailable to men of letters of previous generations, the twentieth-century university would encourage professional scholars such as James to craft their words for the printed page rather than the speaking voice.

Traveling the Chautauqua circuit at the margins of this modern institutional landscape, Rawei could only play a doctor on the lecture platform, and a Samoan one at that. We do not know the personal desires and frustrations that inspired this later invention of his biography. We do know that it occurred during an epoch of higher education that had been profoundly transformed by the emergence of the modern professions and the modern enterprise of academic specialization from which they derived their social prestige and their protocols of learned authority.[20] Where forbears such as George Gliddon sought social influence and moral authority by seeking to bring their learning to general publics, professional scholars such as William James would turn the cosmos into specialized subfields of scholarly research, an orientation to knowledge that served the economic and professional interests of higher education as an industry. It would become the business of academics in both the arts and sciences to "produce" knowledge that could be evaluated and rewarded according to hierarchical norms of expertise and quantitative measures of industry. As with the consolidation of law, medicine, and business as modern professions, those norms depended on the differentiation of learned communities within the university. These norms defined the social value and moral authority of the academy's enterprise—the "public" it served—against measures of public impact or social value available through commerce and mass media.

Since the late nineteenth century, the landscape of learned culture has been dominated by the modern academy in its many guises: large corporate research universities, funded by private endowments and state subsidies and by private and governmental philanthropic foundations; the liberal arts institutions that sustain the economies and cultures of "college towns" large and small; the state university and community college systems that gave access to higher education to millions of men and women.[21] As higher education developed increasingly specialized and intensively capitalized institutions and markets, written and spoken words would find new cultural meaning and social value within the lecture halls and seminar rooms of modern academic enterprise. Through "reform clubs" and other progressive-era organizations and professional networks, educated elites would exert their influence on general publics that, in the earlier decades of the lyceum era, they would have addressed in person. At conferences, learned professionals would speak to one another in their disciplines, producing increasingly specialized expertise. Liberal education would become a booming sector of the cultural consumption within the academy no less than the marketplace, where the mechanics of celebrity and the commercial models of distribution and marketing merchandised general education into an ever-multiplying assortment of products, markets, formats, services, and media.

From its dominance in nineteenth-century America to its demise in the shadow of new institutions of professional knowledge, the lyceum was at the center of changes in public education and mass media that shaped the emergence of a modern intellectual and cultural landscape. The public lecture endowed an oral genre of learned address with a distinctive civic mission and moral authority at an important moment in the maturation of mass communication, on the one hand, and the development of public education and culture as instruments of liberal governance, on the other. In an era when higher education remained both traditional in its curriculum and restrictive in its social mission, the lyceum arguably helped modernize the content and format of humanist education for liberal democracy, in ways that would shape forms of scholarly communication and pedagogy inside the modern academy, while promoting the cultural value and social utility of general learning outside the academy. The history of the public lecture may yet remind us of the centrality of human presence to the art of teaching, illuminating local forms of community and civic faiths in learning required to turn information into knowledge, to build from the virtual cosmos thriving communities in the real world.

NOTES

1. Cited in Carl Bode, *The American Lyceum: Town Meetings of the Mind* (New York: Oxford University Press, 1956), 12.

2. "The organization, length, and style of the lyceum lecture closely resembled that of the religious homily, and sometimes the lecturing was described as lay preaching, the lectures 'lay sermons"; Bode, *American Lyceum,* 31.

3. *Sermons by Reverend Jason Whitman, with a Sketch of His Life and Work* (Boston: Benjamin H. Greene, 1849), xix.

4. On the emergence of lecturing as a professional occupation, see Donald Scott, "The Profession That Vanished: Public Lecturing in Mid Nineteenth-Century America," in *Professions and Professional Ideologies in America,* ed. Gerald L. Geison (Chapel Hill: University of North Carolina): 12–28.

5. George William Curtis, "Editor's Easy Chair," *Harper's Magazine* 10, no. 59 (April 1855): 694–97.

6. Scott, "Profession That Vanished," 25.

7. Ibid., 26

8. For contemporary arguments for liberal education tied to the cosmopolitan capacity for empathy, see Martha C. Nussbaum, *Cultivating Humanity: A Classical Defense of Reform in Liberal Education* (Cambridge: Harvard University Press, 1998).

9. To recognize institutional thinking requires attending not only to mission statements or public relations but also to the broader background of intellectual and moral resources that furnish "presumptions about rightful relationships being played out" and the actions by which people perform "trust in identity amidst assumptions of institutional identity"; Hugh Heclo, *On Thinking Institutionally* (Boulder, CO: Paradigm, 2008), 130. For additional critical perspectives on mechanisms of institutional behavior and their broader social and cultural implications, see Augst and Carpenter, eds., *Institutions of Reading: The Social Life of Libraries* (Amherst: University of Massachusetts Press, 2007); Mary Douglas, *How Institutions Think* (Syracuse, NY: Syracuse University Press, 1986); Jeffrey L. Williams, ed., *The Institution of Literature* (Albany:

SUNY Press, 2001); David Carr, *The Promise of Cultural Institutions* (Walnut Creek, CA: Altamira, 2003); Peter Hall and Rosemary Taylor, "Political Science and the Three New Institutionalisms," *Political Studies* 44 (1996): 936–57.

10. "Our Public Amusements" *New York Tribune,* 23 February 1842.

11. "It is not strange if the same persons do not in many instances for a succession of years attend the evening lecture. The young man who found it pleasant to go with Amanda may, not unnaturally, find it more pleasant to stay at home with Amanda, when she has given him the right to take her to a home. He will, very likely, say to her, as they sit before a crackling fire, that the old interest in Lyceums is over. And she will very likely believe it. Yet for all that, the sale of tickets that year shall be larger in their village than ever"; Edward Everett Hale, "The Examiner," *Old and New* 74 (1871).

12. On literary practices and values that nineteenth-century Americans brought to their leisure, see Thomas Augst, *The Clerk's Tale: Young Men and Moral Life in Nineteenth-Century America* (Chicago: University of Chicago, 2003); and Ronald J. Zboray and Mary Saracino Zboray, *Everyday Ideas: Socioliterary Experience among Antebellum New Englanders* (Knoxville: University of Tennessee Press, 2006).

13. On "middlebrow" culture and its relation to nineteenth-century intellectual and cultural history, see Joan Shelley Rubin, *The Making of Middle-Brow Culture* (Chapel Hill: University of North Carolina, 1992); and Janice Radway, *A Feeling for Books: The Book-of-the-Month Club, Literary Taste, and Middle-Class Desire* (Chapel Hill: University of North Caroline, 1997).

14. George Gilfillan, "Professor Nichol," *Littell's Living Age* 17, no. 208 (6 May 1848): 241–49.

15. Mark Lee Luther, "The Bygone Lyceum," *Dial* 25 (1 November 1898): 291–93.

16. Ibid.

17. On therapeutic ethos in its historical relation to mass consumption in the twentieth century, see T. J. Lears, *Fables of Abundance: A Cultural History of Advertising in America* (New York: Basic Books, 1995); and Richard Wightman Fox and T. J. Jackson Lears, eds., *The Culture of Consumption: Critical Essays in American History* (New York: Pantheon, 1983).

18. For an interpretation of "the enlightenment" from the historical perspective of mediation, including associational forms such as the lecture, see Clifford Siskin and William Warner, *This Is Enlightenment* (Chicago: University of Chicago Press, 2010). On the development of learned societies, see Alexandra Oleson and Sanborn C. Brown, eds., *The Pursuit of Knowledge in the Early American Republic: American Scientific and Learned Societies from Colonial Times to the Civil War* (Baltimore: Johns Hopkins University press, 1976).

19. On the academic history of the lecture form, see William Clark, *Academic Charisma and the Origins of the Modern Research University* (Chicago: University of Chicago Press, 2006).

20. On the history of the professions, see Burton Bledstein, *The Culture of Professionalism: The Middle Class and the Development of Higher Education in America* (New York: Norton, 1976); Samuel Haber, *The Quest for Authority and Honor in the American Professions, 1750–1900* (Chicago: University of Chicago Press, 1991); Rakesh Khurana, *From Higher Aims to Hired Hands: The Social Transformation of American Business Schools and the Unfulfilled Promise of Management as a Profession* (Princeton: Princeton University Press, 2007).

21. On the expansion of higher education in the twentieth century, see Christopher Newfield, *Ivy and Industry: Business and the Making of the American University, 1880–1980* (Durham, NC: Duke University Press, 2004). On images of college education in middle-class culture, see Daniel Clark, *Creating the College Man: American Mass Magazines and Middle-Class Manhood, 1890–1915* (Madison: University of Wisconsin Press, 2010).

About the Contributors

Robert Arbour is a doctoral candidate in the English department at Indiana University, where he studies nineteenth-century American literature. His dissertation is titled "A Sentimental War: American Poetry and the Civil War" and tracks changes in sentimental poetry as a nationalizing mode during and after the American Civil War. He has published essays in the *Explicator, Partial Answers,* and *Texas Studies in Literature and Language.*

Thomas Augst is associate professor and director of graduate study in the Department of English at New York University. He is the author of *The Clerk's Tale: Young Men and Moral Life in Nineteenth-Century America* (2003), coeditor of *Institutions of Reading: The Social Life of Libraries in the United States* (2007), and coeditor of *Cultural Agencies and American Libraries* (2001).

Susan Branson is associate professor of history at Syracuse University. She is the author of *"These Fiery Frenchified Damese": Women, Politics, and Culture in Early National Philadelphia* (2001) and *Dangerous to Know: Women, Class and Crime in the Early Republic* (2008).

Virginia Garnett is a doctoral candidate at the University of Delaware. Her dissertation, "The Podium in Print: How the Printed Lecture Shaped America, 1865–1914," focuses on the relationship between orality and print through examination of the American lecture circuit. More specifically she argues that the lecture, through its ability to be transcribed and circulated in newsprint, challenged popular notions of literature and authorship at the turn of the twentieth century.

Peter Gibian is associate professor of English at McGill University. His publications include *Oliver Wendell Holmes and the Culture of Conversation* (2001), winner of the Best Book Prize awarded by the Northeast American Studies Association for 2001–2, and an edited collection, *Mass Culture and Everyday Life* (1997), as well as essays on Whitman, Poe, Hawthorne, Melville, Twain, Edward Everett Hale, John Singer Sargent, Justice Holmes, Wharton and James, Michael Snow and shopping-mall spectacle, the experience of *flânerie* in nineteenth-century shopping arcades, and cosmopolitanism in nineteenth-century American literature. He is completing a new book exploring the workings of a midcentury "culture of conversation" across the spectrum of talk modes and spheres as it shaped the writings of a wide range of authors and is also completing a major project on the emergence of a "cosmopolitan tradition" in American writing.

Sara Lampert received a PhD in history from the University of Michigan in 2012. She has taught at Presbyterian College in South Carolina, and is currently an assistant professor of American history at the University of South Dakota.

Angela G. Ray is associate professor of communication studies at Northwestern University. Her 2005 book *The Lyceum and Public Culture in the Nineteenth-Century United States* treats the development of the lyceum lecture system, with a special emphasis on the ways that social reformers adapted their messages for this commercial medium. The book received awards from the National Communication Association, the Rhetoric Society of America, and the American Forensic Association. Ray's scholarship has also appeared in journals such as *Argumentation and Advocacy*, the *Quarterly Journal of Speech, Rhetoric and Public Affairs,* and *Women's Studies in Communication.*

Evan Roberts is an assistant professor of history at the University of Minnesota and previously taught at Victoria University of Wellington. He is a social and economic historian of both New Zealand and the United States in the late nineteenth and early twentieth centuries. His current major research projects examine married women's work in the United States and health and living standards in New Zealand. His ongoing interest in connections between New Zealand and the United States can be seen in publications on New Zealand and American department stores and recent conference papers on New Zealand migration to America.

Paul Stob is assistant professor in the Department of Communication Studies at Vanderbilt University. His research focuses on rhetoric and intellectual culture during the Gilded Age and Progressive Era in America. He is especially interested in the way American intellectuals have used popular forums—lecture halls, periodicals, and books—to construct democratic communities of thought. His work has appeared in such journals as *Rhetoric and Public Affairs,* the *Quarterly Journal of Speech, Philosophy & Rhetoric,* and *Argumentation and Advocacy.* His first book, *William James and the Art of Popular Statement,* has recently been published by Michigan State University Press.

Tom F. Wright is a lecturer in American literature at the University of Sussex, England. He has published on nineteenth-century literary and cultural history, including articles on Ralph Waldo Emerson, Thomas Carlyle, John B. Gough, Herman Melville, and the painter Richard Caton Woodville. He is completing a book-length study of the transatlantic dimension to antebellum lecture culture.

Mary Saracino Zboray is a visiting scholar in the Department of Communication at the University of Pittsburgh. She has coauthored, with Ronald J. Zboray, *Voices without Votes: Women and Politics in Antebellum New England* (2010), winner of the Eastern Communication Association's Everett Lee Hunt Award; *Everyday Ideas: Socioliterary Experience among Antebellum New Englanders* (2006), winner of the Association for Education in Journalism and Mass Communication's History Division Book Award and the International Reading Association's E. Jennifer Monaghan Award; and *Literary Dollars and Social Sense: A People's History of the Mass Market Book* (2005).

Ronald J. Zboray is professor of communication, affiliate faculty in women's studies, and director of the graduate program for cultural studies at the University of Pittsburgh. He has received several fellowships and other awards, including a 2012 twelve-month fellowship from the National Endowment for the Humanities, for his coauthored book project on print media use during the American Civil War. He is author of *A Fictive People: Antebellum Economic Development and the American Reading Public* (1993), coeditor of the *Emma Goldman Papers Microfilm Edition* (1990), and, since 1996, coauthor of four additional books and many articles with Mary Saracino Zboray.

Index